Lightning
at Hoover's Gap

Lightning
at Hoover's Gap

The Story of Wilder's Brigade

Glenn W. Sunderland

Thomas Yoseloff

New York ▪ South Brunswick ▪ London

Thomas Yoseloff, Publisher
Cranbury, New Jersey 08512

Thomas Yoseloff Ltd
108 New Bond Street
London W. 1, England

498–06795–5

Printed in the United States of America

Foreword

IN WRITING THE STORY OF COL. WILDER'S LIGHTNING BRIGADE I have provided a great deal of detailed information for the benefit of the Civil War enthusiast who has a good general knowledge of the war and the people involved in it. Yet at the same time I have attempted to interject enough general information so as to make it understandable and interesting to the average reader. Only time will tell whether or not this has been done successfully. In any case it is not intended to be a history as such but a factual account of the exploits of a group of Midwesterners who turned out to be more than just another brigade of Union soldiers. They were different. And they were different because of their brigade commander. Col. Wilder was not a West Pointer nor did he have any other military experience prior to the outbreak of the rebellion. His military success stemmed from his burning desire to be a winner and from his successful background as an engineer and businessman.

The chapter titles are the titles of songs that were popular during the Civil War and they lead Wilder's Brigade from the dark days of late '62 through Kentucky, Tennessee, Mississippi, Georgia and Alabama to the victorious end of the war.

This brigade of tough, lean, Midwestern farm boys and their resourceful and enterprising leader injected new theories and methods into the Union Army that completely changed the concept of mounted warfare during the Civil War. It is a lesson in leadership and a tribute to the resilience and physical stamina of our ancestors.

G. W. S.

Acknowledgments

FOR THE CHRONOLOGY OF DAILY MOVEMENTS OF THE BRIGADE the writer relied primarily on B. F. McGee's *History of the 72nd Indiana Volunteers,* The *Official Records, Adjutant General's Report-State of Illinois,* and *Henry Campbell's Diary.* My special thanks to Mr. Eli Lilly of Indianapolis for lending me his copy of the Campbell Diary as well as photostats of some of Col. Wilder's letters.

Many of the verifications of movements as well as details of specific actions and incidents were taken from regimental histories, personal narratives and biographies, most of which were obtained from state and university libraries. My deepest appreciation is extended especially to Dr. Bowman of the University of Chattanooga Library for his hospitality and assistance on two personal trips to the Wilder Section of his reference library.

To Bob Brissenden and Mrs. Carolyn Roberts for hand-me-down personal recollections of personal incidents, and to Mrs. Loretta Wiman for her editing assistance, my sincere appreciation.

Letters and diaries provided a great deal of personal color and my heart-felt thanks is extended to Mrs. Elmer Kello for the Letters of Andrew Bleakley; to Mrs. Helen Nale and her mother, Mrs. Rose Funkhouser, for the Letters of Capt. John Funkhouser; to Mrs. Nell Harper for the Letters of Tighlman Jones; to Dr. L. M. Hammand for the Letters of William Hammer; and to Mrs. Leah Manhart for the Diary of Forrest Farley.

Last but not least, I am deeply indebted to my father, Glenn H. Sunderland, who was raised by his grandfather, a veteran of Wilder's Brigade, and who provided a considerable amount of information as well as a great deal of encouragement.

G. W. S.

Contents

Introduction

WHEN THE CIVIL WAR OPENED WITH THE FIRING ON FORT Sumter in April of 1861, the Regular Army of the United States numbered only about 16,000 men. The balance of the some 3,500,000 men who served in both the Union and Confederate Armies, with the exception of a small number of conscripts, were volunteers. There were mechanics and carpenters, storekeepers and clerks, and men from many and varied other occupations, but at least half of them were farm boys who were accustomed to the rigors of outdoor life and to whom hard work was nothing new.

Organization of the armies was the same as had been used for some years. A company at full strength contained one captain, two lieutenants and ninety-eight enlisted men. Ten companies made a regiment. Army organization called for three regiments to a brigade, but because most regiments were usually badly depleted from battle losses and disease four or more were quite common. Usually three brigades made up a division, two or more divisions made up a corps, and two or more corps made an army.

Although brigades, divisions and corps were assigned numerical designations, they normally were referred to by the names of their commanders. Union armies were named after rivers in the areas in which they operated such as the Army of the Potomac, Army of the Ohio and Army of the Cumberland. The Confederate armies were named after geographic areas such as the Army of Northern Virginia and the Army of Tennessee. Regiments were the units most often used to identify a man's outfit and they almost always had a numerical designation and the name of the state where they were organized. For example, Pvt. Wilson Henderson, during the Chickamauga Campaign, was a member of Company A, 98th Illinois Regiment, Wilder's Brigade, Reynold's Division, Thomas' Corps, Army of the Cumberland.

Regiments were usually raised in a local area; the company officers and non-coms were elected by the men of the regiments. Battle flags in many cases were designed and sewn by the officers' wives and the regiments marched off to war amid the playing of brass bands and numerous speeches by local dignitaries.

Many emotional reasons have been given over the years as to why Northerners and Southerners fought so viciously on their respective sides. The simplest explanation seems to be that the South was fighting to defend her right to live under the social and economic system to which she was accustomed, and she resented the North's infringement on that right. The North, on the other hand, was fighting to preserve the Union that had grown and prospered under a new form of government in a new world.

In any case the American Civil War was by far the bloodiest contest in which American men were ever engaged. At a time when the total population of the United States was only 31,000,000, more than 618,000 soldiers were killed or died while on duty. This astonishing figure accounts for almost 20 per cent of the men engaged. In comparison the casualty statistics for World War II show 405,000, or about 4 per cent of those engaged. More Americans died in the Civil War than in all of America's other wars combined.

Immediately after the war began, volunteers for army duty were enlisted for three months' service. Later the enlistments were extended to nine months and then to three years. On July 2, 1862, with enlistments dragging, President Lincoln made a request from Northern governors for 300,000 new enlistees for three years' service or for the duration of the war which he said should "not be more than one year." The response to Lincoln's request was enormous and the Union Army grew to gigantic proportions.

By late 1862 the task of clothing, feeding and arming an army of this size had become as well organized as could be expected considering the wide dispersion of the troops and the transportation available. The Union Army was well equipped. The exotic uniforms seen at the beginning of the war had disappeared—replaced by practical, useful clothing. The large Sibley tent had been replaced by the two-man dog or "pup" tent. Each soldier, in addition to his musket, carried a percussion pouch and cartridge box fastened to his belt, a canvas haversack for rations slung over one shoulder and a canteen over the other. He was also issued a heavy blanket, a rubber blanket and a knapsack. Long marches soon taught the new soldier that superfluous equipment and possessions could not be tolerated. General Sherman stated that he did not believe that "a soldier could be loaded down too much, but, including his clothing, arms and equipment, he can carry fifty pounds without impairing his health or activity."

The Confederate Army, not as large or as well equipped, was fighting with a deep-felt purpose. The Rebels claimed that "one southerner could whip five yankees," and because of this mental attitude and the excellent quality of their military leadership, the Confederates were giving a noble account of themselves.

December of 1862 found Washington, D. C., in a state of gloom, both politically and militarily. The war was not popular. The people in the North had finally come to realize that the rebellion was going to be a long full-scale war instead of the three-month-struggle they had expected after the fall of Fort Sumter. President Lincoln's Republican Party had lost several congressional seats in the off-year elections in November. These newly elected congressmen were clamoring for an end to the war no matter what the concessions.

But Lincoln had military problems that far outweighed his political troubles. His armies in the East, although always outnumbering the Confederates, were hesitant about taking the initiative in the conflict; and when the two armies did meet the results usually were disastrous. With all his maneuvering around with the leadership of the Army of the Potomac, Lincoln had not been able to find a winner. The Union's first major battle under General McDowell at Bull Run had ended in disaster before the very eyes of the picnicking elite of Washington who had come out to witness the "suppression of the rebellion." The Seven Days Battle under General McClellan had been a dismal failure. General John Pope then got his chance in August of 1862 at the Second Battle of Bull Run only to experience the same result as the first encounter there. In September, under McClellan again, the Army of the Potomac, after one of the bloodiest battles of the Civil War, finally won a questionable victory by a very narrow margin at Antietam. However, McClellan, whose head was continually filled with political dreams, failed to follow up his advantage and Lincoln replaced him with General Burnsides. In mid-December Burnside's Army was mercilessly slaughtered in the foolhardy assaults on Marye's Heights at Fredericksburg, Virginia, suffering almost three times the casualties sustained by the Confederates.

But Lincoln had winning generals in Grant and Rosecrans who were situated west of the Appalachians, and it was to the west that the President looked for salvation. Grant, the hero of Fort Donelson and Shiloh, was moving south toward Vicksburg, and Rosecrans, the North's most consistent winner, was readying his newly created Army of the Cumberland for the Battle of Stones River at Murfreesboro, Tennessee.

The North's major tactical problem was the ineffectiveness of the Union Cavalry. The Confederate Cavalry was brilliantly led by J. E. B. Stuart and Mosby in the East and by Morgan, Wheeler and Forrest in the West. Rebel cavalry outnumbered Union cavalry three or four to one in most areas. The Rebel horse soldiers cut Federal communications and destroyed their supply trains—in some cases completely encircling the Union forces on their raids. And when it came to battle they weren't too proud to dismount and fight with rifles like infantry.

Union Cavalry, chained to tradition, could not cope with them. The West Point trained Union command held to the obsolete theory that cavalry, armed primarily with pistol and saber, should be used mainly for scouting and for mass saber charges. Such charges may have been practical in years past, but the mortal fate of the famed British "Light Brigade" at Balaclava in the 1850's should have been an omen of things to come—saber charges were virtually useless in the comparative wilderness of the American continent.

This imbalance of mounted troops would soon be reversed, however, and the man most responsible for changing the rules of cavalry warfare and sparking the Union Cavalry to their eventual superiority was not a West Pointer, but a businessman colonel from Indiana, John T. Wilder. Col. Wilder's Brigade, although not professional soldiers, learned to fight by fighting; theirs was the first military unit in the history of warfare *to use horses only as a means of transportation and* TO FIGHT, DISMOUNTED, WITH REPEATING RIFLES.

Lightning
at Hoover's Gap

1

"How Are You, John Morgan?"

UNION GENERAL WILLIAM STARKE ROSECRANS, IN DECEMBER, 1862, had his Army of the Cumberland, 56,000 strong, headquartered at Nashville, Tennessee. Thirty miles to the southeast at Murfreesboro was his adversary, Confederate General Braxton Bragg, with the customary Rebel inferiority of numbers, 51,000 men.

Both Rosecrans and Bragg had graduated in the upper 10 per cent of their West Point classes, and both had resigned from the army in the 1850's to enter private business. When the war began, Bragg, a North Carolinian by birth and a Louisianan by residence, cast his lot with his native southland. Rosecrans returned to active duty as Colonel of Engineers from his home state of Ohio. Both Rosecrans and Bragg were tall and intelligent with strong senses of duty and both possessed endless resources of boundless energy. But both of them were also burdened by the same personality problem—an irritable disposition and violent temper. Despite the things that they had in common Rosecrans and Bragg were destined to pursue and challenge and fight each other over the wooded hills and valleys of Tennessee and Georgia for the next ten months.

Rosecrans was meticulous in his battle preparations. By late December he was adding the finishing touches to his plan for an offensive against Murfreesboro by re-orienting his command organization. One of the results of this re-organization was the appointment of Colonel John T. Wilder to brigade command. Col. Wilder's new command, bivouacked a few miles northeast of Nashville, was made up of the 17th, 72nd and 75th Indiana Infantry Regiments, the 98th Illinois Infantry Regiment and the 18th Indiana Battery of Light Artillery. The 75th Indiana

17

was soon replaced by the 123rd Illinois and the 92nd Illinois was attached to the Brigade for the Chickamauga Campaign, but for the most part, the units which rode as the famous "Lightning Brigade" for the remainder of the war were the 17th and 72nd Indiana, the 98th and 123rd Illinois and the 18th Indiana Battery.

The 17th Indiana Infantry was Wilder's own regiment. It was mustered in at Indianapolis, June 12, 1861, with Col. Milo S. Hascall in command. With Capt. Wilder commanding Company A, the regiment moved immediately to West Virginia and participated in the defeat of Gen. Robert E. Lee at the battles of Cheat Mountain and Greenbrier. In November they were transferred to the Army of the Ohio under Gen. Buell. In 1862 they took part in the sieges of Corinth and Munfordville, and in October the Battle of Perryville in Kentucky.

The 72nd Indiana Infantry was mustered in at Lafayette on August 16, 1862. Their regimental commander, Col. A. O. Miller, as a captain in the 10th Indiana had fought at Rich Mountain, West Virginia, and at the battles of Mill Springs and Shiloh. The 72nd moved to Louisville in early October and subsequently participated in the Kentucky campaign that forced General Bragg and his Confederate army back into Tennessee.

The 98th Illinois Infantry was made up of farm boys from the clay dirt section of southern Illinois. They were mustered in at Centralia, Illinois, September 3, 1862, under Col. John J. Funkhouser and were immediately ordered to Louisville, Ky. While enroute their train was wrecked by a misplaced switch near Bridgeport, Illinois, supposedly thrown by one of the "Copperheads" that were numerous in that area, killing a captain and seven men and injuring seventy-five. Under Gen. Dumont they marched from Louisville to Frankfort, Kentucky, as a feint for Gen. Buell's Perryville campaign.

The 123rd Illinois Infantry was from central Illinois and was mustered in at Mattoon under Col. James Monroe, a veteran of Belmont, Fort Donelson and Shiloh. After mustering in on September 6, 1862, this regiment moved to Kentucky and one month later, with practically no training, was engaged in the Battle of Perryville. Both their Brigade Commander, Gen. Terrill, and their Division Commander, Gen. Jackson, were killed, the regiment losing 36 killed and 180 wounded.

The 18th Indiana Battery of artillery was mustered in at Indianapolis, August 24, 1862. They were commanded by Capt.

Eli Lilly, the Greencastle, Indiana druggist, who after the war founded the Eli Lilly Co., one of the nation's largest manufacturers of drugs and pharmaceuticals. In the fall of '62, Lilly's battery was involved in the defense of Louisville and the expulsion of Bragg from Kentucky.

Col. Wilder, thirty-two years old, grew up in the Catskill Mtn. region of New York State. He came from a fighting family. His great-grandfather, Seth Wilder, lost a leg in the Battle of Bunker Hill in the Revolutionary War. His grandfather, Seth Wilder Jr., replacing his disabled father, participated in the Battles of Saratoga, Monmouth and Stony Point where he received a bayonet wound. In the War of 1812 Wilder's father, Reuben Wilder, fought at Plattsburg and Sackett's Harbor.

After receiving an average education John Wilder, a bright and ambitious young man, traveled west, arriving at Columbus, Ohio, at the age of nineteen. He obtained a job in a foundry where he learned drafting, pattern-making and mill-wrighting. He learned his trades well and received many promotions, but in 1857 he moved to Greensburg, Indiana, where he invented many pieces of hydraulic machinery which he patented. By the spring of 1861 Wilder had become a nationally recognized expert in the field of hydraulics.

At the outbreak of the Civil War, Wilder set to work casting two six-pound cannon at his foundry at Greensburg and recruited a company of light artillery for the first Indiana three-year regiment. However, the artillery company did not fit into the regimental plans, and Capt. Wilder and his company were mustered in as Company A of the 17th Indiana Infantry Regiment. Within a month he was promoted to lieutenant-colonel and a few months later to colonel in command of the regiment.[1]

Now they were together—the brigade that was to set the pattern for modern mounted warfare, and their able ingenious leader.

Rosecrans was building up his supplies for the impending Battle of Stones River which would be fought at Murfreesboro, Dec. 30-Jan. 2. His army was being supplied from Louisville on the Ohio River some 200 miles to his rear. He was concerned about the safety of his communications and rightly so. Confederate cavalry General John Hunt Morgan, whose audacity and agrressiveness had earned him the nickname "Rebel Raider," had been ordered personally by Confederate President Jefferson Davis to move north to destroy Rosecrans' supply lines and to stimulate a more vigorous activity among the growing Copper-head population in Kentucky and in the southern parts of Illinios, Indiana and Ohio. This was done against the better judgment of General Braxton Bragg, commander of the Confederate Army headquartered at Murfreesboro. Bragg knew that a battle was imminent and that without Morgan and his troops he would have to fight the battle without his customary cavalry superiority. But Jefferson Davis was the supreme commander and Murfreesboro was in gay holiday mood. In fact Davis was in Murfreesboro not on military matters but to attend one of the social highlights of the Christmas season—the wedding of John Hunt Morgan, a newly promoted brigadier general.

Gen. Morgan had been raised in the "blue grass" section of Kentucky. Both the Morgans and the Hunts, his mother's family, were members of the blue grass aristocracy and at a young age he became an excellent horseman astride those fine Kentucky bred horses that filled the stables of Lexington. He attended Transylvania College, the same school that Jeff Davis and Albert Sidney Johnston attended before entering West Point, and at the age of twenty-one he saw action at Buena Vista in the Mexican War with the 1st Kentucky Cavalry. Between the two wars Morgan married and lost his wife, successfully oper-ated a general merchandise business, and organized a militia company called the Lexington Rifles. Kentucky, as a border state, tried unsuccessfully to maintain neutrality after the out-break of the rebellion. Even families were split in their loyalities —some of them providing soldiers to both armies. On the night of September 20, 1861, Morgan declared his loyalty to the south by sneaking his company of Lexington Rifles out of town and reporting to General Buckner's Confederate camp near Bowling Green. He immediately launched his career of daring raids, scouting, and night-fighting, doing it the way he liked—as an independent command. By December, 1862, Morgan had al-ready executed two of his dashing cavalry raids into Kentucky, capturing many prisoners and destroying several Union supply depots.

During his recent stay in Murfreesboro, the thirty-seven-year-old Morgan, straight, tall and resplendent in his cavalry officer's uniform, had attracted the attention of young Mattie Ready, daughter of a former congressman. After a whirlwind court-ship a wedding date was set for mid-December. The invitation list included almost the entire leadership of the Confederate

Army in the west. Gen. Bragg himself was there. Also Generals Cheatham, Hardee and Breckinridge. Lt. Gen. Leonidas Polk, Episcopal Bishop of Louisiana, performed the ceremony. Immediately after the wedding Jefferson Davis held a conference with Morgan and that very night Morgan and his brigade began preparations for their third raid into Kentucky. On Dec. 30 Bragg entered the Battle of Stones River without a large part of his cavalry force.[2]

Morgan left Alexandria, forty miles east of Nashville, on the 22nd with a well-mounted force of 3000 cavalrymen. The next day General John J. Reynolds, Wilder's division commander, received a message from General Rosecrans' headquarters: "Try and ascertain the strength of the enemy. . . . Concentrate your forces and fight like the devil."

General Reynolds did not have to be reminded of the necessity of concentrating his forces in the face of a Morgan raid. Only three days before he had taken over command of this division on December 10, Morgan had captured an entire brigade of the division at Hartsville, only ten miles from where the balance of the division was camped at Castillian Springs. The next day, December 24, Reynolds replied to Rosecrans: "Have this moment heard from Hall (another brigade commander) and Wilder. They are ready and so are we, and we will fight like the devil. . . ."

But before the Union command could get organized Morgan had moved past them and well into the heart of Kentucky. General Boyle, commanding the District of Western Kentucky, sent out a force of infantry and cavalry which he had collected from his various outposts. Colonel Harlan and his infantry brigade were sent by rail from Gallatin, Tennessee, to Munfordville, Kentucky, where they arrived on the evening of the 27th only to find that Morgan had that very day captured the entire 91st Illinois Infantry Regiment at Elizabethtown, thirty miles farther north. General Reynolds and his division moved north from Castillian Springs on foot at daylight on the 26th. The chase was on. Near 20,000 men, including some troops under the command of General Horatio Wright who headed the Department of Ohio with headquarters at Cincinnati, all chasing the wily Morgan and his 3,000 Rebel raiders.

Christmas day had been bright and warm but as Colonel Wlider's men shouldered their muzzle-loaders and headed north the next day a cold drizzling rain set in. The division made fifteen miles the first day and slept in the rain all night north of Gallatin. Reynold's column got underway at seven o'clock the next morning and moved toward Scottsville, Kentucky. Water and mud and rocks were a foot deep along most of the way and by the time they reached Scottsville that night many of the men had worn out their shoes. They spent most of their time in camp that evening treating their raw and bleeding feet. One of Wilder's men reflected, "the most disagreeable thing in the world to a soldier is marching in the rain. He don't mind sleeping in it, but to be continually dripping—knapsack, blanket, rations and everything else wet, growing heavy and heavier every moment—is the very worst of misfortune." There was a great deal of grumbling among the troops that night, especially among the men of the 72nd Indiana. They hadn't been too happy when Colonel Wilder had replaced their own Col. Miller as brigade commander and they were blaming Wilder for all their discomfort.

During the night the temperature dropped radically and next morning the men found themselves frozen to the ground. Although getting a late start they reached the Big Barren River by two o'clock in the afternoon only to find that the bridge had been burned by Morgan and his men. It took the division three hours wading through waist deep ice cold water to cross the river; they camped on the other side. A private of the 98th Illinois recalled, "There were pieces of ice floating in the river. I stepped in a hole and went in over my head. I didn't know how to swim and my pack was so heavy that it held me down so I walked on the bottom of the river bed until I came to shallower water and my head came out so I could breathe."[3] The force moved to Glasgow on the 29th where they camped until the morning of the 31st.

Wilder's Brigade was out of rations and Col. Wilder allowed the men to forage on the 30th. They brought in an abundance of food including hogs, turkeys, chickens, corn meal, flour and a sizeable quantity of applejack that they had taken from a still. That night they built crackling fires, ate their first good meal since leaving Castillian Springs, and consumed more than enough applejack to make them forget their uncomfortable rain-soaked march to Glasgow. On the 31st, the division moved in the direction of Munfordville and went into camp at five o'clock in the evening near a place called Bear Wallow.

In the meantime General Morgan had torn up several miles

of railroad tracks within 18 miles of Louisville and was heading back toward Tennessee. On the 29th, Col. Harlan and his large brigade of five infantry regiments with artillery had located Morgan and skirmished with him but Morgan had escaped after losing only two men and a wagon.

Morgan's scouts had reported the presence of Reynold's force to the south of him so on New Year's Day he attempted to move around Reynold's right without being noticed. Union pickets spotted him, however, and Wilder's Brigade was dispatched to intercept him. It moved out at the double-quick but Wilder's infantrymen, sloshing through the mud, were no match for Morgan's well-mounted troopers. Then in a vain attempt to overtake the Confederates Colonel Wilder mounted a detachment of the 17th Indiana on some of the wagon train mules. This decision proved to be disastrous. The mules bucked, jumped on each other's backs and tried to run under each other's bellies in order to dispose of their riders. Sgt. McGee of the 72nd Indiana described it, "It was worse than a battery of grape and canister and the mule line had to be abandoned, upon which they untangled, shook their tails and were soon at their respective wagons eating hay as solemnly as hypocrites."[4]

The attempt to catch Morgan was a complete failure. Morgan returned to his base, having taken 1877 prisoners and destroying over $2,000,000 worth of Union property. Next day the Federal force gave up the chase and were loaded into railroad cars at Cave City and transported to Nashville where they arrived after dark on the 3rd. On debarking they heard the news of the Union's "glorious victory" at Stone's River. Actually this battle had been fought on near even terms but the Confederate Army had withdrawn several miles to Tullahoma and the Union forces occupied Murfreesboro.

On Monday, January 5, the division left Nashville and marched to Murfreesboro as escort for a supply train of almost a thousand wagons containing rations and ammunition for Rosecrans' army.

During the four day trip from Bear Wallow to Murfreesboro Col. Wilder did a lot of thinking about the way Morgan had eluded him at Bear Wallow on New Year's Day. The colonel wasn't the kind of man to take a beating lying down; he was always quick to figure a way to improve on a bad situation. For example, he had noticed that his men were not efficient in camp duties when on bivouac; he also realized that the bayonet was a useless weapon except in the hands of highly trained regulars. He had solved both of these problems with a single solution—he had issued each man in his brigade a hatchet with a two-foot long handle, the possession of which had earned them the nickname of "The Hatchet Brigade."

From Bear Wallow to Cave City to Gallatin, Nashville and Murfreesboro Col. Wilder wrestled with the problem of how to catch a well-mounted cavalry force such as Morgan's and how to defeat him after he was caught. By the time he reported to Gen. Rosecrans in Murfreesboro he had come up with a solution. He would mount his infantry to make them mobile, and in order to maximize their combat capability he would fight them on foot with the best weapon available.

2

"I Can Whip the Scoundrel"

COL. WILDER IMMEDIATELY REQUESTED AUTHORITY FROM ARMY Commander Gen. Rosecrans to mount his Brigade. His request met with eager approval. Rosecrans had suffered an enormous loss of wagon trains in the hands of Bragg's Cavalry during the battle at Murfreesboro in spite of the fact that Morgan had been away at the time.

"Old Rosy," as Rosecrans' men like to call him, knew logistics. Thus far in the war he had demonstrated a remarkable ability for anlyzing problems, planning their solution and guiding the execution of these plans with efficiency and thoroughness. He now realized that with his supply line growing longer and Bragg's diminishing in length, his cavalry deficiency was causing his logistic problem to become even more acute.

On January 14, Rosecrans wrote to Gen. Halleck, General-in-Chief of the Army, in Washington:

"I must have cavalry or mounted infantry. I could mount infantry had I horses and saddles . . . with mounted infantry I can drive the rebel cavalry to the wall and keep the roads open in my rear. Not so now . . . Will you authorize the purchase of saddles and horses for mounting, when requisite, 5,000 or more infantry?"[1]

In early February Rosecrans gave Col. Wilder permission to mount his brigade. For the remainder of the spring Rosecrans' requests to Washington continued, but as late as May 10, his command listed only one brigade of 2,000 mounted infantry— Wilder's.[2]

When Col. Wilder received word that he could mount his men he didn't wait for requisitions to clear War Department red tape for the issuance of government horses. He moved his

25

Brigade through Dekalb and Wilson Counties, Tennessee, in the Cumberland Valley and "persuaded" the Confederate sympathizers of the area to part with their horses. By the middle of March the entire Brigade was mounted.

These newly mounted infantrymen were then issued cavalry uniforms. The Army Uniform Regulation of 1861 called for the stripes and piping on cavalry uniforms to be yellow, but Wilder's men did not want to be confused with the regular cavalrymen who thus far in the war had a reputation for always being someplace else when a battle was to be fought. They were a new branch of the service—mounted infantry—and they were proud of it. They immediately removed the yellow trim from their uniforms.[3] The mounting of the Brigade also necessitated a change in drill and bivouac procedures and, in spite of their dislike for regular cavalry at this particular time, they were required to take on several new duties not needed by infantry. Care of the horses was very important—feeding currying, watering. Proper maintenance of saddles, bridles and other horse equipment was necessary and since horses were not as maneuverable as men, proper march procedures had to be learned. Additional personal equipment was issued—picket ropes, horseshoes and nails, halters, nose buckets, curry combs, etc.

February and March of 1863 were spent, with the exception of forays for food and horses, in drilling and carrying on the daily chores of camplife. However, routine duties far from home, especially when the weather was disagreeable, were conducive to a high desertion rate. The Army of the Cumberland had its share of deserter troubles, but by the 1st of March General Rosecrans had initiated a stern "crackdown" policy. One Sunday in March Col. Wilder, who was himself a firm disciplinarian, made an example of one of his men who had deserted and been brought back into camp by a scouting party. Wilder had the man's head shaved, and the letter "D" branded on his right cheek with a red-hot iron; he was then marched out of town past the whole division to the tune of the "Rogues March."[4]

The desertion rate in the Civil War was relatively high, especially during the first two years. A variety of reasons accounted for this—low pay ($13 per month for a private) combined with hardship at home, strong Copperhead feelings of relatives, close proximity of the home in many cases, homesickness, and a general inability to orient themselves to the routine of military life. Leadership, then as now, played an important part in the morale of the troops. Good leadership, especially at the regimental and brigade levels, provided an atmosphere of competence and contentment, thereby reducing the desertion rate. Col. Wilder was a strong leader as evidenced by a comparison between one of his units and another from the same area. Company I, 98th Illinois, Wilder's Brigade, from Jasper County, Illinois, did not have a single deserter during the entire war. However, the rolls of Co. D. 97th Illinois Infantry, consisting mostly of men from the same county, show 18 deserters—almost 20 percent.[5]

Gen. Rosecrans was strict but fair. He administered stern punishment to deserters yet he instituted a liberal furlough system for deserving soldiers during the spring of '63. During this build-up period he set up a rigid drill schedule. He was familiar with the age-old military axiom that busy soldiers are happy soldiers and he kept them busy with exercises and parades. But all this time he was building up his supplies, preparing for the campaign that would begin the minute that he decided his troops were ready and properly supplied.

Secretary of War Stanton and General-in-Chief Halleck in Washington kept the telegraph wires hot, inquiring of Rosecrans as to when he would launch his offensive. The political situation was causing Stanton and Halleck to push for reckless military decisions. But Rosecrans would not be pushed. He knew that the Army of the Cumberland was not ready. He was short of mounted troops. He did not have a sufficient store of rations and ammunition. Rosecrans was in a better position to know the capabilities of his army than were the Army brass in Washington, and because he would not be pushed into an unsound military decision, he soon lost favor with his superiors.

In the meantime, Wilder's Brigade was kept busy. They were out most of the time skirmishing with the enemy cavalry detachments that constantly harrassed Rosecrans' pickets. Because of the cavalry shortage in the Army of the Cumberland Wilder's mounted infantrymen were constantly on the move. While the foot soldiers were being rotated home on furlough the mounted men were worked to the point of continual exhaustion. Some of them suffered from mild cases of homesickness. Even Col. Wilder himself showed signs of it in a letter home to his wife on March 11:

"Not getting any letters from you I conclude to write again

... Our division took a trip to Woodbury, 20 miles east of here last week and routed Morgan's gang. The 17th took a Lieutenant and 18 prisoners, and had one man wounded. . . . I wish you to write me what you think of coming down here to stay awhile. The probability is that our division will remain here some time and I have a first rate house for my headquarters. You could come here, I think, and have a pleasant time for a month or so. Capt. Lilly who commands the battery of my Brigade has his wife and child here and she would be company for you. . . . You do not know how much I wish to see you or I know you would come."[6]

An incident soon occurred, however, that did away with any inclinations Wilder's men may have had toward boredom or homesickness. The Union Army at Murfreesboro had a visitor —Christopher Spencer of Boston, Massachusetts.

At the outbreak of the Civil War most of the shoulder weapons in existence were smooth-bore muzzle loading muskets. Rifled muskets were just coming into use. As the war progressed most new muskets were rifled and some smooth-bores were re-bored to provide rifling. The Minie ball became the most popular projectile. But whether smooth-bore or rifled, the average soldier at best could fire only two rounds per minute from a muzzle loader.

In 1860 Christopher Spencer had patented a repeating rifle. It was a lever action weapon firing a copper-cased cartridge more than a half-inch in diameter. It had a tubular magazine that inserted in the butt of the stock and held seven rounds of ammunition. Christopher Spencer managed to get enough investors interested in this revolutionary new rifle by late 1861 and formed a production corporation. Although he was not able to jar the Army from its antiquated marriage to the muzzle-loading single shot musket, he did finally persuade the Union Navy into ordering 600 of them. These were delivered in December of 1862. Now caught up on production Spencer set out on a sales campaign. He decided that if he couldn't get Chief of Army Ordnance Ripley interested in this new weapon he would try to sell the army commanders in the field in hopes that they would exert enough pressure on Washington that the Army would come through with an order. The middle of March found Christopher Spencer in Murfreesboro, Tennessee, demonstrating his amazing new repeating rifle to the Army of the Cumberland. Naturally they were impressed. Who wouldn't be with a rifle that would fire seven times as fast as the standard army muzzle-loader? But being impressed wouldn't buy weapons. They knew that Army Ordnance wouldn't supply them.

However, this new, accurate repeating rifle was exactly what Col. Wilder wanted for his men. He had sworn to himself two months before that he would mount his Brigade and arm them with the best weapon available. And here it was. He called his men together and asked them if they wanted to carry this sensational new rifle. Of course he got a unanimous "yes." Wilder then did an unheard of thing for an Army officer. He wrote to his bankers in his home town of Greensburg, Indiana and asked if they would loan him money to buy enough Spencer Repeating Rifles to arm his Brigade. They agreed. Each man in the Brigade offered to pay for his own rifle, so they each signed a note for $35. Wilder co-signed them and sent them to the bank in return for the necessary funds. The new guns were ordered and Col. Wilder and his men went back to their scouting and foraging duties with a renewed enthusiasm.[7]

On April 1, the Brigade moved out on eight days' scout. Half of the Brigade moved to Rome, Lebanon and Snows Hill, while the 17th, 72nd and the 2nd Section of the artillery battery went to Rome and Lebanon, then turned off on the Landcastle Road and camped in a valley the night of April 6. No Rebels had been encountered so far on this expedition and on this pleasant spring evening the soldiers' thoughts were on things other than enemy patrols. Henry Campbell, Bugler of Lilly's Battery, not yet eighteen years of age, related in his diary about a scouting expedition of his own that night that supplied his buddies with laughs for days to come:

"In the evening I went over to a respectable looking house about a half mile from camp—thinking I would run my face for a supper. Found quite a good looking girl, dressed in "home spun" superintending the baking of a 'hoe cake,' whose delicious fragrance filled every crack and corner of your nose and caused your mouth to water sufficiently to start a small Niagra. Wishing to make myself as agreeable and entertaining as possible, I turned the conversation to herself, remarking that I had traveled over a great deal of the South but had failed to see a good looking girl until now. 'Pshaw, says she, Yer pokin' fun at me.' I assured her I was in sober earnest and told her that she was, emphatically, the prettiest girl in the State of Tennessee. 'La! says she, you just oughter seen me afore I had the di-a-ree.'

A huge laugh outside the open door advised me that other ears had been listening to the conversation and I immediately vamoosed."[8]

The next day with the Brigade back together the advance guard came upon a detachment of Rebel cavalry. The Brigade advanced at a gallop and continued for about a mile whereupon the enemy formed a line of battle on Snow's Hill. Capt. Lilly set up his artillery battery near a graveyard trained on the road leading up the hill. The 72nd Ind. and 98th Ill. took positions supporting the battery and the 17th Ind. attempted to move around the hill and cut off their retreat; however, the enemy pulled back to Smithville before the 17th could get around, losing only their rear guard of two companies with officers.

Soon after returning to camp at Murfreesboro, Col. Wilder wrote his wife:

". . . just got back from an eight day's trip, with 88 prisoners, 460 horses, 8 wagons, 4,000 bushels of corn, 86 tons hay, and 194 Negroes taken from the rebels—destroyed over 10,000 bushels of wheat and several tons of bacon. Captured $15,000 worth of tobacco. Whipped Wharton's Brigade of Rebel cavalry, all with the loss of two stragglers captured and one man killed by accident. This is the most successful trip that has been made from here—you will see the details of it in the papers. Now do write me if you can't come to see me. I start in the morning to Franklin to unite in an attack on Van Dorn (Rebel cavalry leader). . ."[9]

On April 13, the brigade moved to Lavergne and Franklin but the campaign on Van Dorn did not materialize and they returned to camp the next day.

Wilder's brigade had become the workhorse of the Army of the Cumberland. Most of the cavalry was used up as scouting parties and pickets. Cavalry could not be sent out on long-range raids because, being armed mostly with pistols and sabers, they could not successfully attack an enemy force of any size if they were challenged. Wilder's men, mounted and armed with rifles, were the only unit in the Army of the Cumberland that could be depended upon to operate away from infantry support and be able to attack or defend themselves on an equal basis with their adversaries. Occasionally they were accompanied on their expeditions by another brigade of Reynolds' division, Hall's infantry brigade, and once in a while by a cavalry detachment; but most of the time they operated as an autogenic unit.

One of the few combined expeditions began on April 20 involving Wilder's Brigade, Hall's Infantry Brigade and Col. Eli Long's Brigade of cavalry. The force moved out at 8 A.M., Capt. Lilly of Wilder's Artillery Battery proudly displaying for the first time his newly acquired "Jackass Battery." These were mountain howitzers that he had brought from Nashville to go with his six Rodman guns; they were made especially to fire high trajectories in mountainous country. After camping the first night at Readyville, the division moved to McMinnville. Arriving at 5 P.M. the 17th Ind. captured the picket post and with the 4th U. S. Regular Cavalry Regiment made a charge through the town. Morgan's force, stationed there, scattered in every direction. Hall's infantry brigade was posted in town while Long's cavalrymen captured a train containing a number of Federal prisoners and Wilder's men burned a cotton factory, a railroad bridge and the depot and railroad shops. While the main body of the Union force traveled back to Murfreesboro, the 98th Illinois and Lilly's "Jackass Battery" made a side trip to Lebanon where they burned the home of a Confederate officer accused of stimulating some of the guerilla activities in the area.[10]

The remainder of April and the month of May were spent foraging, raiding and capturing anything of value from the Confederate Armies and the prominent Rebel sympathizers in the middle Tennessee area.

Foraging was a necessary practice for survival of mounted troops. Many of their scouting patrols and raids lasted for several days. They could not carry a large enough supply of food in their haversacks to sustain them for a long period of time and they dared not take their wagons on these dashing raids because of their slowness. Ration issues for scouting and raiding expeditions usually consisted of hardtack, coffee and bacon. Many a time the members of Wilder's Brigade traveled for 8 or 10 days on 3-days' rations. They were expected to supplement their issue from the gardens of the Rebel countryside. Hogs and chickens were favorite forage items. Cattle were taken only when they could be slaughtered and eaten immediately as they didn't lend themselves to salt preservation as well as pork. Sweet potatoes were abundant in the south, and although the northerners soon tired of them, they were plentiful and many a southerner lost his potato patch.

Worn-out horses were also replaced at the expense of southern civilians. Grain, hay and fodder were often procured locally

when in camp and as needed when traveling. Some of the southern populace contrived some ingenious methods for hiding their
possessions and often, on the approach of a detail of Union
soldiers, they would attempt to make a deal in order to save
their most prized possessions. On one occasion, probably a
typical one, a private of the 98th Illinois took a horse from a
Rebel farm. As he was leading the horse from the barn the lady
of the house came out and offered two of her choicest cured
hams if he would only leave the horse. His own mount still
being in good condition, he took the hams and left the horse
much to the joy of his mess-mates.[11]

Most foraging parties were organized and under the leadership of an officer. Unauthorized and individual foraging was
frowned upon, not so much from a moral standpoint, but rather
because of the danger of guerrillas, Rebel civilians or Confederate deserters organized into gangs who preyed on small
groups of Union soldiers.

One of the original members of Wilder's Brigade, the 75th
Ind., for some strange reason, had not wished to be mounted and
the 123rd Illinois of Hall's Brigade had requested to be assigned
in its place. On May 6, the 123rd officially became a part of the
mounted brigade and when Col. Monroe of that regiment reported to Col. Wilder he immediately received movement orders.
He was sent with the mounted men of his regiment and 150
men from the 98th as a reconnoitering force to seek out the
enemy and at the same time search for horses with which to
mount the remainder of Monroe's regiment. In the afternoon
a detachment of 50 men of the 123rd became separated from
the rest of the force and were attacked by a hundred Rebel
cavalrymen. Fortunately, however, the men of the 98th happened along and drove away the enemy, killing one and wounding two.

Col. Wilder told about the McMinnville expedition in a letter
home on May 4:

"Your welcome letter reached me yesterday. I was very glad
to hear from home. . . . I am at last doing something towards
putting down this infamous rebellion. All that Gen. Reynolds
got the credit for doing in the McMinnville expedition was done
by me. He was not within 10 miles of there or of any enemy on
the trip. My command took every prisoner (over 200) and destroyed all the Rebel property that was destroyed. We are doing

more real work than the entire army besides. We were gone 11 days and marched over 50 miles a day the entire time. Gen. Rosecrans says we beat anything he has known of. We captured 678 mules and horses on the trip."[12]

Saddle talk in the Brigade covered many subjects but as the men returned from missions during April and May the talk always turned to speculation of when the "seven shooters" would arrive. Finally on the 15th of May all their pent-up anxiety of waiting exploded in cries of joy. The Spencer repeating rifles that they had bought with their own money arrived. As soon as each man had drawn his weapon and ammunition, they scattered like schoolboys to the woods to try out their "seven shooters" on rabbits, squirrels, turkeys and almost anything else that moved. The Spencer was a rugged, simple-to-operate weapon, and in a very few days the men of Wilder's Brigade had them completely mastered. They anxiously awaited a chance to try them out in the face of the enemy. In a couple of weeks they got their chance.

On June 4, Wilder's Brigade, proudly carrying their new Spencer repeating rifles, moved out toward Liberty, 30 miles to the northeast. At six in the evening the advance guard surprised two regiments of Wharton's Rebel cavalry cooking their supper at Liberty; they chased them out of town and captured 20 men of the 1st Kentucky Cavalry.

So the 1st Kentucky had the dubious honor of being the first military unit in the history of warfare to meet a force armed with repeating rifles. This dubious honor could not have been bestowed on a more deserving outfit. The 1st Kentucky was a good, well-trained, veteran regiment and had been originally organized by President Abraham Lincoln's brother-in-law, General Ben Hardin Helm. After his graduation from West Point, Helm had served under Robert E. Lee in the 2nd Cavalry in Texas. After leaving the service due to ill health, Helm became a lawyer and in 1856 married Miss Emilie Todd, a half-sister of Mary Todd Lincoln. Upon the outbreak of the war, Lincoln offered Helm the rank of major in the Union Army with the post of Paymaster General. Although remaining fast friends, Helm declined Lincoln's offer; he recruited the 1st Kentucky Confederate Cavalry and cast his lot with the South. After being in the thick of most of the fighting in the west he was promoted to brigadier general and given command of Kentucky's famous "Orphan Brigade" of infantry. It was while leading this command in September of 1863 that he was killed at the Battle of Chickamauga.[13]

About dark that same evening, the 3rd, 4th, and 10th Ohio Cavalry joined Wilder's Brigade and encamped with them at Liberty. Harrison's Brigade of Wharton's Confederate Cavalry, consisting of the 1st Kentucky, 8th Texas, 11th Texas, and the 3rd Conf. Regular Cavalry regiments camped a short distance away outside of town.

The following morning, after a brief skirmish, the Rebels fled to the tune of the "seven shooters," leaving much of their equipment behind. It was during this skirmish that Major Connelly of the 123rd Illinois, in referring to his regimental commander, Col. Monroe, made the following observation of the challenge of leadership:

"Now the regiment becomes a machine, and now comes the hour of trial for its commander—he must ascertain where the enemy is the best way he can—he must see and think for the whole regiment. Must direct every movement, and watch every movement of the enemy—he is responsible for the safety and honor of the regiment, and if he makes a mistake disgrace stares him in the face. He must be cool when all others are excited. Must stand when all others are disposed to run."[14]

The incident at Liberty was the first sizeable test of the Spencer rifle against the enemy, but it was only a skirmish. Three weeks later, on June 24, the world's first officially recorded battle in which repeating rifles were used would be fought. It would open Rosecrans' Tullahoma Campaign with a noise that would eventually jar the old-fashioned ordnance people in Washington off of their muzzle-loading seats.

The 23rd of June, 1963, found the opposing forces of Union General Rosecrans and Confederate General Bragg in the following positions: Rosecrans' Army of the Cumberland was at Murfreesboro; Bragg's headquarters was at Tullahoma, thirty-five miles to the south toward Chattanooga; halfway between the two Bragg had his Confederate Army placed east and west; Hardee's Corps was at Fairfield halfway between Murfreesboro and Tullahoma behind a range of mountainous hills; a few miles west of Hardee at Shelbyville was Gen. Leonidas Polk's Corps; the extreme east flank was covered by Wheeler's Cavalry near McMinnville.

Rosecrans' strategy was to send Granger's and McCook's

Corps and Stanley's Cavalry toward Polk's Corps at Shelbyville as a feint and then move around Hardee's right flank with Thomas' and Crittenden's Corps to Manchester. Thomas' 14th Corps was the main Union force and was to move through the ridge of mountains a few short miles northeast of Fairfield.[15]

For five long months the brass in Washington had been pushing Rosecrans to move on the enemy and now he was finally ready.

On the evening of the 23rd the word was put out to the men of Wilder's Brigade to make ready to break camp and move out in the morning. Lilly's bugler, Henry Campbell, recorded in his diary:

"Have just finished clearing up and completing one of the most cheerful and comfortable camps we ever established. Our horses and quarters are always in the shade and the sun can't penetrate through the thick foliage that overhangs our camp. Boys have fixed up their 'dog tent' homes in the highest style of art that a soldier can invent with the very few materials he has to work upon. We made bunks that out done the sailors hammock. They were formed by driving forks into the ground the size of your bunk—then running two poles through coffee sacks and resting the ends in the forks. J. Binford and I, who tented together, made a double bed of this description by running a pole up through the middle. It worked very well except when one got out of bed before the other did, it had the disagreeable habit of letting you down on the ground, or if you rolled about any in the night, it stirred the other side of the house up like a wagon on a corduroy road."[16]

Early the next morning the Tullahoma Campaign began.

3

"Glory Hallelujah"

BRAGG HAD REMAINED AT TULLAHOMA UNMOLESTED FOR AL-
most six months, ever since he had withdrawn there after the
Battle of Stone's River. During that time his corps commanders,
Polk and Hardee, had built strong fortifications at both Shelbyville and Tullahoma. What fighting that had been done during
this period of time had been done by the Confederate cavalry
under the leadership of Forrest, Wheeler and Morgan.

It had been this constant raiding and skirmishing by Bragg's
superior cavalry force that caused Rosecrans to continually request more mounted troops from Washington. But as the day
arrived for Rosecrans to launch his offensive against Tullahoma
he remained at a disadvantage in this department. Although he
outnumbered Bragg by 10,000 infantrymen the Confederate
cavalry had him outmanned by more than 7,000; and at this
stage of the war the Rebel cavalry in the west was the toughest,
most effective, and most ably led body of troops on either side.

As Rosecrans prepared to begin his advance early in the morning of June 24, two other offensives were in progress in other
theatres of operations. Grant had Vicksburg under seige on the
Mississippi River and Confederate General Robert E. Lee, after
having lost the beloved Gen. Stonewall Jackson at Chancellorsville, was moving north toward Gettysburg, Pennsylvania.

At 4 A.M. Wilder's Brigade moved out as the advance of
Thomas' XIV Corps. When Wilder was six miles out of Murfreesboro, the remainder of Reynold's Division started, followed at 7 A.M. by Rousseau's Division and at 10 A.M. by Negley's Division.[1]

A slow drizzling rain soon began and the beating of hooves
and the weight of wagon wheels turned the road into a quag-

mire. With all the discomfort of the march, however, Wilder's men eagerly moved toward what they knew would be a major encounter with the enemy. They had the usual reservations that soldiers have when going into battle, but they had their new Spencer repeating rifles; they had practiced and skirmished with them for over a month. The possession of this new weapon, and knowing what it could do, gave them more than the usual amount of self-confidence.

At 10 o'clock Col. Wilder and his Brigade reached the entrance of Hoover's Gap, by this time being almost nine miles ahead of the remainder of their division. Hoover's is a gap in a range of hills 11 miles south of Murfreesboro dividing the waters of the Duck River and the head waters of the Stone River, through which runs the Manchester Pike.

On duty in the gap was the 1st Kentucky Cavalry, the same regiment that had unsuccessfully skirmished with Wilder three weeks before at Liberty. Wilder's sudden and unexpected advance took the Rebel pickets completely by surprise, driving them back rapidly in disorder.

The main body of the 1st Kentucky was immediately dispatched to meet the attack, but Col. Wilder and his brigade came on in such strength that the Rebels were forced to retreat through the gap. Major Chenoweth of the 1st Kentucky called for a dozen volunteers to act as a rear guard to cover the withdrawal toward the main Confederate camp at Fairfield. These men put up a valiant fight through the seven-mile length of the gap, and when they reached their defensive positions at the south end of the gap only three of them were still in their saddles.[2]

By this time Stewart's Division of Hardee's Corps, stationed near Fairfield, had been alerted and was approaching the south end of the gap, Bate's Brigade in advance, to reinforce the 1st Kentucky. Stewart's Division of infantry was composed of the following brigades:

BATE'S BRIGADE

37th Georgia
4th Batt. Ga. Sharpshooters
58th Alabama
15th Tennessee
20th Tennessee
37th Tennessee
Eufala Alabama Artillery

BUSHROD JOHNSON'S BRIGADE

17th Tennessee
23rd Tennessee
25th Tennessee
44th Tennessee
Everett's Georgia Battery[3]

BATTLE OF HOOVER'S GAP
JUNE 24, 1863

N

HOOVER'S GAP

WILDER

ILL. 98TH

IND. 17TH

ILL. 123RD

IND. 72ND

ILL. 98TH 2CO.

LILLY BATT.

RIVER

DUCK

JACOB'S STORE

G.A. 37TH

TENN. 20TH

ALA. 58TH

TENN. 37TH

IND. 72ND Co. E

BATTERY ALA.

TENN. 15TH

FORK

OF

BATE

GARRISON

MANCHESTER PIKE

One of Major Chenoweth's men wrote afterwards: "One of the twelve men who volunteered for the hazardous duty of covering the 1st Kentucky Cavalry's retreat through Hoover's Gap, Sgt. Cicero Harris, was shot by my side and I did not know it for a half hour or more afterwards. His foot was torn to pieces; yet he made no sign, uttered no complaint, but fought on like the splendid soldier he was till his white death-like face attracted attention and in response to inquiries he told of his wound and his agony. When we got out Major Chenoweth reported to the general and asked the honor of commanding the advance on the enemy, proposing to make it with the three of us who were still unhurt. Of course, his request was denied; and we rejoined our regiment and heard the infantry, as they marched by us in the rain toward the front, 'going,' as they said, 'on a wild goose chase,' curse the cavalry for raising a 'false alarm,' as they called it. Poor dear boys! It was not many minutes before they found what a real alarm it was, and many of them never answered a roll call again. The fight was a sharp one, lasting all the remainder of the day. . . ."[4]

In the meantime Wilder had taken possession of the hills at the south end of the gap, the very position that the Confederates had planned to use for their defense. Wilder's attack had been so rapid, however, that he had run the Rebels two miles past it, Co. E of the 72nd Indiana, in fact, getting so far out that it was cut off from the Brigade by the skirmishers of the 15th and 37th Tennessee Regiments which were moving on Bate's right.

The long roll of the Rebel drummers from the direction of Fairfield, signalling the movement of Stewart's Division, had been heard by the Union troops. Colonel Wilder placed his Brigade in battle positions at the south end of Hoover's Gap.

The 72nd Indiana was stationed to the right of the gap and thrown forward on a hill near a graveyard. Captain Lilly placed two howitzers immediately in front of them. Lilly was ordered to position four of his 10-pound rifled Rodman guns on a secondary hill on the right of the gap facing toward Fairfield, from where the Rebels were approaching. The 123rd Illinois was dispersed in a hollow on either side of Lilly's Battery in support. Two companies of the 98th Illinois took station on a hill on the left side of the gap and four companies of the 17th Indiana were placed a quarter of a mile to the right on a high wooded hill. The remainder of the 98th Illinois and the 17th Indiana were placed in reserve between and slightly behind the 123rd and the 17th.

Wilder's men were already tired and muddy. The artillery horses had given out in the rush through the gap and the men of the brigade had helped pull the battery for a mile through the mud, but these men were anxious to try their "seven shooters" in a real battle and they eagerly awaited the Confederate advance.

General Bate positioned the 15th and 37th Tennessee to hold his right and the 58th Alabama to anchor his left, the Georgia Sharpshooters placed in support of the artillery.

In less than half an hour Wilder's men heard their pickets, stationed in the edge of a woods in front, begin firing briskly, and soon afterwards General Bate's attacking force, the 20th Tennessee and 37th Georgia, screaming their Rebel yell, emerged from the woods.

The mountain howitzers were the first to open up on them, followed by the Rodman guns. The Rodman's had fired only one round when a shell from one of the five Rebel artillery positions came whizzing over their heads and killed the chaplain of the 72nd Indiana, Captain Eddy. Lilly's battery replied with a continuous fire from his 10 pounders. After firing 10 rounds a shell became wedged in his No. 1 gun and it was sent to the rear. Captain Lilly ordered up his third section and just as it got into the line the Rebel infantry, flags flying, came charging across the field in an attempt to take the battery.

Lt. Scott's 1st section gave them a volley of long range canister, but on they came. The Rebels moved up in splendid style, not realizing that they were charging into 1,500 repeating rifles, each capable of firing 14 rounds per minute.

The advancing Southerners moved up the hill, loading and firing their smooth-bore muzzle loaders. The 123rd Illinois rose up from the hollow on either side of the artillery battery and opened a murderous fire on the charging Rebels. The lead regiment reeled, its colors falling to the ground, but in a second the colors were picked up and they moved ahead. Wilder's men were working the levers of their repeaters like pump handles and the Rebels were finally overwhelmed by the continuous sheet of flame from the Spencers and they were forced to fall back.

A brisk artillery duel then ensued and shortly thereafter Lilly's battery sustained its first casualty—Bicken, a driver from the third section, was mortally wounded by a musket ball, fired by a Georgia Sharpshooter.

The Confederates then concentrated their attack on the 17th Indiana on the right end of the line. Bate consolidated his attacking force, and an entire brigade—four regiments deep, led by the 20th Tennessee—charged the lone Indiana regiment on a small wooded hill. The 17th held its fire until the Rebels reached the bottom of the hill and then poured out a continuous volley from their "seven-shooters." Bate's valiant Tennesseeans staggered but filled up their ranks from their reserves and on they came again. The fire from the Spencers was terrifying but those brave men from the South charged to within 50 feet of the 17th before they were forced back to the bottom of the hill. Again the Rebels reformed and again they charged the 17th Indiana, this time assaulting its right flank, led by Col. Rudler and his 37th Georgia. Some of the Indiana men had used up all their ammunition and the 17th began to give ground.

Col. Wilder, seeing the trouble, ordered the 98th Illinois up to support the 17th. The 98th met the Rebels almost to the crest of the hill with a withering storm of lead that halted the Confederate advance and then, without even slowing, led the 17th in a charge that completely doubled up Bate's entire brigade, and the Rebels withdrew in wild confusion.

Although routed by only the 17th Indiana and eight companies of the 98th Illinois, General Bate, in describing this phase of the battle said, "a bloody engagement here ensued with great odds against us, and after a futile but most persistent and gallant effort to dislodge him, Colonel Rudler properly withdrew his command under cover of the bank . . . the enemy turned our already extended left flank, giving an enfilading fire to the Twentieth Tennessee."[5]

The 72nd Indiana's Company E, cut off when it overran its position, returned to the battle line during this phase of the encounter. While being fired at by Rebel skirmishers that were between them and the rest of the brigade the men of Company E discovered three small children—two girls and a smaller boy—trying to find their way out of the woods amid the shower of bullets. Sgt. Wilhite dismounted, helped them over a fence, put the little boy between the girls and headed them toward a house that was out of range of the firing. The company then went about the business of fighting its way back to the brigade.[6]

Gen. Bate reorganized his brigade, brought up his reserves, and he and Bushrod Johnson, who had arrived with his brigade, made preparations for a new attack on Wilder's positions.

In the meantime, Captain Rice, Gen. Reynolds' Adjutant, rode up with orders from Reynolds to withdraw immediately. Wilder's messenger had accurately reported that the brigade was faced by Stewart's entire division and the advance of Thomas' Corps was still six miles to the rear. Col. Wilder, after telling Rice that he could hold this position against any force, refused to comply with the order and stated that he would take the responsibility for the consequences. Capt. Rice threatened to place Wilder under arrest if he did not obey. Wilder declined the order of arrest and Captain Rice returned to the division just as Bates and Johnson launched their next attack.

This last attack of the day was easily repulsed and a short time later Generals Rosecrans, Thomas, and Reynolds rode up. Wilder immediately explained to Rosecrans why he had refused General Reynolds order, and after surveying the situation, Rosecrans turned to Reynolds and said, "Wilder has done right. Promote him. Promote him."[7]

At 7 P.M. the 21st Indiana Battery arrived to support the weary men of Lilly's Battery and a half hour later the infantry, doing their best to hurry through the ankle-deep mud, came up and took positions along side Wilder's riflemen. At dark Rousseau's and Negley's divisions arrived and Wilder's Brigade, having fought a vastly superior force for eight hours, pulled back to rest.

A short time later General Thomas grasped Wilder by the hand and said, "You have saved the lives of a thousand men by your gallant conduct today. I didn't expect to get the gap for three days."[8]

Col. Wilder's mounted infantry and their Spencer Rifles had won the day, and these men had acquired a special feeling for their new weapons. During one of the Rebel charges a corporal of the 17th Indiana was shot through the breast; he had always said that the enemy would never get hold of his Spencer Rifle. Being severely wounded he didn't have the strength to destroy it, so he took out his knife, removed the lock plate and threw it away, rendering the gun useless. He then fell back and died.[9]

A private of the 98th Illinois remembered thinking, as he fired his rapid-fire repeater while driving the Rebels off a hill, that the "poor devils didn't have a chance."[10]

If there had been any doubts among the leaders of the Union Army about the effectiveness of the Spencer Repeating Rifle before this day, they had now been gloriously and resoundingly dispelled. Wilder's men had moved upon the enemy so swiftly and delivered such a terrific fire with their "seven shooters" that General Thomas himself directed that from then on they would be known as the "Lightning Brigade."[11]

In the Battle of Hoover's Gap, against a numerically superior force, Wilder lost only 51 men killed and wounded while the ground was strewn with over 200 Confederate casualties. General Bates commented later that judging from the fire power of the Union force, he thought he was outnumbered five to one.[12]

It might very well be that this performance of the repeating rifle at Hoover's Gap, Tennessee, started the expression that traveled around the Rebel army for the rest of the war: that the "Yankees could load on Sunday and shoot all the rest of the week."

The steady rain continued on all through the night while the Union infantry moved up and strengthened their positions. The next day, June 25, the firing consisted only of skirmishing between the infantry and an occasional exchange of artillery fire.

Thomas' Corps, on the 26th, was ordered to advance toward Manchester, with Reynolds' Division in the lead and Wilder's "Lightning Brigade" in advance of the division. The Confederate commands of Hardee, Polk, Forrest and Wheeler, in order to prevent from being outflanked and surrounded, withdrew toward Tullahoma. Gen. Rosecrans' well-executed flanking maneuver had forced Bragg's Army to abandon its defensive positions between Murfreesboro and Tullahoma; and now he set about outflanking Tullahoma itself. Bragg had expected the Union advance to move south and southwest of Murfreesboro over the wide roads that ran across the level countryside in that direction. That was the reason he had set up the elaborate works and abatis defenses near Shelbyville. But Rosecrans was too smart to plunge head on into such strong fortifications and so far his strategy was working.

The Lightning Brigade camped that night four miles from Manchester, a small town on the "Jack Oak" studded plateau called the "Barrens."

Next morning, preceding the division with the 123rd Illinois in advance, the Brigade moved into Manchester at a gallop. Within five minutes the town was occupied and completely surrounded, the 123rd taking 50 Rebels including a Confederate major. Capt. Lilly set up his artillery pieces covering the roads leading into Manchester until the remainder of Thomas' Corps and part of Crittenden's Corps arrived to relieve them. The Brigade then moved outside of town and made camp.

At 5 A.M. on the 28th the Brigade, with one section of the Jackass Battery, moved out on a raid on Decherd Station south of Tullahoma. The 123rd Illinois was detached on a separate mission to Allisonia. The main body of the Brigade, arriving at Decherd, drove the Rebels from the stockade and proceeded to destroy the railroad track. The primary objective of the raid was the destruction of the railroad bridge over the Elk River, but before Wilder and his men could reach it Col. Dibrell, one of Forrest's trusted cavalry leaders, dispatched nine regiments of cavalry and two artillery batteries, led by the 8th Tennessee Confederate cavalry, to reinforce the garrison at Decherd. Wilder, on seeing the approach of this large Rebel cavalry force and being unfamiliar with the terrain, withdrew toward Manchester.

In the meantime, the 123rd Illinois had set out to destroy the railroad bridge near Allisonia between Tullahoma and Chattanooga. After 30 miles of hard riding they came upon the road leading south from Tullahoma. To their surprise they found the road filled with Rebel wagons, infantry and artillery. General Bragg was slipping away toward Chattanooga.

The Tullahoma Campaign was, strategically, one of the most brilliant campaigns of the Civil War. In only one week General Rosecrans forced Bragg's entire Confederate Army of 46,000 men from middle Tennessee almost a hundred miles into Chattanooga, on the other side of the Tennessee River. It was also one of the least costly—manpowerwise—of any of the successful Union offensives of the war. Rosecrans' Army of the Cumberland sustained only 560 casualties, while Bragg's Rebel Army suffered 1,634, a high percentage of them inflicted by the repeaters of the "Lightning Brigade" at Hoover's Gap.

The Brigade bivouacked near Normandy on the Duck River and spent the next few days resting, foraging and celebrating the news of the Union victories at Vicksburg and Gettysburg.

On July 11, Col. Wilder filed his official report on the Battle of Hoover's Gap:

HEADQUARTERS FIRST BRIGADE, FOURTH DIVISION, FOURTEENTH
ARMY CORPS, CAMP NEAR DUCK RIVER BRIDGE, JULY 11, 1863

MAJOR: I have the honor to submit the following report of the part taken by my command in the late movements resulting in driving the Rebel forces under General Bragg south across the Tennessee River.

On the morning of June 24, 1863 at 3 o'clock a.m., my command moved from camp (six miles north of Murfreesboro), and taking the advance of the Fourteenth Army Corps on the Manchester Pike moved forward to Big Spring Branch, seven miles from Murfreesboro. Here my scouts gave notice of the proximity of Rebel pickets. The command was halted until the infantry closed up, when we immediately moved forward, the Seventy-second Indiana, Colonel Miller, being in advance, with five companies under Lieutenant-Colonel Kirkpatrick thrown out as an advance-guard and a party of twenty-five scouts of the Seventeenth and Seventy-second as an extreme advance-guard. One mile from the creek we came upon the Rebel pickets, who opened fire on the advance, which was returned by the men, driving the Rebels to a hill thickly covered with cedars, where the Rebel reserves were drawn up under cover of the hill, and opened a rapid fire upon our men, who advanced rapidly to the foot of the hill, when Colonel Kirkpatrick deployed one company on each side of the hill and without halting drove the Rebels from their position, capturing two prisoners, without loss on our part. I directed the advance to push speedily forward and take possession of Hoover's Gap, and, if possible, prevent the enemy from occupying their fortifications, which I learned were situated at a narrow point of the gap sixteen miles from Murfreesboro. The orders were handsomely executed by Colonel Kirkpatrick, who dashed forward along the pike, pushing the enemy so fast that they had not time to deploy into their works before he had possession, the Rebels breaking and scattering through the hills with a loss of their battle-flag—a beautiful stand of embroidered silk colors presented to the regiment (First Kentucky) by the sister of General Ben Hardin Helm while in Kentucky under Morgan last year—and several prisoners.

Learning that a regiment of cavalry (Third Kentucky) was stationed at the Garrison Fork of Duck River, one mile further on, and that a brigade of infantry was encamped two miles to the right, I determined to take the entire gap, and, if possible, hold it until the arrival of the infantry column (now some six miles behind us), believing that it would cost us at least a thousand men to retake the ground we now held if it was reasonably contested by the Rebel force close at hand. My whole command was rapidly moved forward to the southern extremity of the gap, and while being placed in position we heard the "long-roll" sounded in the Rebel camp at our right, two miles down the Garrison Fork. The advance pushed on two miles further and captured seven wagons belonging to the Rebels. They were soon recalled, and we were hardly in position before our pickets were driven in by a large force of Rebel infantry from the direction of Fairfield. My dispositions were: the Seventy-second Indiana, Colonel Miller, stationed to the right side of the gap and thrown forward to a hillock on which there was a graveyard; two mountain howitzers at their front on the point of the hillock; four pieces of 10-pounder Rodmans of Captain Lilly's Eighteenth Indiana Battery, stationed on a secondary hill facing towards Fairfield on the right side of the gap, supported by One Hundred and Twenty-third Illinois Colonel Monroe; the Seventeenth Inldiana, Lieutenant-Colonel Jordan, and Ninety-eighth Illinois, Colonel Funkhouser, in rear of a high hill in reserve. I ordered two companies of the Ninety-eight Illinois to take position on the hill at the left of the gap and four companies of the Seventeenth Indiana to take possession of a high wooded hill about a quarter of a mile to our right, and to throw skirmishers forward to some cleared hills to their front, both for the purpose of observation and to prevent a sudden attack from that quarter. The enemy in the meantime advanced rapidly and opened on our left from two batteries a rapid cross-fire, which killed two gunners and the animals of one of the mountain howitzers. They were promptly replied to by Captain Lilly, who dismounted one of their pieces and compelled both of their batteries to change position several times. In the meantime I observed a column of the enemy moving behind some hills toward our right, and immediately ordered the remainder of the Seventeenth Indiana to take position on the wooded hill before spoken of, with orders to look well to their right and send me word if any attempt was made to flank them. They had hardly reached the hill when a heavy and rapid fire was opened from both sides, the Rebels charging boldly up the hill and cheering loudly. Not hearing from Colonel Jordan, but seeing that he was hard pressed, I sent Colonel Funkhouser with the remainder of the Ninety-Eighth Illinois to his assistance. He reached the ground just as the Rebels had succeeded in turning Colonel Jordan's right flank. Colonel Funkhouser immediately deployed his command to the right, thus outflanking the Rebel left, and opened a rapid raking fire upon them, causing them to break in disorder down the hill. The fighting for a few moments had been desperate, most of it at a distance of not over twenty yards between combatants. In the meantime on the left two rebel regiments attempted to take our battery. Col. Monroe by my direction ordered three companies under Lieutenant-Colonel Biggs forward to a ravine about seventy-five yards in front of Captain Lilly's position. They had hardly got in position before the Rebels came over the hill in their front. They delivered a cautious and deliberate fire upon them, and Captain Lilly gave them a few rounds of double-shotted canister from his guns while Col. Miller, Seventy-second Indiana, opened an enfilading fire upon them, which caused them to first fall to the ground to escape the tornado of death-dealing missiles which were being poured into their ranks; but finding no cessation of the leaden hail they crawled back as best they could under cover of the hills and made no further attempt to take our left. They, however, made another attempt with five regiments on our right, but were easily driven back by Colonels Funkhouser and Jordan, with not over 700 men (Seventeenth and Ninety-eighth Illinois) engaged. The Rebels now fell back all along the line and opened a furious cannonading upon our battery, without doing much harm or receiving harm in return, they being under cover of the hills. General Reynolds now arrived with two brigades of infantry, and placed one of them in support of and on a prolongation of our right. About dark we were relieved by a brigade of Rousseau's division, and at 2 o'clock next morning were again in line, and were held in reserve all day. Our entire loss in the action of the 24th June is one commission officer mortally wounded (Lieutenant J. Moreland, Seventeenth Indiana;) enlisted men killed, 12; enlisted men wounded, 47.

The conduct of both officers and men was all that the most sanguine could ask. To speak of individuals when all did their whole duty would be unfair; each officer seemed to appreciate the importance of taking and holding the very strong position of "Hoover's Gap," and the men were eager to obey and sustain their officers. Their conduct was the same, whether in driving in the rebel outposts or defending their position against fearful odds, or when lying in support of our battery exposed to a terrible cross-fire of shot and shell, or when advancing against the Rebel columns —always earnest, cool, determined, ready, and brave, seeming best pleased when necessarily in greatest danger.

On the morning of the 28th we again moved forward, my command on horseback, debouching into the valley of Garrison Fork, and filing over the chain of hills between that stream and McBride's Creek, flanking the Rebel left, and causing it to hastily fall back before the infantry column of General Reynolds, who was advancing on the line of the Manchester Pike. We then moved up McBride's Creek to the table-land, and marched rapidly around the head of Noah's Fork, for the purpose of turning the strong position of "Mat's Hollow," but on arriving at the Manchester Pike, after it reaches the table-land, we found that the infantry column was passing, having met no enemy, they having retreated in the direction of Fairfield. We camped that night six miles from Manchester, and at daylight next morning moved forward, cutting off a rebel picket post, and were in Manchester before the few rebels there knew of our approach. We captured about forty prisoners, including one captain and three lieutenants. Pickets were immediately thrown out, and on the arrival of General Reynolds I dispatched Major Jones, with four companies of the Seventeenth Indiana, and Captain Kilbourne, with a detachment of pioneers, to destroy the trestle work on the McMinville Railroad, four miles from Tullahoma. Their object was fully accomplished and they returned to camp that night.

The next morning we started to get in the rear of Tullahoma to des-

troy the Rebel communications. We moved rapidly to Hillsboro, leaving
two companies of the One Hundred and Twenty-third at that place until
relieved by a brigade of infantry under General Beatty, and from thence
toward Decherd, but on arriving at Elk River found that the incessant
rains had so swollen that stream that we could neither ford nor swim
it, the current being so rapid that our horses were washed down stream.
There was a bridge at Pelham, six miles further up; we turned our course
for that place, sending Colonel Monroe, with eight companies One Hundred
and Twenty-third Illinois, down Elk River to destroy, if possible, the
road and railroad bridges over Elk River at Estell Springs, with orders,
if successful, to come down the railroad and join me at Decherd or below.
On his arrival at the railroad he found a division of infantry guarding
the bridge and a large wagon train. He immediately fell back to Hillsboro, finding it impossible to accomplish anything further, being pursued
by a force of Rebel cavalry without any loss to himself, although skirmishing with and holding them in check for several miles. The next morning
he moved forward and safely joined us on the top of Cumberland Mountain.

On leaving the direct road to Decherd and going in the direction of
Pelham, we were compelled to ford streams that swam our smallest horses,
and compelled us to carry our howitzer ammunition on the men's shoulders
across the streams. When near Pelham we learned that a party of Rebels
were at the bridge, with the intention of destroying it on our approach.
I immediately ordered the advance, under Lieut.-Col. Kitchell, Ninety-
eighth Illinois, and about thirty scouts of the different regiments, to go
forward on a run and prevent the destruction of the bridge. They dashed
forward, not only saving the bridge but taking two of the party prisoners,
and capturing a drove of seventy-eight mules, which were sent back to
Hillsboro in charge of a company. We soon reached the south fork of
Elk River, and found the water deep enough to swim our tallest horses.
The stream, though rapid, could, by crossing diagonally, be swam; and,
by tearing down an old mill, we made a raft that, by being towed with
our picket ropes, floated our two mountain howitzers over. The crossing
occupied about three hours. We immediately moved forward toward
Decherd, half fording, half swimming another stream on the way. We
reached the railroad at 8 o'clock in the evening, and immediately attacked the garrison, of about eighty men, who, protected by a stockade
and the railroad cut, made a pretty good resistance. We soon dislodged
them, however, when they took a position in a deep ravine with timber
in it, completely protecting them, while our men had to approach over
a bare hill to attack them, exposing themselves to a sharp fire at sixty yards
range. I ordered up our howitzers, and a couple of rounds of canister
silenced them and drove them out. We immediately commenced destroying
the railroad track and waterworks on the Nashville and Chattanooga
Railroad, and blowing up the trestle work on the branch to Winchester.

The railroad depot was well filled with commissary stores, which we burned; we also destroyed the telegraph instruments.

A large force was by this time approaching from the north side, and having destroyed about 300 yards of track, we left. After skirmishing with their advance-guard, and capturing some four or five prisoners, who, on being questioned separately, stated that six regiments of infantry were about to attack us, believing I would have but little chance of success in a fight with them, on account of the darkness and our total ignorance of the ground, we moved in the direction of Pelham, and after going about six miles off the road into the woods, at 2 o'clock, and bivouacked without fires until daylight, when we started again up the Cumberland Mountain, on the Brakefield Point road, determined to break the road if possible below Cowan. When partly up the mountain we could plainly see a considerable force of infantry and cavalry near Decherd. We moved forward to the Southern University, there destroying the Tracy City Railroad track. From there I sent a detachment of 450 men, under Colonel Funkhouser, of the Ninety-eighth Illinois, to destroy the railroad at Tantalon, and went forward myself in the direction of Anderson, intending to strike the railroad at that place. Colonel Funkhouser reported to me that three railroad trains lay at Tantalon loaded with troops; and my scouts reported two more trains at Anderson. Both places being only approachable by a bridle path, I deemed it impossible to accomplish anything further; besides, the picket force left at the railroad near the University were driven in by cavalry, who preceded a railroad train loaded with infantry. They were now on my track, and in our rear. I collected my force, and determined to extricate them. Leaving a rear guard to skirmish with and draw them down the mountain, I started on the road to Chattanooga. When about eight miles from the University, during a tremendous rain, which obliterated our trail, I moved the entire command from the road about two miles eastward into the woods, leaving the rear-guard to draw them forward down the mountain, which they did, and then escaped through the woods and joined us, some not coming up until next morning.

As soon as the rebel column had passed us, we struck through the mountains, without guides, in the direction of Pelham, and came out on the place we intended to strike, and reached the foot of the mountain at Bilham's Cave, over a very rocky and steep road. We bivouacked at 10 o'clock P.M., and the next morning at daylight started for Manchester, just getting ahead of Forrest, who, with nine regiments of cavalry and two pieces of artillery, aimed to intercept us at Pelham. We reached Manchester at noon, having been in the saddle or fighting about twenty hours out of each twenty-four for eleven days, and all the time drenched with rain, our men half starved, and our horses almost entirely without forage. Yet our officers and men seemed willing and cheerful, and are now only anxious for another expedition, if by such they can accomplish any good. We did not lose a single man in our expedition to the rear of Tullahoma. If our course had not been impeded by the streams, flooded beyond all precedent, we must have captured one or two railroad trains, one of them having General Buckner and staff on board. We should have had ample time to have thoroughly torn up the railroad in daylight, at several points, whilst, on account of the darkness, we were compelled to follow the main roads, and the time lost in going via Pelham enabled the rebels to throw a large force in pursuit of us.

I am, very respectfully,

> J. T. Wilder,
> Col. 17th Ind., Com'g Brigade[13]

4

"The Brass Mounted Army"

THE CONFEDERATE ARMY WAS NOW SAFELY BEHIND THE TEN-
nessee River, headquartered at Chattanooga, an important rail
and water transportation center. General Bragg was in friendly
territory in a city where he could keep his army well supplied
from the Southern arsenals in Alabama and Georgia and from
the ripening fields and gardens of the local area.

Gen. Rosecrans' Army of the Cumberland, on the other hand,
had stretched its line of supply another hundred miles. From
July 1 to August 16 it spent its time building up supplies and
replacing horses and equipment that had been expended during
the Tullahoma Campaign. Wilder's Lightning Brigade had
authority to keep itself supplied with horses off the country, thus
during this time it conducted numerous raids in the vicinities of
Wartrace and Decherd where it captured several hundred horses
and mules.

Early in July the Brigade was enlarged by the addition of the
92nd Illinois, Col. S. D. Atkins commanding. The 92nd, as a
part of Granger's Corps, had participated in the movements
against Van Dorn's Confederate Cavalry in March and April
and in the engagement at Guy's Gap during the Tullahoma
Campaign. Col. Atkins' request to get out of Granger's Corps
was granted by Gen. Rosecrans and his desire to mount his regiment and arm it with repeating rifles was fulfilled when he was
assigned to the Lightning Brigade. On July 22 a detachment of
200 men from the 92nd joined the 98th Illinois under Col. Funkhouser in an expedition to procure horses for the new regiment.
In four days they captured 1,700 head of horses and mules and
rounded up 800 colored men who were mustered into a colored
regiment. The expedition produced enough horses to mount all

51

the men of the 92nd. By this time the government had begun buying some Spencer rifles and the 92nd soon became a full-fledged member of the lightning Brigade when it received its "seven shooters."

From the 1st of July to the 28th the Brigade's base camp was in the Duck River Valley at Normandy, seven miles northwest of Tullahoma. This little valley contained an abundance of ripe apples, blackberries and garden vegetables, and forage for the horses was lush and bountiful.

The Brigade moved out July 12 on a seven-day expedition to the west. Wilder and his men passed through Shelbyville at noon and camped at Farmington the first night. Both of these towns were predominately Union and Wilder's men were greeted by cheers and the waving of Union flags. Five miles southwest of Farmington was the strong Confederate town of Lewisburg and on the morning of the 13th the Brigade dashed into the public square before the townspeople knew there was a Union force within 40 miles. They opened the stores and burned down the jail that had been used to hold arrested Union sympathizers. Next day they moved to Columbia, the home of President James K. Polk, and captured three Rebel lieutenants and 30 privates, Lt. Col. Gantt of the 9th Battalion Tennessee Cavalry escaping. Shortly after daylight on the 16th, the Brigade entered Centerville, county seat of Hickman County, where they found Col. Gantt and he surrendered after being wounded in the arm and leg. Wilder and his men were now 80 miles west of their base at Normandy and they proceeded back to camp, picking up Negroes, prisoners and horses on the way.

During the return trip, the 98th Illinois and the 72nd Indiana went on a scouting expedition to destroy the saltpeter works at Lynchburg, Tennessee. Sometime, amid the dust and smoke of razing this gunpower ingredient plant, Corporal John T. Haynes of Co. I, 72nd Indiana captured an old fighting cock which he promptly named "Methuselah." The game old bird traveled hundreds of miles thereafter as mascot of the regiment. He furnished hours of amusement for the men and fought dozens of fights, but as long as he was with them he never lost a bout.[1]

On the 28th Wilder moved his brigade headquarters to Decherd, 20 miles to the south, where it remained until the 16th of August. During this period, Gen. Rosecrans was conducting a battle of letters with Washington. General-in-Chief Halleck, President Lincoln and Secretary of War Stanton were all pushing

Rosecrans to launch his offensive against the Confederates at Chattanooga. Rosecrans was requesting more men, more horses and more time, but he and Stanton had a personal feud going and he wasn't getting much satisfaction.

General Halleck had proved himself to be an incompetent field commander but possessed a certain though often exaggerated amount of administrative ability. Secretary Stanton had been a relatively competent attorney-general under President Buchanan and, although opposed to slavery, had upheld the constitutional rights of slaveholders. Both Halleck and Stanton no doubt felt that they were contributing something of value to the cause but sitting in Washington, engulfed in the swirl of politics, telling a field commander hundreds of miles away his situation and his needs, they were very possibly stepping outside their realms of knowledge and ability.

It hadn't taken long for the exploits of Wilder's Brigade to become known throughout the army. Every infantryman in the Union Army was clamoring to be mounted and armed with a Spencer Rifle. There was a large number of men who had signed up for two-year enlistments and their time was about up. Several governors offered to re-enlist these two-year regiments if Washington would guarantee that they would fight with Rosecrans as mounted infantry and carry repeating rifles. Since Rosecrans was short of mounted troops because of the long supply line that he had to maintain and protect, this proposition interested him.

In mid-July Gen. Rosecrans sent Gen. Rousseau and Col. Sanderson of the 15th U. S. Infantry to Washington to make a deal for these two-year veterans and to procure more horses and Spencers. Their proposition met with cold opposition from Halleck and Stanton but President Lincoln was favorable. The next day Lincoln told Rousseau that Stanton wished to see him and when he arrived Stanton informed him that his entire division would be mounted on horses and would be equipped with the best repeating rifles. However, a few days later Stanton changed his mind. He announced that Rousseau's Division would be mounted on mules and the repeaters would not be delivered until January.[2]

Stanton had set himself up as a self-styled military genius and maybe he really thought that, militarily, this was not the thing to do; but more likely he had just received one of those irritating letters from Rosecrans and this announcement was made in a fit of anger. Rosecrans had thus far in the war displayed all the attributes of an excellent field commander but now he was showing his only bad side—his uncontrollable temper. His letters to Stanton were biting and sharp and quite possibly these were the cause for Stanton's withholding of horses and repeaters.

In any case Stanton was apparently fed up with Rosecrans, and before Rousseau and Sanderson left dejectedly for Tennessee, Sanderson heard Stanton say, in referring to Rosecrans' requests for more men, horses and repeaters: "He shall not have another damned man!"[3]

On August 16, the Army of the Cumberland began its movement against Chattanooga that culminated at the Battle of Chickamauga late in September, and Col. Wilder's Lightning Brigade was to play a critical part in the operations. In fact from the 16th of August when they left Decherd until October 24, the men of the Brigade never had time to pitch their pup tents. Each mess group would, at night, hitch their horses in a circle and cook, eat and sleep on the ground in the middle of the circle.

Rosecrans' Army was divided into three corps—the 14th under Gen. Geo. Thomas, a Virginian who had married a Northern girl and remained loyal to the Union; Gen. Alexander McCook, who had nine brothers and a father in the Union Army, commanded the 20th Corps; and the 21st Corps, led by Gen. Thomas L. Crittenden, who had a brother in the Confederate Army and whose father, a veteran of the War of 1812, had been governor of Kentucky and a U.S. Senator.

The Union strategy was practically the same as it had been for the Tullahoma Campaign—to feint an attack at and above Chattanooga while the main part of the army crossed the Tennessee River below Chattanooga and moved around Bragg's rear.

Wilder's Brigade left camp at 1 o'clock in the afternoon with 10 days' ration of hardtack and forage and ascended the Cumberland Mountains. The road up the mountain was steep and slippery from the rain that had begun falling that morning and the men cursed the winding of the mountain road and the mud thrown up into their faces from the hooves of horses in front of them. But this was the last rain that they would see for a long time and before it rained again they would see times when they would give a month's pay to travel under these same conditions. Near the top of the mountain they passed through the cloud that was producing the rain and when they reached the top they found themselves on dry land.

From the summit of the mountain the men beheld a beautiful sight. One of Wilder's soldiers described it: "We were above the cloud of rain where the sun was shining brightly, making hundreds of rain bows on the sides of the mountain beneath us. Occasionally the cloud would break away and let us catch a glimpse of the most beautiful landscape underneath, all gleaming like silver as the sunlight shone on the rain. Towards evening it cleared away and afforded us such a landscape that no pen could describe. We went into camp on the edge of the mountains at a place called University Springs, a spring of pure water right on top of the mountain. The state of Tennessee intended to start a college here before the war."[4]

Although officially attached to Reynold's Division of Thomas' Corps, the Lightning Brigade was assigned to Crittenden's Corps for the advance on Chattanooga and this corps was given the task of making the Confederates think that the entire Union Army was going to cross the river above Chattanooga. The Brigade moved to Tracy City on the 17th, then moved on across the mountains and camped on the 19th in the beautiful Sequatchie Valley. This valley lies between the Cumberland Mtns. and Walden's Ridge and is about 3 miles wide and 80 miles long. After three days of travel in jack oak country the men welcomed the peaches, apples and fresh corn that this fertile little valley yielded.

The Brigade moved out at 6 A.M. on the 20th and crossed Walden's Ridge, arriving at Poe's Tavern at 10 o'clock that evening. At daylight the next morning the 98th Illinois and the 1st section of Lilly's Battery were sent north to Harrison's Landing on the Tennessee River to prevent the Rebels from crossing. Two companies of the 17th Indiana were ordered to examine the river near the mouth of North Chickamauga Creek and the remainder of the Brigade moved south toward Chattanooga, with Major Connolly and two companies of the 123rd Illinois as scouts. When the scouts reached the bank of the river directly across from Chattanooga they surprised a ferry boat on their side of the river, capturing 12 Rebels and 60 head of mules.[5]

A short time later the rest of the Brigade arrived and Captain Lilly unlimbered his guns to begin shelling the city. The appearance of Union troops completely surprised the residents of Chattanooga—they didn't know there was a Yankee within miles.

Although it was a weekday the city had a Sunday appearance. Jeff Davis, president of the Confederacy, had been there the day before visiting Gen. Bragg and had suggested a prayer service for the Southern cause. The old church at the corner of Market and 7th Streets was jammed with worshipers, both civilian and military, and a guest minister from Huntsville, Alabama, was leading the service.[6]

Lilly's guns, positioned on Stringer's Ridge, a series of hills overlooking the river, opened up on two Confederate steamboats, the "Paint Rock" and the "Dunbar." At the sound of the first shot the city went into wild confusion. People on the streets ran to seek shelter in the forts. Soldiers scurried to their duty stations. By the time the "Paint Rock" had been sunk and the "Dunbar" had been disabled the Rebels were beginning to return the fire.

The first Confederate reply came from a James Rifle, firing a 15-lb. shell, situated to the Union right on a hill across the river. Then a Rebel battery to the left opened up, but neither of these batteries, 12 lb. Howitzers and 6 lb. rifles, had sufficient range to reach the Yankee emplacements and their shells exploded only halfway up the hill. Lilly's 2nd section fired at the Rebel forts to the right and the 3rd section fired at the forts to the left. With only 4½ degrees elevation both of these sections could reach the Rebel positions and they maintained a continuous and accurate fire.[7]

The line of sight from one of Lilly's guns to one of the Rebel batteries passed directly over the church where the minister from Alabama was conducting divine services. When the first Union shell passed over the church the congregation became quite nervous, but General Cheatham who was in the church arose and assured them that there was no danger—that it was only their own men having target practice. The people in the church were calmed momentarily and the preacher, requesting the congregation to join him, knelt at the altar in prayer with his back to the audience and his eyes closed. Captain Lilly's gun fired again and this time the shell tore part of the coaming off the church roof, but the devout minister prayed on. After a lengthy and emotional prayer the minister arose, turned and opened his eyes only to find that the entire congregation had quietly filed out and deserted him.[8]

By 4 P.M. all nineteen Rebel guns had been silenced; only one Union gun was firing and most of the men were resting on the ground. An unusual incident then occurred as described by one of Lilly's artillerists: "I was sitting down just in front of the No. 5 gun watching the effects of the shot with the captain's glass. No. 6 had just fired their gun and at the same instant exactly that the report of our gun rang out through the air and while everyone's attention was engrossed in watching the shot strike, the Rebels fired a shot from a 32-lb. James Rifle that they had been mounting during the time when they were silent. . . . The shell whizzed over my head, under the axle of No. 5, striking the ground near the trail just at the spot where Corporal McCorkle was lying asleep. It cut his leg entirely off below the knee, ricocheted and struck the lead horse of the limber square in the breast, passing entirely through him endways—striking the next horse just above the chest, passing clear through him— hit the next horse in the throat, splitting his backbone from one end to the other, making its exit just above the tail. The wheel horse in the rear escaped by having his head down close to the ground eating grass, but unfortunately his mate had his head around in rear of the off-swing horse and the shell struck him in the side of the head just below his ears, carrying his brains entirely out. The shell then passed over the caisson, struck a tree and fell to the ground. The horses were killed so suddenly that their mates never moved. . . . McCorkle was carried in a blanket to an ambulance and sent back to Poe's Tavern, where after lingering a few days, he died and was buried in the Chickamauga Valley."[9]

The 32-pounder fired but four rounds, however, before Captain Lilly quieted it also, "one of his shells exploding in the embrasure from which the gun was being fired, killing a captain and three men."[10]

Next day the Confederates got some guns up and sporadic firing continued on both sides. By evening of the 22nd Lilly was short of ammunition and Colonel Wilder, in a message to Rosecrans' headquarters, requested 200 percussion shell, and 1,000 friction primers.

Stringer's Ridge, from which the Union artillery was firing, was about a mile from the edge of the river. Halfway down the hill between the summit of the ridge and the river was a small frame house. On Sunday the 23rd Col. Wilder, with two Brigade officers and Lt. Newell of the Topographical Engineers, went down the hill to this little house in order to get a closer look at the city. As with most houses built on hillsides, the back of the house rested on the ground while the front was standing on stone pillars three or four feet high. Unknown to the officers, quietly sleeping in the shade under the house was a big old brood sow. Col. Wilder and the others sneaked down the hill and entered the house from the rear, but they failed to escape the watchful eyes of the Confederate artillery spotters. They had barely gotten settled down in the house when the Rebels cut loose at them with a 32-pounder. The first shot landed under the house and exploded, killing the sow and demolishing the house, but Col. Wilder and the officers were not hurt and they scurried back up the hill with Lt. Newell leading the pack. As Newell sped over the brow of the ridge, Capt. Rice of Wilder's staff shouted, "Hello, Newell, what's the matter with you!" Without slowing his gait or missing a step, Newell replied, "O, there's nothing the matter with me but it was terribly hard on the old sow!"[11]

Gen. Crittenden had left the Lightning Brigade, Minty's Cavalry, and Hazen's and Wagner's Infantry Brigades to feign crossings and harass the enemy at and above Chattanooga while he took the rest of his corps below the city to cross the Tennessee with Thomas and McCook.[12]

Col. Wilder reported that his men "then commenced making feints as if trying to cross the river at different points for 40 miles above town, and succeeding in deceiving them as to induce them to use an entire army corps to prevent the execution of such a purpose, they worked every night fortifying the south bank of the river at every feasible crossing for miles above." To make the fake crossing even more realistic Wilder put his men to work hammering and sawing and throwing boards into streams so that the Rebels would think they were building pontoons. Every night they would build numerous camp fires so the enemy would think a large force was camped in that area awaiting the order to cross. This sham was kept up until the main Union Army had crossed below Chattanooga and Bragg's Confederate Army, at the threat of being out flanked, had withdrawn from the city.[13]

While Rosecrans was making his movement to take Chattanooga the Army of the Potomac, which had stopped Lee's Confederate Army at Gettysburg, moved into Virginia. But Gen. Meade, in the manner typical of the Union leadership in the East, didn't really want to bring Lee to fight. He moved his well-supplied, well-disciplined Army of the Potomac too slowly and hesitantly and Lee pulled his army back into strong positions along the Rapidan River. Meade then sat along the Rappahannock and looked at Lee all fall and winter and the Army of the Potomac would not fight again until President Lincoln brought a fighter from the west, Gen. U. S. Grant, in the spring of 1864 to lead the Army of the Potomac to the victories it so richly deserved.

For the remainder of the year the fight for the salvation of the Union would be carried to the Confederacy by the more aggressive leadership of the western armies.

By Sept. 4, Rosecrans had his main force across the Tennessee River and hidden behind Lookout Mountain below Chattanooga. As at Tullahoma his strategy worked, and his flanking movement caused Bragg to withdraw his Southern troops from Chattanooga toward Ringgold and LaFayette, Georgia. Before daylight on Sept. 9, Col. Atkins and the 92nd Illinois, who had remained under Gen. Reynolds' command, were ordered to move into the city. By mid-morning the 92nd was in the streets of Chattanooga. Although they encountered no organized Confederate resistance they did come under the occasional firing of Wilder's men from across the river who did not realize that Union troops had entered the city. One of Atkins' men signalled Wilder that they were the 92nd Illinois and shortly thereafter the Stars and Stripes were flying from the highest building in Chattanooga. The remainder of Crittenden's Corps then crossed the river, the Lightning Brigade in advance.[14]

In the area south of Chattanooga are four mountainous ridges running approximately north and south, each separated from the other by a valley through which runs a creek that empties into the Tennessee River at the north end. The western most of these ridges is Raccoon Mountain. Across Lookout Valley to the east is Lookout Mountain which stretches for 100 miles south from Chattanooga. Between Lookout Mountain and Missionary Ridge to the east is Dry Valley through which runs Chattanooga Creek. This creek joins the Tennessee River near the city of Chattanooga located at the north end of Dry Valley. On the east side of Missionary Ridge is Chickamauga Creek, running generally

north and south. To the east of Chickamauga Creek, opposite
the southern end of Missionary Ridge, is Pigeon Mountain, the
area between these two ridges called McLemore's Cove.

The Union command was convinced that Bragg and his Confederate Army, since withdrawing from Chattanooga, was retreating toward Rome, Georgia, and that is exactly what Bragg
wanted them to think. He knew that if he could trick them into
reckless pursuit he could defeat them in detail. Rosecrans had
his three army corps widely and dangerously dispersed. Mc-
Cook's Corps was forty miles south of Chattanooga near Alpine.
Thomas' Corps was halfway between McCook and Chattanooga.
Negley's Division of Thomas' Corps was in McLemore's Cove
and Wood's Division of Crittenden's Corps was at Lee and Gordon's Mill on Chickamauga Creek several miles north of Negley. The main part of Crittenden's Corps, including Wilder's Brigade, was between Chattanooga and Ringgold, Georgia, 15 to
20 miles northwest of Lee and Gordon's.

Rosecrans suddenly became suspicious of Bragg's movements,
and shortly before noon on the 11th, he ordered Crittenden's
Corps, with the Lightning Brigade in advance, to move toward
Lee and Gordon's Mill between Chattanooga and Lafayette.

Confederate General Forrest and his cavalry, who had been
protecting the Tennessee River north of the river for Bragg
prior to the evacuation of Chattanooga, discovered Crittenden's
isolated corps north of Ringgold and requested infantry from
Bragg to support an attack. Bragg had the Union forces where
he wanted them but for some unexplainable reason he did not
take advantage of his opportunities. He declined to send infantry to Forrest. On the morning of the 11th Forrest moved
to hamper and delay the advance of Crittenden's Corps down
the railroad in the direction of Ringgold.

At 1 o'clock in the afternoon Wilder's advance troops, the
92nd Illinois, ran into Rebel pickets stationed in a woods a mile
from Ringgold. The 92nd dismounted and engaged them briskly; with the help of the 3rd section of Lilly's battery and the
17th Indiana they soon forced the Rebel pickets back toward
Ringgold. The Brigade then moved on through Ringgold toward
Dalton, Georgia, but soon ran into a strong enemy force posted
across a narrow valley near Tunnel Hill. This body of enemy
troops turned out to be Scott's Brigade and Armstrong's Brigade of Forrest's Cavalry Corps with Gen. Forrest personally
in command.[15]

General Nathan Bedford Forrest, although lacking in formal military education, was the South's most brilliant cavalry leader. He had been born to a poor family in the backwoods of middle Tennessee. At the death of his father young Nathan, although only sixteen years old, took charge of the family affairs. He worked hard at farming and livestock trading and by the time he was nineteen the family was relatively prosperous. He then went into partnership with an uncle in the mercantile business at Hernando, Mississippi, where he built a flourishing and highly profitable business. In 1851 he sold out and moved to Memphis where he engaged in the real estate business and slave trading. In 1859 he closed out his real estate holdings and slave business in Memphis and devoted all his time to two large plantations he had accumulated in Coahoma County, Mississippi. By the time the war started his plantations were yielding him an annual income of over $30,000 per year, a sizeable fortune in those days. In June of 1861, at the age of forty, Forrest joined the 7th Tennessee Cavalry as a private. A short time later, the governor of Tennessee gave him authority to raise a battalion of cavalry of his own and by October he was a Lt. Colonel with a battalion largely equipped with his own money. The next spring Forrest refused to be surrendered at Fort Donelson and got his men out during the night before it was surrendered to Gen. Grant. In April he fought gallantly in the Battle of Shiloh where he was wounded.[16]

Forrest was a natural born military tactician. He almost always did the right thing at the right place at the right time. He had a reputation in the Union Army of being almost unbeatable.

As Forrest's pickets were being driven back toward Tunnel Hill, he positioned his artillery on a small hill in the center of the valley. His dismounted cavalrymen were stationed on each side with their flanks extending to the steep hills on either side.

As the Lightning Brigade approached, Col. Wilder sent the 17th Indiana forward as skirmishers while the 123rd Illinois was deployed to the left side of the valley and the 98th Illinois to the right. Lilly's Battery was set up on either side of the valley with the 72nd Indiana in support. This brought the Rebels under a crossfire and after about an hour the Confederates withdrew to strong positions on a range of hills near Dalton called "Buzzard's Roost."

In the encounter at Tunnel Hill General Forrest received another wound. Although it was not serious enough to cause Forrest to leave the field, it caused a great deal of exultation among the Union troops when they learned of it. The effect of the wound on Forrest was merely faintness from pain and loss of blood, but it caused him to do what he never did except when sick or wounded—take a drink of whiskey.[17]

The Brigade camped that night in the area—close enough to Forrest's men that the men of Companies E and K, 72nd Indiana on picket duty could hear Forrest's pickets talking in the darkness.

While the Lightning Brigade, in covering Crittenden's left flank, had been engaged with Forrest near Tunnel Hill, the balance of Crittenden's Corps moved west across Chickamauga Creek toward Lee and Gordon's Mill.

On the 12th the Brigade moved back to Ringgold and then toward the LaFayette Road. Halfway between Ringgold and Lee and Gordon's Mill, at a place called Rock Spring, the skirmishers of the 17th Indiana ran into an ambush set by the Rebels who were hiding in the dense underbrush alongside the road. The first volley from the Confederate positions took its toll in the Union ranks, but Col. Wilder ordered up the 72nd Indiana to the left and right of the 17th and they charged the Rebels with their Spencer Rifles. The Confederates, the Sixth Georgia Cavalry and Rucker's Legion of Forrest's command under General Pegram, gave ground momentarily but soon recovered.

Gen. Pegram described the fight as "almost literally hand to hand" in the heavy woods. After two hours of desperate tree to tree combat the pressure of the repeating rifles forced the Rebels into an open field and they retreated toward LaFayette, leaving fifty killed and wounded.[18]

When the Brigade reached the LaFayette Road the deep dust indicated that a large force had recently traveled past the crossroads. Supposing that it had been the balance of Crittenden's Corps, Col. Wilder sent a scout to them to deliver some dispatches. However, this body of troops turned out to be Pegram's Division of cavalry again and the scout was captured.

Before the Brigade had moved much farther they came upon General Pegram's Division drawn up in line of battle. At the same time a cavalry force, probably Scott's Brigade, was pushing Wilder's rear guard and Armstrong was attacking Wilder's left flank. The woods was too heavy to make use of artillery so with the 72nd Indiana holding the left flank and the 123rd

Illinois holding the rear, Wilder boldly attacked Pegram with the 98th Illinois and the 17th Indiana, driving them south down the LaFayette Road. In the meantime, Wilder discovered a Confederate infantry brigade under General Strahl holding the Gordon's Mill Road on his right—the Lightning Brigade was surrounded!

It was almost dark. The 72nd Indiana, the 123rd and 98th Illinois and Lilly's Battery were formed in line of battle across the LaFayette Road while the 17th Indiana pressed in the inhabitants of the area to act as guides in finding a way out—threatening them with death if they failed. Several men were sent into the woods to build campfires in order to deceive the enemy into thinking that they were camping for the night.

Shortly after dark the 17th Indiana scouts found a weak spot in the Rebel lines between Strahl's infantry and the force in the rear. Col. Wilder, leaving a strong line of skirmishers to protect his front, left, and rear, attacked Strahl with the balance of his command. Strahl's left was driven back, opening the road to Napier's Gap, and with the 17th Indiana leading the way the Lightning Brigade escaped by that route through Pea Vine Ridge. The column moved over ditches and fences, through dense undergrowth, crossed and recrossed roads, and after 8 miles of extremely difficult travel joined Crittenden's Corps at midnight with the loss of only one man captured.[19]

By 1 o'clock in the morning the men had unsaddled and settled down on their blankets for much needed sleep. At 3 A.M. they were aroused by heavy picket firing. After only two hours of rest the Brigade remounted and moved out to investigate. They discovered, much to their amusement, that it was not picket firing at all, but Forrest's men firing at the phony campfires they had set in the woods as decoys.

After breakfast on the 13th the members of the Brigade scattered out over the countryside for forage. One group of foragers from the 72nd Indiana who had strayed a considerable distance from camp were picked up by Gen. Rosecrans' body guard and arrested as stragglers. They were taken to headquarters and the General was informed that they had falsely claimed to be Colonel Wilder's men. The General replied, "Impossible! Wilder's whole command is captured and now on its way to Libby Prison." General Rosecrans then came outside his tent to take a look at them. When he was assured that they actually were from the 72nd Indiana, he said, "Wilder's men beat the devil, anyhow; take them to Wilder—he's the only man that can manage them."[20]

The next day the Brigade moved south to Crawfish Springs to join Gen. Reynolds and the remainder of the division. There they saw their clothes for the first time in three weeks.

While Wilder's Brigade was making its escape from the Rebel trap on the night of the 12th, Confederate General Braxton Bragg was having troubles of his own. On this same evening Bragg sent the following order to Gen. Polk:

"General: I enclose you a dispatch from General Pegram. This presents you a fine opportunity of striking Crittenden in detail and I hope you will avail yourself of it at daylight tomorrow. This division crushed and the others are yours. We can then turn again on the force in the cove. Wheeler's Cavalry will move on Wilder so as to cover your right. I shall be delighted to hear of your success."[21]

Lt. Gen. D. H. Hill, CSA, wrote later: "Gen. Polk did not make the attack on the 13th as ordered. Although he had Crittenden outnumbered he set up defensive positions and requested reinforcements. Crittenden had marched and countermarched his corps for a week in the face of superior enemy strength and for a period of at least two days had his divisions divided 10 miles apart. But uncertainty of the Union Army movements and lack of mutual confidence between Bragg and his immediate subordinates caused the Confederate commander to miss several opportunities to destroy the divided corps of Rosecrans' army individually."[22]

Rosecrans received word that Longstreet's Corps of Lee's Army of Northern Virginia had left Virginia en route to reinforce Bragg and he again wired Halleck in Washington for more troops. But Halleck didn't believe that Bragg was being reinforced; or he didn't want to believe it. He had plenty of inactive troops that he could have sent to Rosecrans' aid. Grant at Vicksburg had plenty of men to spare. Burnside at Knoxville was free. But Halleck hesitated; by the time he decided that Lee really was sending support to Bragg and he ordered Burnsides, who didn't move, to Rosecrans' assistance, it was too late.

The Army of the Cumberland was about to be the first Union Army since the outbreak of the rebellion to enter a major battle outnumbered by the Confederates—and deep in enemy territory at that.

By September 17, Rosecrans had almost gotten his widely scattered forces together. Both the Union and Rebel Armies were in line of battle with the Northerners on the west side and the Confederates on the east side of Chickamauga Creek.

Col. Wilder's Lightning Brigade was camped at Alexander's Bridge, a broken down wooden bridge across Chickamauga Creek, two miles east of the Chattanooga-LaFayette Road. A mile and a half farther north at Reed's Bridge was Col. Robert H. G. Minty and his brigade of Federal Cavalry. Both Alexander's and Reed's Bridge were north of the northern end of the Union battle line. Wilder and Minty were ordered to prevent the Rebels from outflanking the Union forces on the left.

Early on the 18th Confederate General Braxton Bragg issued his order for battle:

"1. Bushrod Johnson's column (Hood's), on crossing at or near Reed's Bridge, will turn to the left by the most practicable route and sweep up the Chickamauga toward Lee and Gordon's Mill.

2. Walker, crossing at Alexander's Bridge will unite in this move and push vigorously on the enemy's flank and rear in the same direction.

3. Buckner, crossing at Tedford's Ford, will join in the movement to the left and press the enemy up the stream from Polk's front at Lee and Gordon's.

4. Polk will press his forces to the front of Lee and Gordon's Mill and if met by too much resistance to cross will rear to the right and cross at Dalton's Ford or at Tedford's, as may be necessary, and join the attack wherever the enemy may be.

5. Hill will cover our left flank from an advance of the enemy from the cove and, by pressing the cavalry in his front, ascertain if the enemy is reinforcing at Lee and Gordon's Mill, in which event he will attack them in flank.

6. Wheeler's Cavalry will hold the gaps in Pigeon Mountain, and cover our rear and left, and bring up stragglers.

7. All teams, etc., not with troops should go toward Ringgold and Dalton beyond Taylor's Ridge. All cooking should be done at the trains; rations when cooked will be forwarded to the troops.

8. The above movement will be executed with the utmost promptness, vigor and persistence."[23]

The stage was now set for the bloodiest battle of the Civil War. The Union Army effective strength was 58,222 while the

Confederate Army, strengthened by the arrival of five brigades with General Longstreet, numbered 66,326.[24]

SEPTEMBER 1863

UNION ARMY OF THE CUMBERLAND

Gen. Wm. S. Rosecrans

14th Corps—Gen. Thomas

Baird's Division
  Scribner's Brigade
  Starkweather's Brigade
  King's Brigade

Negley's Division
  Beatty's Brigade
  Stanley's Brigade
  Sirwell's Brigade

Brannan's Division
  Connell's Brigade
  Croxton's Brigade
  Van Derveer's Brigade

Reynold's Division
  Wilder's Brigade
  E. King's Brigade
  Turchin's Brigade

20th Corps—Gen. McCook

Davis's Division
  Carlin's Brigade
  Heg's Brigade

Johnson's Division
  Willich's Brigade
  Dodge's Brigade
  Baldwin's Brigade

Sheridan's Division
  Lytle's Brigade
  Laiboldt's Brigade
  Bradley's Brigade

21st Corps—Gen. Crittenden

Wood's Division
  Buell's Brigade
  Harker's Brigade

Palmer's Division
  Cruft's Brigade
  Hazen's Brigade
  Grose's Brigade

Van Cleve's Division
  Beatty's Brigade
  Dick's Brigade
  Barnes' Brigade

Reserve Corps—Gen. Granger

Steedman's Division
  Whitaker's Brigade
  Mitchell's Brigade

Detached Brigade
  McCook's

Cavalry Corps—Gen. Mitchell

E. McCook's Division
  Campbell's Brigade
  Ray's Brigade
  Watkins' Brigade

Crook's Division
  Minty's Brigade
  Long's Brigade

SEPTEMBER 1863
CONFEDERATE ARMY OF TENNESSEE
General Braxton Bragg

Right Wing—Gen. Polk

Polk's Corps—Gen. Polk
  Cheatham's Division
    Jackson's Brigade
    Maney's Brigade
    Smith's Brigade
    Wright's Brigade
    Strahl's Brigade
  Hindman's Division
  (assigned to Longstreet)

Hill's Corps—Gen. Hill
  Cleburne's Division
    Wood's Brigade
    Polk's Brigade
    Deshler's Brigade
  Breckinridge's Division
    Helm's Brigade
    Adam's Brigade
    Stovall's Brigade

Walker's Reserve Corps
(Gen. W. H. T. Walker)
  Walker's Division
    Gist's Brigade
    Ector's Brigade
    Wilson's Brigade
  Liddell's Division
    Govan's Brigade
    Walthall's Brigade

Left Wing—Gen. Longstreet

Buckner's Corps—Gen. Buckner
  Stewart's Division
    Bate's Brigade
    Clayton's Brigade
    Brown's Brigade
  Preston's Division
    Gracie's Brigade
    Kelly's Brigade
    Trigg's Brigade
  Hindman's Division
    Anderson's Brigade
    Deas' Brigade
    Manigault's Brigade

Hood's Corps—Gen. Hood
  McLaw's Division
    Kershaw's Brigade
    Humphrey's Brigade
  Johnson's Division
    Johnson's Brigade
    Gregg's Brigade
    McNair's Brigade
  Hood's Division
    Law's Brigade
    Robertson's Brigade
    Benning's Brigade

CONFEDERATE CAVALRY

Wheeler's Corps—Gen. Wheeler

Wharton's Division
  Crew's Brigade
  Harrison's Brigade

Martin's Division
  Morgan's Brigade
  Russell's Brigade
  Roddey's Brigade

Forrest's Corps—Gen. Forrest

Armstrong's Division
  Armstrong's Brigade
  Dibrell's Brigade

Pegram's Division
  Davidson's Brigade
  Scott's Brigade

REGIMENTAL BREAKDOWN OF UNITS MOST INVOLVED
WITH WILDER AT CHICKAMAUGA

September 18:

Liddell's Division (Walker's Corps)

Govan's Brigade

2nd Arkansas Infantry
5th Arkansas Infantry
6th Arkansas Infantry
7th Arkansas Infantry
8th Arkansas Infantry
13th Arkansas Infantry
15th Arkansas Infantry
1st Louisiana Infantry
Sweet's Miss. Battery

Walthall's Brigade

24th Mississippi Infantry
27th Mississippi Infantry
29th Mississippi Infantry
30th Mississippi Infantry
34th Mississippi Infantry
Fowler's Alabama Battery

September 19:

Hood's Division (Longstreet's Corps)

Robertson's Brigade

3rd Arkansas Infantry
1st Texas Infantry
4th Texas Infantry
5th Texas Infantry

Benning's Brigade

2nd Georgia Infantry
15th Georgia Infantry
17th Georgia Infantry
20th Georgia Infantry

McNAIR'S BRIGADE (Johnson's Division)

1st Arkansas Mounted Rifles
2nd Arkansas Mounted Rifles
25th Arkansas Infantry
4th and 31st Arkansas Battalions
39th North Carolina Infantry
Culpepper's S. C. Battery

September 20:

Hindman's Division

Manigault's Brigade

24th Alabama Infantry
28th Alabama Infantry
34th Alabama Infantry
10th South Carolina Infantry
19th South Carolina Infantry
Water's Alabama Battery

Dea's Brigade

19th Alabama Infantry
22nd Alabama Infantry
25th Alabama Infantry
39th Alabama Infantry
50th Alabama Infantry
17th Alabama Battery Sharpshooters
Robertson's Battery

Anderson's Brigade

7th Mississippi Infantry
9th Mississippi Infantry
10th Mississippi Infantry
41st Mississippi Infantry
44th Mississippi Infantry
9th Mississippi Battery Sharpshooters
Garrity's Alabama Battery

5

"Root Hog or Die"

CONFEDERATE GENERAL BRAGG'S BATTLE PLAN WAS WELL conceived. Crittenden's Union Corps was the northernmost of Rosecrans' forces and its left flank extended to just south of the Viniard house. Bragg's plan to cross the Chickamauga on the 18th at two places to the north of Crittenden was sound. By crossing at Alexander's Bridge with Walker's Corps a half mile to the north and at Reed's Bridge with Bushrod Johnson's division and Forrest's Cavalry a mile and a half farther up the Confederates would have the Union Army outflanked to the north and could sweep down on the Federals between the Chickamauga and Mission Ridge while Buckner, Polk and Hill attacked from the east. Walker and Johnson had the defenders of these two bridges, Wilder and Minty, outnumbered five to one and Bragg's plan, successfully executed, would cut off Thomas' Corps, still far to the south in McLemore's Cove. Since McCook and his 20th Corps was still near Crawfish Springs Crittenden would be caught in both flank and frontal attacks and outnumbered more than two to one. If these assaults were effectively perpetrated the Union Army would be cut off from Chattanooga and chewed up piece by piece, and Bragg's hopes to annihilate Rosecrans' glorious Army of the Cumberland on the 18th would be fulfilled.[1]

But Bragg had underestimated the capabilities of the Irish-born Col. Minty and of Col. Wilder and his Lightning Brigade. By noon these two mounted brigades of 1,500 men each were being attacked by a total Confederate force of nearly 16,000, ably led by Walker, Johnson and Forrest.

While most of Wilder's men were eating their noon meal some men who had been on the east side of the creek picking wild

70

grapes came running into camp shouting that a Rebel cavalry force was coming up the road. A lookout was sent up one of the tall trees situated near the Alexander house. He reported a large column of dust on the road to the east that appeared to be a sizeable enemy force advancing toward the bridge.

The Brigade was immediately deployed in line of battle along the densely wooded bank of Chickamauga Creek while Lilly's Battery was positioned on a knoll 400 yards northwest of the bridge near a log house that had been occupied by a family named Alexander. Just as the Brigade was about formed for battle a messenger arrived from Col. Minty and reported to Col. Wilder that Minty's Brigade had been attacked by a large enemy force and that if not reinforced they would have to abandon their position. Wilder, knowing that if Minty withdrew from Reed's Bridge, he himself would be outflanked, sent Col. Miller with the 72nd Indiana, one section of Lilly's battery and seven companies of the 123rd Illinois to render assistance.

Col. Robert H. G. Minty, one of the many foreign born officers in the Civil War, had served as an officer in the British Army in the West Indies, Central America and in Africa before retiring and settling in Michigan in 1853. In September, 1861, he was commissioned a major in the 2nd Michigan Cavalry and in July of 1862 was promoted to Col. of the 4th Mich. Cavalry. On September 18, 1863, Minty commanded a splendid cavalry brigade made up of the 4th Mich. Cavalry, 7th Penn. Cavalry, 4th U.S. Regular Cavalry, 3rd Ind. Battalion Cavalry and one section of the Chicago Board of Trade Battery of artillery.

Minty's Brigade had taken position on the east side of Chickamauga Creek and had been attacked at 7:30 in the morning by Johnson's Division and Forrest's Cavalry. Until almost noon Minty had held his own but the weight of superior numbers had finally caused him to give ground. He had fought a desperate delaying action back to Reed's Bridge and at the time he sent to Wilder for help the bridge was still in his possession.

The Lightning Brigade, for all practical purposes, now had two regiments and two sections of artillery with which to defend Alexander's Bridge. Chickamauga Creek at this point was narrow but deep with very steep banks. The entire area along both sides of the creek was densely wooded. The 17th Indiana was deployed to the left and the 98th Illinois to the right. A total of less than 1,000 men to hold off Walker's entire corps of two divisions plus part of Forrest's cavalry and artillery that had

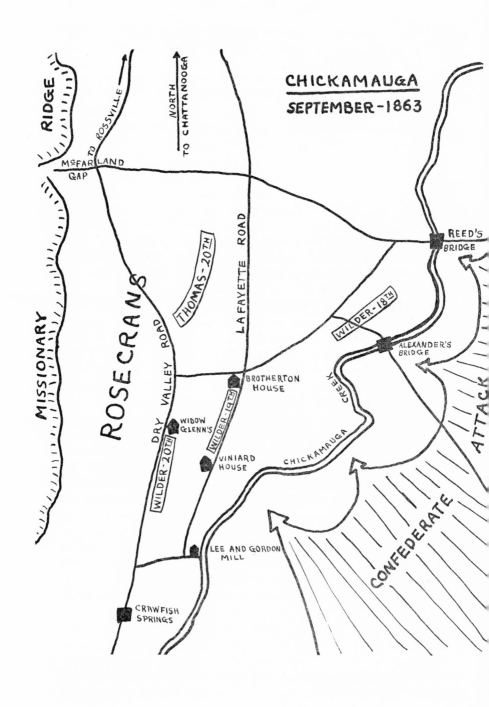

CHICKAMAUGA
SEPTEMBER - 1863

come down from Reed's Bridge, led personally by Gen. Forrest. The Confederate force numbered almost 8,000.

As the Rebels approached Wilder's position Lilly's battery opened up with percussion shell and long range canister with much effectiveness. After a short time Forrest's artillery set up two guns on the east side of the creek and opened fire. The first round fired by the Rebel gun produced one of the first heroes of the battle. The shell struck the ground just in front of Lilly's No. 2 gun, riccocheted and hit the corner of the Alexander house and bounced back among the cannoneers, the fuse still burning. One of Lilly's men, Sidney Speed, coolly picked up the live shell and threw it over the log house where it exploded harmlessly. One of Speed's buddies said later, "I don't think I will ever forget the awful, unearthly screeching that shell made as it approached us."[2]

Gen. Walker then ordered Liddell's Division to take the bridge with Walthall's Brigade of Mississippians in advance and Govan's Brigade in support, with Walker's own division in reserve. Walthall launched a ferocious attack on the bridge but the "seven shooters" drove them back with heavy losses. Walthall again attacked and again was repulsed. Govan's Brigade then moved up to reinforce Walthall's left, his skirmishers being driven back by two companies of the 98th Illinois posted in a dense thicket on the extreme right of the Union line. The fight for the bridge lasted almost five hours.

At a little after 4 P.M. Minty sent word that the weight of superior numbers had forced him to abandon Reed's Bridge. This information plus the fact that Walker had sent part of his corps downstream to ford the creek made Wilder's position untenable and he destroyed the bridge and withdrew toward the Viniard house.

A. P. Adamson of the 30th Georgia, Wilson's Brigade of Walker's Division recalled later, "Walker's Division had orders to cross the Chickamauga at Alexander's Bridge, but on arriving there he encountered strong resistance, and found the bridge so badly destroyed that he had to go some distance down the river to Byram's Ford where a crossing was effected late in the night."[3] Adamson's term "strong resistance" was almost an understatement in view of the fact that Liddell lost 105 men while Wilder's losses were negligible, the 98th Illinois losing only one man killed. Most of the Confederate loss was sustained by Walthall's Brigade, the 29th Mississippi suffering the most heavily. Although Wilder had been badly outnumbered the Spencer rifles had evened up the odds. Gen. Liddell, in referring to his losses, said, "I can only account for this disproportion from the efficiency of this new weapon."[4]

The Confederate artillery shelled Wilder's position at the bridge while Walker moved his corps downstream and by the time he reached Wilder's position the Lightning Brigade was gone. This delay gave Wilder time to form a line of battle in a cornfield located on a small hill a short distance east of the Chattanooga-Lafayette Road.

Just as they got in position the 72nd Ind. and the 123rd Ill. returned with Minty's command and were placed in line on the left. Minty dismounted his men also and formed on Wilder's right. Thus Wilder and Minty were the extreme left flank of the Union Army and extended Crittenden's Corps from Chickamauga Creek to the Viniard house on the Chattanooga Road. Wilder then found General Crittenden and Gen. Wood at the Viniard house and reported to the Corps Commander that the large Rebel force was approaching. Crittenden did not believe him. In a few minutes Capt. Vale of the 7th Pennsylvania Cavalry reported to the Viniard house and delivered the same message from Col. Minty. Crittenden asked in reply, "Who is it that's coming? What have you been fighting out there?" The captain replied, "Buckner's Corps, Hood's Division of infantry and artillery and some of Forrest's Cavalry." Crittenden scoffed at the idea and said, "Wilder here," turning to him "has come in with the same outlandish story; there is nothing in this country except Pegram's dismounted and Forrest's mounted cavalry, with a few pieces of artillery; they have been firing on me all day but could not cross the creek."[5]

Captain Vale did not have his information exactly correct, but he was partly right. The original attacking forces at the bridges were Walker's Corps, Bushrod Johnson's Division and Forrest's Cavalry, but the force now pursuing Wilder and Minty was made up of Bushrod Johnson's Division and Hood's Division, both under the command of Gen. Hood. Hood and his division, now commanded by Gen. E. McIver Law, had just arrived as the van of Longstreet's Corps that had been sent from the Army of Northern Virginia by Gen. Robert E. Lee to reinforce Bragg's Army of Tennessee.

About this time Minty rode up and reported, and Crittenden said, "Well, Wood, as Wilder has been chased in from Alexander's and Minty from Reed's Bridge, I suppose we will have to get ready for a little brush."[6]

Gen. Wood then moved an infantry brigade up to the line where Wilder's and Minty's men were skirmishing. On arriving, Wood said, "Well, Wilder where is the enemy?" Wilder answered. "Ride forward, General, ten paces, and you will see for yourself." As the infantry brigade moved around Wilder's left to form a line of battle in front, Gen. Crittenden, with a grimace toward Wilder, addressed its commander, "And, Colonel, we expect to hear a good report from you." Wood, who had been Gen. Grant's first roommate at West Point, laughed at the implied compliment. Wilder swore under his breath and Minty gritted his teeth.[7]

The infantry advanced into the woods and was suddenly assailed by a tremendous fire of musketry in both front and flank. The infantry brigade broke completely to pieces and rushed back over Wilder's and Minty's men in disorganized panic. Wilder called to Minty so that Gen. Crittenden could hear, "Well, Colonel, the General has got his report." Without waiting for orders, he and Minty ordered their men to attack while Gen. Wood, exclaiming, "By Gad, they are here!" galloped off towards Lee and Gordon's Mill.[8]

The advancing Confederates were now within thirty yards of the rail barricades behind which Wilder's and Minty's men had taken positions but when these two Union brigades opened up with their Spencers, Hood's men pulled back. Hood then ordered another advance and this one was also thrown back by Wilder and Minty along with two regiments of Dick's Brigade, Van Cleve's Division that had been brought up as reinforcements. The fighting continued on this line for two hours after dark. At 4 A.M. Wilder and Minty were relieved in the line by Palmer's Division. The Union troops then moved west across the Chattanooga Road and took position in the edge of the woods, leaving the picket and skirmish line where it was.

The night of the 18th was extremely cold—made worse by the fact that no fires were allowed. The misery of the night was intensified when no meal was issued, not even feed for the horses.

All night long Wilder's men were kept awake by the sound of marching feet and the creaking of wagon wheels. Rosecrans was rearranging his three army corps. Thomas was marching his 14th corps north beyond Crittenden so as to extend the line northward in order to neutralize Bragg's flanking maneuver.

The movement of Thomas' Corps lasted all night and by morning the northern extremity of the Federal battle line overlapped
that of the Confederates.

For the first but not the last time during the battle of Chickamauga the Lightning Brigade, along with Minty's cavalry, had
saved the Union Army from annihilation. Without the valiant
stand on the Chickamauga by the "seven shooters" the Rebels
would have swept down the Union flank and the battle would
have been lost on the 18th according to the Confederate battle
plan. They had held off the Rebel advance against over-whelm-
ing odds that whole day and until after dark. This hard-fought
action gave Rosecrans the time he needed on the night of the
18th to move his troops to a more advantageous position. On
the morning of the 19th Wilder found himself, instead of being
the extreme left of the army, stationed in the right center.

The moving around of the Union Army during the night had
been done partially on a division basis and the corps commanders
did not have all their troops together. Wilder, who was attached
to Reynold's Division, Thomas' Corps, found himself between
Van Cleve's of Crittenden's Corps on the left and Davis' Div.
of McCook's Corps on the right, just west of the Chattanooga-
LaFayette Road north of the Viniard House.

Saturday morning, Sept. 19, broke bright and clear in northwest Georgia. Thomas' 14th Corps was now the left wing of
the Union forces and was facing east along the east side of the
Chattanooga Road. Thomas' right crossed the road and joined
the left of Wilder who was on the west side of the road. The
road at this point angled slightly southeast. The Lightning Brigade was in line along a fence with a densely wooded area to
their rear and an open field in front. A large deep ditch ran
through the field almost paralleling the road. The ground sloped
gently downward from 100 to 300 yards from the ravine to the
west where Wilder's men were positioned behind hastily constructed defenses.

The Lightning Brigade breakfasted on roast sweet potatoes,
and two ears of corn were issued for each of the horses which
were grouped to the rear.

The battle on the 19th began on the Union left with Brannan's and Baird's Divisions of Thomas' Corps engaging Forrest's Cavalry and Walker's Corps who had remained in the
area between Reed's Bridge and Alexander's Bridge on the east
side of the Lafayette Road. The battle thundered southward

as division after division became hotly engaged with the enemy. Shortly after noon the battle reached the segment of the line where Wilder's men waited, dismounted, with their Spencer rifles at the ready, seven cartridges in the magazine and ten refills in their cartridge cases—160,000 rounds of .52 caliber ammunition that could be expended in five minutes.

By 1 P.M. the necessities of battle movement had left a gap of almost half a mile between Van Cleve on Wilder's left and Davis on his right. To the Lightning Brigade fell the almost impossible task of supporting two widely separated divisions that were being attacked at almost the same time.

Shortly after 2 o'clock Hood's Division, led by Robertson's Brigade, attacked Davis on Wilder's right.

General Davis had come up through the ranks. He fought as a private in the Mexican War. Commissioned in the Regular Army in 1848 Davis had been at Fort Sumter during the bombardment on April 12, 1861. He had two brigades on the line, his third being on guard duty in the rear. His left brigade under Col. Heg, a Norwegian who had raised the 15th Wisconsin Infantry made up of Scandinavians, was made up of the 25th Ill., 35th Ill., 8th Kansas, 15th Wisconsin and the 8th Wisconsin Battery. Davis' right brigade was commanded by Brig. Gen. Carlin. Carlin, from Illinois, was a West Pointer who had been an Indian fighter in Utah before the war. His brigade consisted of the 21st Illinois, 38th Ill., 81st Ind., 101st Ohio and the 2nd Minnesota Battery.

Hood hit Davis like a whirlwind, killing Col. Heg on the first volley, and Davis' men were driven back in confusion. Col. Wilder, noting that the 8th Wisconsin Battery was about to be flanked, ordered Collonels Monroe and Miller with the 123rd Illinois and 72nd Indiana to move to the right and charge the enemy. These two regiments saved the battery and with Davis' division, which had recovered from the initial assault, drove the Rebels back across the road.

Col. Wilder then discovered that another enemy force was flanking him on the left under cover of the woods. Gen. A. P. "Old Straight" Stewart, West Pointer and former mathematics professor, had sent his tough Confederate division against Van Cleve.

Van Cleve had returned to active duty at the outbreak of the war as Colonel of the 2nd Minnesota Infantry. At fifty-four he was the oldest Union division commander on the field at Chickamauga. Van Cleve had two brigades on the field, his third, Barnes', being on its way from Lee and Gordon's Mill to take position on Davis' right. Sam Beatty's brigade, consisting of the 79th Ind., 9th Ky., 17th Ky., and 19th Ohio, was on the left of the line. German-born Col. Dick's Brigade, made up of the 44th Ind., 86th Ind., 13th Ohio and 59th Ohio, was the right of the division. Van Cleve had his division on the east side of the Lafayette Road just south of the Brotherton House.

Stewart ordered Clayton's Brigade of Alabamans to initiate the assault on Van Cleve. Clayton's attack was resisted successfully by Beatty and Dick and the two forces fought on even terms for over half an hour. Stewart then sent Brown's Brigade into the fight. The weight of Brown's attack and the threat of Dick being outflanked caused Van Cleve's Brigades to fall back. Only a desperate counterattack by Dick's brigade through the smoke-filled woods that had caught fire during the fighting saved them from utter disaster. About that time Gen. Reynolds put three regiments of Edward King's Brigade into the line on Van Cleve's right. One of these regiments was the 75th Indiana, once a member of Wilder's Brigade, and though this regiment of 800 men had never before been in battle they gave a good account of themselves the remainder of the day, suffering very heavy losses. Neither side gained any ground for a short time and then Gen. Stewart threw in his remaining brigade led by Gen. Bate. Bate's fresh but battle-hardened veterans launched such a strong attack that Van Cleve's Brigades along with King's broke and withdrew to the west side of the LaFayette Road. Before Van Cleve could get organized in line of battle in his new position Bate assaulted him again. The Federals resisted them momentarily but a second thrust drove the overpowered Union brigades west almost to the Widow Glenn's house where Rosecrans had his headquarters. Stewart's offensive, led by Bate, had almost cut the Union line completely in two and outflanked Wilder on his left; but the Confederate success was to be short-lived. Bate would be subdued by Wilder and his Lightning Brigade for the second time in three months.

Col. Wilder ordered the 98th Illinois and 17th Indiana to change front and charge Stewart's left flank, and charge they did, with two guns of Capt. Lilly's artillery battery at the edge of the timber setting the stage for the assault. The enfilading of Bate's left flank by the repeating rifles and Lilly's two guns soon broke the Rebel assault and they withdrew to their original position.

Hood then ordered Robertson's Brigade of Texans, supported by Fulton's Brigade of Bushrod Johnson's Div. in another furious assault on Carlin. Carlin's Brigade gave way and was temporarily driven back past the Viniard House.

William Fletcher of the 5th Texas, after the long tiring ride from Virginia and the dusty march from the railroad station, had fallen asleep after being lined up in the woods east of Viniards. Fletcher was awakened by a buddy when Davis' forward regiments had begun an advance. The Texans were then ordered to charge—yelling and firing on the run. Carlin's men, in the haste of their retreat, got jammed up behind a rail fence at the Viniard House and when they moved along the fence in order to run through a gap between the fence and the house they were stacked up as if entering a funnel. Fletcher thought at the time, "Oh, for a shotgun loaded with buckshot!"[9] He then ran around the house so as to get a shot at the retreating Federals as they came out of the funnel but as he rounded the house he was hit in the foot by a Yankee Minie ball. Carlin's Brigade again recovered and drove the Texans back across the road.

At the same time Robertson was carrying his attack to Carlin, Hood had launched an even larger offensive against Heg on Carlin's left. Benning and his Georgians hit Heg's Brigade head on; Gregg's Brigade followed by McNair's Brigade of Bushrod Johnson's Div. hit Heg's left flank and Davis' entire division began to disintegrate.

When Gregg's and McNair's men came storming around Heg's left the Lightning Brigade was ordered up to stop them. As the Confederates advanced, two of McNair's regiments, the 25th Arkansas and the 39th North Carolina, got up front with Gregg's regiments. When Wilder's charge struck them in flank it caught these two regiments in a terrible enfilading fire with both the "seven shooters" and Lilly's Battery inflicting severe losses on them. The firing of the artillery was so intense and so rapid that Capt. Lilly himself made several trips to the caisson on horseback to bring up ammunition to the guns, with the enemy sharpshooters doing their best to pick him off on every trip. This torturous attack caused Johnsons's offensive to completely fold up, and he withdrew to the east side of the LaFayette Road into the woods.

Wilder then moved his men back and to the right to support Davis again. Hood was planning another attack this time with Robertson's and Benning's Brigades having Trigg's fresh brigade of Preston's Division on their left.

Just before Hood launched his last assault of the day Sheridan arrived with two brigades to relieve Davis. As Sheridan approached Wilder's Brigade on his black horse, his staff officer carrying the general's battle flag, shouted, "Make way for Sheridan, make way for Sheridan!" Wilder's men opened ranks and let the general and his staff pass through. As Davis moved off the field to the left, Sheridan swung his division around as if on dress parade and placed them in line of battle over the brow of a hill about 200 yards in front of the Lightning Brigade.

Sheridan ordered his men to advance into the woods which they did in splendid style but in less than two minutes, amid the roar of musketry and the Rebel yells, they came pouring back out of the woods with the Rebels hard on their heels. As Sheridan approached Wilder's lines in retreat, the men of the Lightning Brigade could not keep from yelling, "Make way for Sheridan, make way for Sheridan!" A sgt. of the 72nd Indiana said, "He passed through our line, his men following him, like a swarm of locusts." Sheridan's demoralized troops swarmed to the rear. The pursuing enemy, however, had not forgotten how the Lightning Brigade had handled them before with their Spencers and they halted their pursuit before they reached Wilder's position behind the brow of the hill. The Rebels moved skirmishers forward and they began sharpshooting at any of Wilder's men who exposed themselves.[10]

Four hundred yards in front of Wilder's position was a log cabin, behind which the Confederate sharpshooters had crawled in order to get more advantageous shots at the Lightning Brigade. Pretty soon a big Rebel carrying his weight in coats and blankets that he had taken from Sheridan's dead, stepped out from behind the log cabin. Wilder's men began shooting into the dirt between the man and the cabin. At each volley he would run farther from the house, and each time he would start to run for the house another volley would scare him farther away. Wilder's men yelled and shouted at him as if they were beginning a charge. When he finally started to run toward a woods 200 yards to the north the Yankees began firing in earnest and he fell dead a short distance from the woods.[11]

In the meantime heavy firing to the north and east of Wilder's position had gradually moved to the north and west indicating that the Union line to the north was giving ground. The line in front of the Lightning Brigade was relatively quiet but they were ready—Lilly's battery had each gun double-shotted with canister—the Spencer-armed regiments at the ready, waiting for the attack they knew was sure to come.

Just before dark, they came—Robertson, Benning and Trigg, their bayonets fixed, charging the frail works behind which Wilder's men waited. The first shot from the battery was the signal for the brigade and when Lilly opened up with his battery the entire brigade cut loose with their "seven shooters." The Rebels promptly answered by screaming their Rebel yell and charging at the double quick, attempting to overpower the Union line. But the Lightning Brigade was strong as as a rock and by the time the Rebels got close to the Union works their line was so thin that it virtually disappeared. The survivors took refuge in the ditch in front from which they were soon driven by Capt. Lilly. Lilly had moved two guns forward and set them in such a position that he could rake a wide ditch from end to end. Triple-shotted canister filled the ditch with enemy killed and wounded. The effect of Lilly's crossfire was so devastating that he later commented, "At this point it actually seemed a pity to kill men so. They fell in heaps; and I had it in my heart to order the firing to cease, to end the awful sight."[12] The brigade then made one tremendous charge and drove the enemy back at least a half-mile. During this Union drive, Gen. Crittenden was saved from capture by a brisk advance by the 72nd Indiana in a heavily wooded area.

The night of the 19th was a nightmare. Henry Campbell, of Lilly's Battery, recalled that "both armies rested on their arms in the same positions they fought. Each soldier as he prepared to catch what rest he could get thanked God that he lived through such a day of hell. No fires were allowed and consequently no supper except hardtack and raw bacon—thankful to be alive to eat that. Watered the horses by detachments from a pond near by (later called "Bloody Pond")—nothing but cornstalks to feed them. They have been standing in harness since Friday morning and are nearly worn out."[13]

There were many times during the Civil War when as night fell after a battle soldiers from the opposing sides would meet between the lines and talk and trade tobacco, whiskey or coffee. But this was not the case on this night. The night was uncomfortable. It was cold and dry and the air was full of dust and the smoke from the many grass fires and was accented by the acrid odor of sulfur from the two million charges of gunpowder that had been fired that day. But worse than that, it had been a vicious, bloody and violent battle that day that had lasted until after dark, and the wrath and anxiety and bitterness induced by the heated battle had not subsided.

A great many badly wounded men of both armies lay between the lines that could not be moved because of the constant sniping fire that kept up through the night. Rebel and Union wounded lying side by side, unable to help each other and unable to receive help. One of Wilder's men said that "the cries and groans from these poor fellows were perfectly awful, they were more dreadful than the storm of bullets that showered on us all day."[14]

September had been extremely dry. Water was scarce at best, but making it worse was the fact that the Confederate troops had possession of Chickamauga Creek. The only water within the Federal lines was at Bloody Pond near the Widow Glenn's and three miles south at Crawfish Springs. A few scattered wells and springs were in the battle area, but with 120,000 tired and dirty soldiers camped in the area there was no relief for the terrible thirst.

After the success of Wilder's Brigade at Hoover's Gap, the Union Army had begun mounting other infantry regiments and arming them with Spencer Rifles. Early on the night of Sept. 19, one of these newly mounted regiments, the 39th Indiana of McCook's Corps, gathered up all the empty canteens they could find and began hauling water from Crawfish Springs to the suffering Union soldiers. By midnight they had delivered over 1,000 canteens of water to the Federal camps.

For years after the war the veterans of Chickamauga, at reunions and local get-togethers, relived that agonizing night of Sept. 19. They were never able to forget the terrible thirst, or the smoke from the powder-dry grass and vegetation set on fire by artillery shells, or the unseasonable coldness, or the cries of the wounded lying between the lines. Many of the wounded were burned alive in the grass fires. Pvt. Henderson of the 98th Illinois recalled years after the war, "we spent almost as much time fighting the fires as we did fighting the enemy." And the unbearable tiredness and fatigue. Some of the Union troops had marched all night on the 18th and then fought all day on the 19th. Both sides had suffered heavy casualties during the day and both sides knew, as they lay on their arms that night, that the next day would be even worse.

Late that evening Gen. Rosecrans called a conference of his division and corps commanders to discuss the day's battle just ended and to issue orders for the next day. Thomas, Crittenden and McCook were all there. General "Pap" Thomas had trouble staying awake. He had gotten no sleep the night before while he was moving his corps to the north end of the Union line. But Rosecrans respected Thomas' military ability and he frequently asked his opinion concerning the alignment of troops for the next day. Each time Thomas would recommend strengthening the Union left.

During the previous day Johnson's Div. of McCook's Corps and Palmer's Div. of Crittenden's Corps had been moved to the left and placed under Thomas' command. Thomas now had all but ten brigades of Rosecrans' Army. Rosecrans then issued orders for the 20th. Thomas was to hold his position of the day before. McCook's two divisions under Davis and Sheridan were to close up on Thomas in the area around the Widow Glenn's house and Crittenden's two divisions under Wood and Van Cleve were to take position near where McCook and Thomas joined so as to be able to reinforce or support either of them. Wilder and his brigade were to take position south and west of McCook on the west side of the Dry Valley Road in reserve.

In the past Rosecrans had always displayed a great deal of self confidence in his decision making. He had a reputation of being an excellent military strategist. His mind worked rapidly and accurately. However, as his officers left headquarters that night, some of them felt that he seemed to be irritable and unsure of himself.

While Rosecrans was having his meeting there was also activity in the Confederate camp. Gen. Longstreet, who had become Robert E. Lee's right arm since the death of Stonewall Jackson, arrived from the Army of Northern Virginia with two more of Lee's brigades, those of Humphrey and Kershaw. These, along with Robertson's, Benning's and Law's Brigades, who had arrived with Gen. Hood on the 18th, made a total of five brigades of reinforcements for Bragg from Lee's eastern army. Three other brigades enroute from the east did not arrive until after the battle.

When Longstreet departed from Virginia, Gen. Lee had told him, "General, you must beat those people," and had Lee been in northwest Georgia on Sept. 20, he would have seen that Longstreet did not disappoint him.[15]

As the two armies lined up for the battle on the morning of the 20th they were in the following order from North to South:

UNION	CONFEDERATE
Baird's Division	Breckinridge's Division
Johnson's Division	Cleburne's Division
Palmer's Division	Cheatham's Division
Reynold's Division	Walker's Corps
Brannan's Division	Stewart's Division
Wood's Division	Bushrod Johnson's Division
Van Cleve's Division (Recessed)	Hood's Corps
Negley's Division (Recessed)	Hindman's Division
Davis' Division	Preston's Division
Sheridan's Division	

General Granger with the Union Reserve Corps was at Rossville toward Chattanooga. Van Cleve was behind Brannan, and Wilder was a half-mile south and west of Sheridan in reserve.

General Bragg divided his army into two wings under the commands of Gen. Leonidas Polk and Gen. Longstreet. Polk had the right of the Confederate line consisting of Breckinridge's Cleburnes, Cheatham's Divisions and Walker's Corps. The left wing under Longstreet was made up of Stewart's and Bushrod Johnson's Divisions, Hood's Corps, and the divisions of Hindman and Preston. Forrest's Cavalry was on the extreme right under the direct command of Bragg.

When the sun rose on the 20th the dawn haze made it look large and red and as bloody as the battlefield on which it shone. As on the previous day, the battle began at the north end of the line. Bragg had ordered the attack to begin at the break of day, but between the dilatory attitude of Polk and the bull-headedness of Gen. Hill, the attack was not initiated until 10 o'clock in the morning. As the church bells called the people of Chattanooga to church on this Sunday morning, the second day of this bloodiest of all battles began.

Baird's and Johnson's Divisions became desperately engaged with Breckinridge, Cleburne and Forrest, and shortly thereafter as on the 19th the battle gradually rolled south as division after division entered the fighting. Thomas sent to Rosecrans for reinforcements.

Gen. Rosecrans had stated that Thomas must hold the road that ran through the Rossville Gap to Chattanooga at all costs and that he would reinforce him with the whole army if necessary. At 10:30 Rosecrans answered Thomas' request for help by ordering Van Cleve's Division and two brigades of Sheridan's Division to move north and support Thomas.

At about this time, Capt. Kellogg of Thomas' staff came riding down behind the Union lines toward army headquarters. Brannan's Division, which was between Reynolds' and Wood's Division, was stationed in a dense woods on the west side of the LaFayette Road. Capt. Kellogg could not see Brannan's men through the heavy foliage and when he arrived at Rosecrans headquarters he mistakenly reported that Brannan was not in line and that Reynolds' flank was exposed.

Gen. Garfield, Rosecrans' Chief-of-Staff, who was later to become President of the United States, was busy with another matter so Rosecrans turned to Major Bond, another staff member, and told him to write an order to Gen. Wood. The misinformation carried to headquarters by Capt. Kellogg and the resulting order sent to Gen. Wood set off a chain of events that caused the near-destruction of the Union Army.

> "Headquarters,
> Department of Cumberland
> September 20th—10:45 A.M.
>
> Brigadier-General Wood, Commanding Division:
>
> The General commanding directs that you close up on Reynolds as fast as possible, and support him.
>
> Respectfully, etc.,
> Frank S. Bond,
> Major and Aide-de-Camp."

Earlier that morning Rosecrans had ordered Negley to move north to reinforce Thomas and ordered McCook to fill the gap left by Negley. Negley received this order at 2 A.M. but had not moved yet at 7 A.M. Rosecrans personally went to find out the reason for the delay. Negley's excuse was that Gen. Wood had not yet moved to replace him in the line. Rosecrans, who had been boiling with anger at Negley and McCook over their reluctance to move, then vented his pent-up wrath on Wood. He severely admonished him in strong and vile language in front of his staff for not having promptly and unquestioningly carried out an order.

Now, at shortly before 11 A.M., when Wood received the order to close up on Reynolds, he remembered the embarrassment of Rosecrans' outburst that morning. He knew that Brannan's Division was in position between his own division and that of Gen. Reynolds and that the only way he could close up on Reynolds was to pull back out of line and cross behind Brannan.

Gen. Wood also knew that pulling out of line in the face of the enemy was a dangerous maneuver, but he had been severely rebuked once that day for not immediately executing an order from headquarters and he wasn't going to let it happen again. He immediately ordered his division consisting of Harker's and Buell's Brigades to move out, leaving a gap in the Union line between Brannan and Davis.

Meanwhile, Confederate Gen. Longstreet was aligning his divisions for an attack on the Union right. At the time Wood received the order to move, Longstreet was preparing to give his order of attack. Longstreet had his assault force organized in column with the front two brigades wide, consisting of McNair's and Fulton's of Bushrod Johnson's Division. Immediately behind these two brigades was Johnson's other brigade commanded by Gregg. Behind Johnson's men were aligned Hood's old division made up of Law's Brigade, Robertson's of Texans and Benning's Georgians. The rear of the column was Kershaw's and Humphrey's Brigades under Kershaw. The main assault column contained 11,000 men. On the immediate right was Stewart's Division and on the left was Hindman's Division supported by Preston's making Longstreet's total attacking force 23,000 seasoned Confederate troops. At 11:10 A.M. Longstreet ordered his attack.

On orders from headquarters Van Cleve was moving his division laterally behind Brannan to go to Thomas. Two of Sheridan's brigades were also moving laterally behind Davis to go to Thomas' assistance. And Wood was pulling back to cross behind Brannan and close up on Reynolds.

Longstreet had no knowledge of these Union orders and movements. The fact that he attacked at this particular time was pure coincidence, but it could not have occurred at a more opportune time for the Confederates.

The spearhead of the Rebel attack hit where Wood had left the gap in the line. Bushrod Johnson's division followed by Hood literally rolled over Van Cleve and Wood as they were moving north in column. Hindman's Division, consisting of the brigades of Deas, Anderson and Manigault hit Davis and Sheridan. Davis' two brigades were driven right over Sheridan's men adding to the confusion. And into this melee piled Van Cleve's runaway artillery horses. The entire Union right was routed and they retreated in wild confusion, sweeping Rosecrans and two of his corps commanders, Crittenden and McCook, from the field. Thousands of Federal soldiers were killed or captured during the onslaught; some were trampled by horses amid the catastrophe as the divisions of Van Cleve, Wood, Davis and Sheridan virtually disintegrated. The total collapse of the Union right was complete—except for one lone Union brigade, the Lightning Brigade commanded by Col. Wilder.

When General McCook ordered two of Sheridan's brigades to the left shortly before noon he had ordered Col. Wilder to "close up on his right, and keep the line connected, and occupy the ground left vacant by him, as he was going to move to the left." The Brigade was moving up the hill at Widow Glenn's in line of battle from the southwest when Hindman's assault hit Sheridan. Half of Battery G, 1st Missouri Light Artillery, had been stationed at the Glenn House by Gen. Sheridan, supported by the 27th Illinois Infantry. The 27th was driven off and the battery captured by the Rebels as the Lightning Brigade approached the hill. Col. Wilder ordered Col. Funkhouser and his 98th Illinois to change front to the left and charge them. The 98th charged on the run, drove the Rebels off and retook the battery, Col. Funkhouser falling severely wounded in the assault but cheering his men on even after he fell.

When General McCook received the order to dispatch two of Sheridan's brigades to the aid of Thomas, he sent one of his staff members, Col. Thruston, to Crawfish Springs to order the cavalry up to strengthen his position. McCook was being left with only three brigades, all of them badly depleted by the losses incurred during the fighting around the Viniard House on the 19th. Col. Thruston had no more than started when Longstreet launched his overwhelming attack on the Union right.

Col. Thruston hurriedly delivered his orders at Crawfish Springs and returned to the vicinity of the Widow Glenn's. On his way back he came upon Col. Harrison and his 39th Indiana regiment of mounted infantry, and he led them at a gallop toward the Widow Glenn's. There they joined Col. Wilder and his Lightning Brigade.

The other regiments of the brigade and the 39th Indiana

then came up and took their places in the line and Col. Wilder ordered the Brigade forward. As they passed over the brow of the hill they were met, not fifty yards away, by "six solid lines of gray, coming with their hats down, their bayonets at a charge, and the old familiar Rebel yell."[16] Manigault's Brigade of Hindman's Division was driving to take the Dry Valley Road. The Lightning Brigade met them with a volley from their repeating rifles, but they kept coming. A second volley and then another and the deadly fire of the "seven shooters" continued until it became a steady chatter of lead. Finally the Rebel ranks, thinned by the terrible stream of fire broke and fled to the woods on the opposite side of the field.

Col. Wilder ordered his men to hold their fire until the command was given.

Manigault's Brigade had been badly hurt but his gallant Alabamans and South Carolinians would not give up easily. They reformed in the shelter of the timber and then launched another ferocious attack on the Glenn Hill. When they got to the point at which they had broken before, Col. Wilder gave the command to fire. The devastating fire of the Spencers again drove them across the field and into the woods. Three more times the Rebels attacked and each time they were hurled back in wild confusion. After the last attack Col. Wilder ordered his Brigade to advance and the Lightning Brigade charged, led by the 17th Indiana and the 123rd Illinois, and while the rest of the Union right was fleeing toward Chattanooga, the Lightning Brigade pushed Manigault's Brigade three-quarters of a mile and across the LaFayette Road, "taking two guns from the enemy, still loaded with canister, which were emptied into their fleeing ranks."[17]

Manigault's routed brigade retired into the woods on the east side of the road to lick its wounds and reorganize, having lost over 200 men captured and a large number killed and wounded, mostly from the 24th 28th and 34th Alabama Regiments.

While the Lightning Brigade was driving Manigault back Hindman's two other brigades, Deas' and Anderson's had reached the Dry Valley Road north and west of the Widow Glenn's on Wilder's left and rear. Wilder then pulled back his attacking force and hit Hindman's troops in the left flank. The Lightning Brigade, with the 17th Indiana carrying a captured Alabama battle flag, charged Deas and Anderson viciously and a short but sharp fight ensued around "Bloody Pond" until Hindman, rejoined by Manigault, moved on north toward Snodgrass Hill.

Gen. Thomas, on learning of the flight of the right wing of the Union Army, had pulled his left wing back onto Snodgrass Hill facing south and east and set up defenses to resist the Rebel attack. Hindman, Johnson and Hood, after breaking the Union right, turned north and moved to attack Thomas from the south. Johnson and Hindman were now between Wilder and Thomas, and the remainder of the Federal troops were in flight to Chattanooga.

The Lightning Brigade, the only unit still on the field on the Union right, was winning its part of the battle and Col. Wilder decided to cut through Hindman and Johnson and go to Thomas' assistance. Although these two Rebel divisions outnumbered Wilder five to one, he knew that by piling his 2,000 repeating rifles into their rear he could break through to Snodgrass Hill. He sent a messenger to Gen. Sheridan who was on his way to Chattanooga almost a mile to the rear and asked him to rally his men and come and join in the assault.

While waiting for an answer from Sheridan, Wilder gave his men a brief rest. Neither men nor horses had had water for hours and dead men and dead horses nor the blood and mud of "Bloody Pond" detained them from quenching their agonizing thirst in the pond. Some of them waded into the pond. Others knelt at the edge and drank beside men who had fallen dead of wounds while drinking.

Although Sheridan was not being pursued, he refused to join Wilder and advised him to follow him to Chattanooga.

Col. Wilder positioned his Brigade in a hollow square with two regiments across the front leaving an opening for Lilly's artillery, one regiment on each side and one regiment across the rear. Wilder issued his order to attack and the Brigade had moved 100 yards when a hatless, red-headed man rode up and asked what unit he had. Col. Wilder answered, "1st Brigade, 4th Division, of the 14th Corps, Wilder's Brigade of Mounted Infantry on foot."

The newcomer who was a civilian in a highly emotional state, introduced himself as Charles A. Dana, Assistant Secretary of War. He excitedly told Wilder that the entire Union Army had been crushed, that Rosecrans had been killed or captured and that the disaster was as bad or worse than the Battle of Bull

Run. Dana requested that Wilder escort him to Chattanooga.[18]

Col. Wilder informed Dana that Gen. Thomas was holding Snodgrass Hill and that all was not lost. But Dana was hysterical. Three times he repeated his name, "Charles A. Dana, Assistant Secretary of War," and three times he repeated his request for escort to Chattanooga by Wilder and his Brigade.

Finally Wilder agreed to send some of his scouts with Dana to Chattanooga and added that he intended to break through Bragg's Army and render assistance to Thomas. To the scared civilian, who had been sent to Rosecrans' headquarters as Secretary Stanton's political spy and stooge, Wilder's desire to help Thomas was preposterous. Dana ordered Wilder not to make the charge and to leave the field and proceed to Chattanooga.

Dana, as Assistant Secretary of War, had the authority to issue the order, and although Wilder was infuriated by the situation, he refrained from making the attack. In reference to this incident, Col. Wilder said later:

"I had decided to cut our way through Bragg's Army on Sunday to join Thomas on Snodgrass Hill, and was only prevented from attempting it by peremptory orders from Charles D. Dana, Assistant Secretary of War, who, having lost his way to Chattanooga, had just come up as I was forming the Brigade in five lines, columns of regiments to make the charge which I firmly believe would have resulted successfully. I would have struck them in flank and rear with five lines of Spencer Rifles in the hands of the steadiest body of men I ever saw."[19]

Although Wilder obeyed Dana's order not to make the attack he did not leave the field as Dana had insisted. He moved his Brigade slowly down the Dry Valley Road toward McFarland's Gap, protecting the evacuation of the wagon trains and ambulances from Crawfish Springs to Chattanooga. A short time later Gen. Thomas learned that Wilder's Brigade was intact and still full of fight.

He sent a message to Wilder to take a position on his right to prevent Rebel cavalry from getting in his rear during the Confederate infantry assaults on Snodgrass Hill. The Lightning Brigade remained in this position until daylight the next morning when Thomas, having moved his troops back to Rossville, ordered Wilder to withdraw, which he did—his Brigade being the last to leave the field.

The resistance of the Lightning Brigade and its Spencer Rifles amid disaster on the Union right and its savage attack on Hindman had delayed Bragg's attack on Thomas at Snodgrass Hill for three hours. Gen. Longstreet told Wilder after the war that "the steady and continued racket of these guns led him to think an army corps had attacked his left flank." The delay on the Confederate left perpetrated by Wilder's attack caused Gen. Bragg to lose valuable time in attacking Thomas. Gen. Longstreet wrote later: "It is my opinion that Bragg thought at 3 P.M. that the battle was lost. . ."[20]

This gave Thomas the time he needed to organize his troops and defenses and Thomas told Wilder on the next day that the gallantry of his Spencer-armed brigade quite possibly saved the Union Army from complete annihilation.

Twice during the Battle of Chickamauga the Lightning Brigade saved the Union Army from disaster. First at Alexander's Bridge on the 18th when they held off an entire Confederate Army Corps, thereby giving Rosecrans time to cover his left flank. And secondly on the Union right on the 20th, the Brigade resisted and attacked Hindman's Division so savagely that Thomas was able to make a stand at Snodgrass Hill and earn the nickname that lived with him the rest of his life: "The Rock of Chickamauga." Two months later Gen. Thomas recommended Wilder for promotion to Brigadier General:

"Headquarters
Department of the Cumberland
Chattanooga, November 27, 1863
Brig-General Lorenze Thomas,
Adjutant—General, U. S. Army
General: Enclosed herewith I have the honor to transmit the report of Col. John T. Wilder, Seventeenth Indiana Volunteers, commanding Brigade of mounted infantry, of the Cumberland before and after the evacuation of Chattanooga by the rebel army, including the battle of Chickamauga, and up to the time of the assembling of the army at Chattanooga.

For his ingenuity and fertility of resource in occupying the attention of the entire corps of the rebel army while our army was getting around its flank, and for his valor and the many qualities of a commander displayed by him in the numerous engagements of his Brigade with the enemy before and during the battle of Chickamauga, and for the excellent service rendered by him generally, I would respectfully recommend him to the President of the United States for an appointment of Brigadier General.

I am, sir, very respectfully, your obedient servent,
George H. Thomas,
Major-Gen., Commanding"[21]

The distaster at Chickamauga was a crushing blow to the North. It ruined, at least temporarily, the careers of both Crittenden and McCook, and it caused Rosecrans to be shelved for the remainder of the war. The exploits of Col. Wilder's Lightning Brigade and the stand by Gen. Thomas on Snodgrass Hill were the only bright spots in the Union performance. But the North's setback was only temporary and under new leadership they would soon avenge the loss at Chickamauga.

6

"Riding a Raid"

ON THE 21ST ROSECRANS' BATTERED ARMY BEGAN TO DIG IN FOR the defense of Chattanooga. It had its back to the Tennessee River and Bragg's Confederate Army had possession of Missionary Ridge that runs north and south to the east of Chattanooga, and of Lookout Mountain to the southwest. Bragg did not follow up his victory by attacking the defeated Union Army in Chattanooga and came under much criticism from Longstreet and Forrest at the time because of it. Many historians have since assailed his judgment on this matter but Confederate General John B. Gordon defended Bragg's decision:

"A calm review of the situation, and the facts as they existed at the time, will demonstrate, I think, that his failure to follow and assault General Rosecrans in his strong works at Chattanooga was not only pardonable, but prudent and wise. The Confederate victory at Chickamauga . . . was achieved after two days of desperate fighting and at tremendous cost, while the Confederates had inflicted heavy losses upon the Union Army, they had also suffered heavy losses. Of the thirty-three thousand dead and wounded, practically one-half wore gray uniforms. For every Union regiment broken and driven in disorder from the field, there was a Confederate regiment decimated and shattered in front of the breastworks . . . General Bragg's right wing had been partially shattered in front of the Union field works in the woods at Chickamauga, and his left wing held in check till near nightfall at Snodgrass Hill. It seems to me, therefore, that these facts constitute almost a mathematical demonstration—at least a moral assurance—that his army must have failed in an immediate march across the open plain through the network of wire spread for Confederate feet, in the face of wide-sweeping

Union artillery, and against the infinitely stronger works at Chattanooga."[1]

While the Union Army was retreating back to Chattanooga on the evening of the 20th and all through that night, the Lightning Brigade remained on the field to protect the movement of the wagon trains through the Rossville Gap.

Early on the morning of the 21st, the 98th Illinois left for Bridgeport, Alabama, on the west side of the Tennessee River as guard for 2,000 prisoners; the remainder of the Brigade crossed the river and moved northeast of the ctiy to Friar's Island. This is the same place that they had crossed on September 9, when they had entered the evacuated city. Here they set up an outpost to prevent the Rebels from crossing the river and attacking the Union supply lines.

As the Brigade moved through Chattanooga the battering that the army had taken on the 19th and 20th was shockingly apparent. Broken caissons and limber chests, splintered artillery and damaged wagons were everywhere. Although many of the severely wounded had been captured, the roads were filled with thousands of walking wounded. Rosecrans' Army of the Cumberland appeared to be doomed to eventual subjugation. Even the ordinary soldier realized that the beseigned Union Army could only be supplied by moving wagon trains from middle Tennessee across the Cumberland Plateau and that the Confederates would try to starve them out by attacking their wagon trains.

For the next week the men of Wilder's Brigade spent their time in strengthening and fortifying their position at Friar's Island. The 98th Illinois returned on the 25th. On the 28th Wilder's Brigade was relieved by infantry and was assigned to the 2nd Cavalry Division under Gen. Geo. Crook. Crook was a regular army officer. He had been wounded in 1857 by a poisoned arrow. After the war, Crook, known as "Gray Fox" by the Indians, became the most successful Indian fighter in the army. In 1876 he commanded one column of a three-pronged attack on the Sioux Nation in which Gen. Custer and his command were annihilated.

The 2nd Cavalry Division consisted of Col. Eli Long's Brigade of cavalry, Minty's Brigade and Wilder's Brigade of Mounted Infantry, now under the command of Col. Miller, 72nd Indiana, Col. Wilder having gone on sick leave after Chickamauga. To Crook's Division fell the task of protecting the Tennessee River for over 50 miles north of Chattanooga. On the opposite side of the river were the Rebel pickets, patrolling up and down the Tennessee.

Guarding one of the fordable points on the river was the 4th Ohio Cavalry of Long's Brigade. On the opposite bank was Terry's Texas Rangers (8th Tex. Cavalry) of "Fighting Joe" Wheeler's Confederate Cavalry Corps. These two regiments felt like they were acquainted with each other after having had a skirmish during the Battle of Chickamauga. One of the Ohioans called over, "Johnny Reb, where is Old Ironsides today?" The Rebels called back asking about the whereabouts of the Col. of the 4th Ohio, whereby a Yank answered, "Oh, the devil, you know where we left him over at Chickamauga." The men arranged a truce and promptly proceeded to take a swim, tell a few yarns, trade tobacco for coffee and have a good time in general. These brief truces were common during the Civil War. They could not be condoned by the commissioned officers so they were almost always arranged when no officers were present. However, Capt. Blackburn, Co. F., 8th Tex. Cavalry, commented that "if the terms of peace had been left to the men who faced each other in battle day after day, they would have stopped the war at once on terms acceptable to both sides (except the civil rulers) and honorable to all alike."[2]

While the 4th Ohio was exchanging pleasantries with the 8th Texas, the 72nd Indiana of Wilder's Brigade, on not so friendly terms, was skirmishing with the 4th Georgia Cavalry farther upstream.

Wilder's Brigade left Friar's Island at 8 A.M. on the 30th of September and moved north in the direction of Poe's Tavern along the foot of Walden's Ridge. They camped that night on the bank of Sales Creek, 16 miles north of Poe's. That night Wheeler's Confederate Cavalry force crossed the Tennessee River 20 miles to the north near Washington with 6,000 men.

General Wheeler was a small, wiry man, dark eyed and serious. When given an assignment he planned and executed it with determination and persistence. He followed military procedures to the letter. Not flashy like Forrest and Stuart, Wheeler was serious and businesslike in his movements and attacks. He was to become the only officer to serve as a corps commander in the United States Army after having served as a Confederate Corps Commander in the Civil War, leading an army corps in Cuba in the Spanish-American War at the age of sixty-two.

Born in Augusta, Georgia, in 1936, of transplanted New Eng-

land parents, Wheeler was educated in the east and entered
West Point in 1854 while Col. Robert E. Lee was Superintendent. He was assigned, upon graduation, to a regiment of
Mounted Rifles at Fort Craig, New Mexico. When Georgia se-
ceded from the Union Wheeler resigned from the Regular Army
and took a commission in the Georgia forces. A short time later
he was made colonel of the 19th Alabama Infantry. After giving
an excellent account of himself at Shiloh, Wheeler was given

WHEELER'S RAID
SEPT. 30 – OCT. 8, 1863

command of a cavalry brigade and shortly after the Battle of
Perryville, at the age of twenty-six, was promoted to brigadier-
general and named Bragg's Chief of Cavalry.

Now, in the fall of 1863, Gen. Bragg, in preparing for the
raid into middle Tennessee, order Gen. Nathan Bedford Forrest
to turn over his cavalry command to Gen. Wheeler. But this was
a case of bad judgment on Bragg's part. "Forrest had demonstrated a remarkable ability to command large bodies of cavalry
on independent expeditions. Wheeler could not claim this special
talent, but did his best work when operating in close conjunction

with the main army. It seems therefore, that Bragg, who apparently had a positive genius for making mistakes, rid himself of the one leader who might have had a chance to impair permanently Rosecrans' communications. A union of the two commands at this time seems to have been a necessary move, but it also appears that temporarily at least Forrest should have been the commander; not only because he was better fitted for this type of work, but for the additional reason that Wheeler's troops apparently showed no resentment in being commanded by Forrest while the same could not be said in reverse order."[3]

Forrest protested to Bragg about turning over his troops to Wheeler, and Bragg threatened to arrest him if he did not obey the order immediately. Forrest then, after threatening Bragg with his life if their paths ever again crossed (which they did not), left for a conference with President Davis at Montgomery, Alabama, where he was given an independent command in Mississippi and western Tennessee.

When Gen. Wheeler and his combined command crossed the Tennessee River on the night of Sept. 30, his forces consisted of:

Wharton's Division	*Martin's Division*
Crew's Brigade	Morgan's Brigade
Harrison's Brigade	Russell's Brigade

Davidson's Division (Forrest's)

Davidson's Brigade
Scott's Brigade
Hodge's Brigade

Col. Minty of Crook's Division had less than half his command in the area where Wheeler crossed, and Wheeler's advance guard quickly drove in the pickets of the 4th Michigan. Minty then gathered together about 400 of his men, consisting of detachments of the 4th Michigan, 7th Penn., and the 4th U. S. Regular Cavalry, and attempted to make a defense. However, Wheeler's overwhelming numbers soon drove Minty off, and the rebels had possession of the west side of the river.

That night it rained for the first time since August 16—44 days, and the rain continued almost every day for the next thirty days, making the roads practically impassable.

Daylight came late on October 1st. It was cloudy and drizzly, and Wheeler began his movement westward over the mountains toward the Sequatchie Valley.

At noon word got to Rosecrans' headquarters in Chattanooga that Wheeler had crossed the Tennessee. He immediately issued orders to Gen. Crook to give chase with his 2nd Cavalry Division and to Col. Edward McCook to move his 1st Cavalry Division north from Bridgeport, Alabama.

The Lightning Brigade received their movement orders shortly after noon and got underway at 2 P.M. They traveled up river six miles to where two roads led up the ridge. When they got to the point where Wheeler had gone up the mountain, they had difficulty in determining which road to take. The rain had turned to a full-scale storm and the water came down the mountain in torrents, washing out all signs of Wheeler's tracks. The men of the Lightning Brigade had just fought a ferocious and bloody three-day battle at Chickamauga and now, with practically no rest, they were off on a ten-day running battle with Wheeler. They had been issued five days' rations on the 18th of September, and it would be 22 days before they would be issued any more. They had managed to procure some bacon from the countryside after Chickamauga, but as they hurriedly moved after Wheeler, there was no time to stop and cook it. As they moved along on their horses, they ate the bacon raw out of their haversacks and cupped their hands to catch rain water for drinking. Finally at dark, the Brigade, with the 72nd Indiana in advance, started up the ridge by the right-hand road. For five hours they struggled up the mountain road dismounted, leading their horses through ankle-deep mud, the driving rain blinding them and soaking them to the skin. Lilly's Battery had the worst of it. They had only enough good horses to fit out three guns, and the horses were not teamed with their usual partners; consequently they did not pull together very well and the guns had to be double-teamed on the slippery slope. At 10 P.M. with the battery half way up the mountain, the 72nd Indiana came out on top of the ridge above the rain only to find that they had taken the wrong road. Since the two roads were separated on the ridge by a deep gorge, there was nothing to do but to move the entire Brigade back down the mountain. By this time the wind had shifted to the north and the temperature had dropped considerably. It was a cold, drenched, tired command that reached the bottom of the ridge at daylight.

After feeding the horses the Brigade started their ascent up the other road. A detail from the 123rd Illinois was assigned to help Lilly's Battery up the steep mountainside and by noon the Brigade reached the top, being met there by Gen. Crook and the balance of his command.

The division was now a full day behind Wheeler and they moved across the flat top of Walden's Ridge as rapidly as possible. The roads on top of the ridge were dry and the division made the 12 miles across the top in good time. The descent on the west side was made by the middle of the afternoon. On reaching the Sequatchie Valley the column halted long enough to feed and curry the horses, and to give the men time to eat what rations they had with them. From the direction of Dunlap they could hear the sound of exploding ammunition.

Gen. Wheeler was familiar with the geography of the Sequatchie Valley. When Generals Bragg and Kirby Smith had invaded Kentucky in the summer of 1862, Wheeler and his cavalry force had moved through this valley, capturing several Union outposts. On reaching the valley for this raid, Wheeler dispatched Wharton's and Davidson's Divisions to seize the Union supply depot at McMinnville, and moved with Martin's Division to attack a Union wagon train near Dunlap.

Charles Schultz had come to America from Germany to make his fortune. He settled in Olney, Illinois, and entered the general merchandise business. As was customary for the more agressive businessmen during the Civil War, Schultz got into the sutler business, which could be described as a traveling "PX". Normally one sutler was assigned per regiment. It was a private enterprise, and the sutler, by shuttling wagons between his source of supply and the regiment with which he was doing business, kept a supply of personal items, canned delicacies, tobacco, etc. available to the men of the regiment. The sutler was also the best way to get a letter back home. Although the sutlers no doubt charged the limit on their wares, they did provide a necessary service to the soldiers. In many cases they issued credit until payday which was often several months away. Mr. Schultz was sutler for the 38th Illinois Infantry, and among the several hundred wagons enroute to Chattanooga through the Sequatchie Valley on this day were his sutler wagons containing $11,000 worth of merchandise. When Martin's Division hit the wagon train, they drove the escort into the hills, took what supplies they could carry with them and set fire to the rest, including Charles Schultz's stores.[4]

Wheeler then crossed the Cumberland Mountains with Martin and joined Wharton and Davidson at McMinnville.

After feeding Crook's Cavalry moved across the valley and began its ascent of the Cumberlands just at dark. The mountain road was every bit as bad as the one they had taken up Walden's Ridge—muddy, covered with loose stones and very steep. Capt. Lilly had to have help from the brigade to get his battery up. A detail of 25 men was assigned to each gun and caisson, and they literally pulled the double-teamed horses up the slope. The ascent of the long column was slow and tedious, hampered by weather that was damp and cold. Each time the column would halt, which was often, the men would dismount and build warming fires with rails from the fences. By the time they were halfway up the mountain they could see a trail of fires six to eight miles long. Sgt. McGee said "We never saw so much fire in one night, and we burned up enough rails to fence a county."[5] At 10 P.M. the division reached the summit of the Cumberlands and went into camp, having traveled 20 miles in severe weather and crossed two mountain ranges in 24 hours. There was no feed for the horses that night.

The division moved at daylight on the 3rd with the two cavalry brigades, Long's and Minty's, in advance. The column made good time on the roads across the top of the mountains, and moved the 50 miles to the western slope by 3 o'clock in the afternoon. At the point where the road begins its descent down the west side of the mountains, the advance cavalry overtook the rear guard of Wheeler's force. Wheeler's men retreated down the mountain slowly after harassing the Union Cavalry in their descent and killing two of Crook's cavalrymen.

On reaching the cove at the foot of the mountain, Crook found the Confederates in line of battle across the mouth of the cove. It was Crew's Brigade of Wharton's Division behind rail barricades. The 4th U. S. Regulars of Minty's Brigade were ordered to make a charge and drive the Rebels out. They formed their line, drew their sabers, and made ready for the charge— but did not charge. One of Wilder's men recorded, "We afterwards learned that it was because they were barefooted, having traded their boots off over at Mount Washington; and upon reflection we remembered that, as we come up the valley, we noticed all the women wore boots."[6]

Just before dark the 17th Indiana and 98th Illinois were ordered to dismount and move against the enemy. These two regiments moved forward through the windings of Thompson's Cove in the dim light of dusk until suddenly, only eighty yards in front of them, a voice called out gruffly, "Who are you?" Major Jones of the 17th Indiana answered, "Who are you?" The voice called out, "We're Rebels, come on over." The 17th and 98th were then ordered to charge and the fire leaped from the Spencers; the Rebels immediately pulled out leaving their killed and wounded.[7] The 17th Indiana captured a stand of national colors belonging to the 4th Alabama Cavalry, but before a general attack could be made, it got too dark to see and the Brigade rested on the line all night.

Though the night was very cold, no fires were allowed and they passed the bitter night without food or sleep. Men nor horses had had any food for 24 hours. The command was out of rations and the barren country they had just crossed had yielded nothing in the way of forage. The horses had eaten only the dried corn stalks they had found on the descent down the lower part of the mountain slope. Orderly Miller of Lilly's Battery offered 50 cents for a piece of hardtack but couldn't get anyone to take the offer.[8]

Reveille was at 4 A.M. on the 4th and at daylight they discovered that the Rebels had pulled out during the night. Gen. Crook then started his division off toward McMinnville, the Lightning Brigade in advance. As they passed through the place where the Rebels had been camped, they found the ground covered with opened pickle bottles and empty sardine and oyster cans, the remains of the sutler's stores that the Rebels had taken from the wagon train in the Sequatchie Valley. The sight of such luxuries to these men who had not eaten in more than a day, fired their anger and made their desire to catch the Rebels even more intense.

But their hunger was soon relieved when the column, moving toward McMinnville, passed through a rich, fertile country untouched by the ravages of the war. The column rested for a short time about noon to let the men dig potatoes from a nearby field. Since the Lightning Brigade had the advance, they got the choice forage. By the time they got through this part of the country, the saddles of Wilder's men were weighted down with ham, sides of bacon, chickens and bags of sweet potatoes.

At 3 P.M. the division reached McMinnville just as the Rebels were leaving on the other side of town.

Wharton's and Davidson's divisions had arrived at McMinnville earlier in the day and captured and paroled the garrison there that consisted four companies of the 4th Tennessee Union Infantry. They then set about looting the town. They found the blankets and overcoats belonging to the Union 1st Cavalry Division that had been stored there for the summer. They ravaged the stores and pilfered the homes of the loyal Union citizens. While this pillaging was going on, Gen. Wheeler arrived with Martin's Division and he tried, as he said, "unsuccessfully," to stop it. Only the approach of Gen. Crook and his Union Cavalry caused the Rebels to cease and leave town.

The Confederate sympathizers of the area, on hearing that the Rebels were in town, came in with wagons to load up all the coffee and sugar that Wheeler's men could not carry with them. But before they could get loaded and out of town, the Union troops entered and not only took the coffee and sugar from them, but also took their horses.

The Union troops then moved on through town at a gallop, and a half a mile out met the enemy's rear guard. The 4th U. S. Cavalry was sent to the front and they drove the enemy ahead at a trot without stopping the column. The column followed the enemy so closely that they finally drove the rear guard back on Harrison's Brigade of Wharton's Division which was in the rear of the main body. Col. Harrison deployed his men in line of battle in a thick woods on the far side of a field. Lilly's battery, unlimbered in an orchard, started firing percussion shell into the woods.

Company F of the 8th Texas was on the left of its regiment in the line when Capt. Blackburn suddenly realized that Lilly's battery was firing directly over his company and the shells were getting lower all the time. In looking for a reason for this, he found that he had four men mounted on white horses and they had somehow gotten grouped together, thereby providing a perfect target for the Union artillery. Capt. Blackburn requested permission from Col. Harrison to dismount his men but the request was denied. Blackburn disobeyed the denial and ordered his men to dismount, lie on the ground and keep their bridle reins in their hands. Just as the order had been executed, a shell hit one of the white horses, tearing off its shoulder. It undoubtedly would have killed or severely wounded its rider had he been mounted.[9]

Col. Miller then ordered the 17th Indiana and the 72nd Indiana to make an attack, with Co. B of the 72nd under Capt.

Herron out as skirmishers. These two regiments charged into the woods and put the Rebels on the run, capturing several as they were attempting to mount their horses. Capt. Blackburn had possibly saved a life by disobeying orders, but the fact that several dismounted men were captured shows that Col. Harrison knew what he was doing.

The enemy had been driven about a mile when a Confederate officer came galloping down the road on a white horse. He was waving a white handkerchief. Lt. Col. Kirkpatrick of the 72nd Indiana stepped out on the road as he approached and called out, "What the devil do you want?" The Rebel officer said, "I want to make some arrangements about burying our dead." Col. Kirkpatrick madly roared back, "This is not the time or place to make such arrangements. Get out of here you son of a b————!" The officer wheeled his horse and rapidly left. One more charge by Wilder's two regiments sent the Rebels scurrying toward Murfreesboro.[10]

By this time it was dark and the division camped in the area which was six miles from McMinnville. Before retiring early, Crook's men made coffee for the first time in three days.

General Crook guessed that Wheeler's next objective would be Murfreesboro. The Union Army had a sizeable supply depot there, guarded by only two regiments of infantry under Gen. Ward. At daylight on the 5th, Cook renewed his pursuit of the Rebels toward Murfreesboro across the "Barrens" or Cumberland Plateau. Roads on the plateau were in good condition and the force made good time, passing through Woodbury at 2 P.M. and arriving at Readyville at 5 P.M. Wheeler had a strong rear guard force posted across the pike from Readyville to Murfreesboro. In order to avoid it, so he could get to Murfreesboro ahead of the main Confederate body of cavalry, Crook moved his command north to the Liberty Pike and then towards Murfreesboro. By this time, however, Wheeler had arrived in front of Murfreesboro and demanded its surrender. While awaiting Gen. Ward's reply, Wheeler's scouts reported Union Cavalry at his rear and Wilder's Brigade flanking him on his right, and he immediately retreated from Murfreesboro, this important supply center being saved without a shot being fired. At sundown the Brigade camped on the Stone River, northwest of town near the fortifications that had been built for the battle fought there in December of 1862.

By now Wheeler and his huge cavalry force had traveled 200

miles since crossing the Tennessee River on September 30. With the exception of the wagon train in the Sequatchie Valley, which McCook's 1st Cavalry Division had been sent to protest, Crook and his 2nd Division had prevented Wheeler from creating any great amount of destruction; but he had not been able to get Wheeler in a position where he would have to stand and fight.

On October 6, Wheeler moved his cavalry corps toward Shelbyville. During this movement Wharton's Division burned all the railroad bridges between Murfreesboro and Wartrace. Wheeler temporarily divided his force on his way to Shelbyville, and while Martin's Division skirmished with the 5th Iowa Cavalry which was garrisoned at Manchester, Wharton and his men, captured a large Union wagon train and a quantity of military stores at Christiana and Fosterville. As Wheeler approached Shelbyville, the small Federal garrison fled, leaving a large quantity of supplies and ammunition which were taken by the Confederates.

That morning Gen. Crook's column did not get underway until almost 8 o'clock. From daylight until that time was taken up with feeding and caring for the horses, eating breakfast and drawing rations of hardtack, coffee and sugar. They were expected to procure meat and vegetables on the road. The men had been in the saddle for six days on an issue of two day's rations, and when the company officers attempted to draw rations that morning, they were able to get only a three day's ration of hardtack plus some of the coffee and sugar captured at McMinnville.

The column moved slowly down the Shelbyville Pike and by the middle of the afternoon it began to rain. Moving through this beautiful, middle Tennessee country, the Union troops could not help but admire the fine southern mansions and plantations along the route. They camped that night four miles from Shelbyville in a thicket filled with briar patches while Col. Miller sent the Brigade scouts ahead to find where the enemy had camped.

That same evening Gen. Joe Wheeler had ordered Davidson's Division to camp on the Duck River near Warner's Bridge between Shelbyville and Farmington. Martin's Division camped two miles farther downstream to the northwest and Wharton's Division was two miles below Martin's. Wheeler knew that Crook's Division and McCook's Division, which had caught up with Crook at Murfreesboro, were in the area and he told Davidson that if he were attacked he was to fall back on Martin. The scouts from the Lightning Brigade found Davidson's

Division and reported to Col. Miller that they were camped two miles on the other side of Shelbyville.

That night the rain came on stronger and the wind blew hard and gusty. The men constructed "raider's bunks" for protection from the weather. A man from the 72nd Indiana described this:

Here it was that we first learned how to put up a raider's bunk, and as it served us a happy purpose on many occasions we will describe it. The raider's bunk was constructed of six rails and two men could put one up in less than a minute. With the addition of a rail at each side and our gum blankets thrown over them, the bunk had ample room under it for six men to sleep and keep dry, no matter how hard it rained. Lay three rails down parallel with each other and two feet apart. Lay a rail across these a foot from the ends, on top of the two outside ones and under the center one. Now raise this end of the three rails three feet high and cross two rails over the end of the center one, and under the ends of the outside ones, and the work is done.[11]

Gen. Crook was less than six miles from the enemy with only two-third of his division, Minty and his brigade having been side-tracked near Readyville by a skirmish with Wheeler's rear guard. Minty and his brigade were still several miles to the north.

Crook moved his troops out at 6 A.M. on the morning of the 7th, the Lightning Brigade in advance, followed by Eli Long's Brigade of cavalry. They took the pike that led directly to Farmington. McCook's 1st Division was ordered toward Unionville, ten miles north of Farmington.

Wheeler's men had completely sacked Shelbyville when they moved through on the evening of the 6th, destroying everything they could not carry off. When Crook's column arrived there at 7 A.M., they were greeted with cheers and waving handkerchiefs of the sympathetic Union citizenry.

Before the small Union garrison had evacuated Shelbyville on Wheeler's approach, they had partially dismantled the court house and blocked the streets leading to it with the debris, possibly with the idea of making a stand until they realized the size of the Rebel force.[12]

When Wheeler's men entered Shelbyville, they found many shops and sutler's stores well stocked with goods. Much of the merchandise was owned by Northern camp followers who were forced to leave it behind rather than risk capture themselves. One of Wharton's men said,

Such plunder was considered as legitimate for capture as a United States mule or wagon, and to many it was much more acceptable. No Southern sympathizer would be granted this privilege. Commanding officers would attempt to restrain in a degree but efforts were generally futile; and the result was that, after a raiding party had left a place, not much was left to commence business on again. . . . A couple of ladies had come to town that morning to make some purchases. When they saw what had happened, they waved their handkerchiefs and cheered lustily for Jeff Davis. The soldiers gathered around them, filled their buggy full of goods, and then escorted them out of the town.[13]

Crook's troops moved through Shelbyville without stopping and continued towards Farmington. Davidson's Confederates were a few miles down the pike, and he sent Scott's Brigade back toward Shelbyville on a side road that paralleled the pike a mile to the north, hoping to come in on the Union rear after they had passed the point where this road came back to the main pike. However, a boy from one of the loyal Union families in the community approached Col. Miller and told him of this maneuver. The brigade then took the right-hand fork in the road that would lead to the dirt road on which Scott had doubled back. They had hardly gone a quarter of a mile when the 17th Indiana at the head of the column came upon the Rebels lying dismounted in the brush and fence rows along the road.

The 17th Indiana and the 98th Illinois dismounted and charged the Rebels with their seven shooters. Scott's men resisted stubbornly at first, but the overpowering fire from the Spencers soon got the best of them and they pulled back 200 yards and reformed their line across the road. Before they could get properly formed, the 17th and 98th hit them again. They immediately broke under the withering fire and ran to their horses, leaving their dead and wounded where they lay. An entire company of 200 men of Scott's Brigade who were cut off from their horses, were captured by the 98th Illinois and taken into custody by Capt. Robinson, Co. C., 72nd Indiana. The Rebels who were able to get mounted attempted to pass through a narrow lane where the 17th and 98th poured a destructive flanking fire into them, killing many men and horses. The 17th and 98th pursued the retreating Confederates at the double-quick with the 72nd Indiana close behind and the 123rd Illinois bringing up the rear.

Col. Hodge, a graduate of the United States Naval Academy, arrived with his brigade to reinforce Scott but found Scott's

Brigade in wild retreat. Col. Hodge gave this account of the situation at the time:

Being ordered by General Davidson to lead them and to take command of the rear in person, I countermarched with my brigade and was proceeding at a gallop with my command back, when ahead of me I encountered the whole of Scott's Brigade crowded in frightful and horrible confusion, wild and frantic with panic, choking the entire road and bearing down upon me at racing speed. It was too late to clear the way; they rode over my command like madmen, some of them stopping only, as I am informed, when they reached Tennessee. I was ridden over and my horse knocked down, but succeeded in extricating myself and Captain Larmer's company, 27th Virginia Battalion, which I threw into position behind a fence running at right angles with the road, and opened fire upon the enemy, who were fiercely charging the rear of the panic-stricken crowd.[14]

Col. Kirkpatrick of the 72nd Indiana, at the head of his regiment, shouted to his men, "Hurry up boys or you won't get a smell." His men followed him on the run in their attempt to get into the fight. The pursuit had become a regular foot race with the 17th and 98th firing on the run and the 72nd and 123rd running to catch up. The regimental color bearer for the 72nd ran out of breath, but Capt. Thomson picked it up in his strong hands and with the colors in one hand and his sword in the other he encouraged his men to renewed energy, "Come on, Seventy-Second!"[15]

Col. Hodge managed to get some semblance of a battle line formed, and Gen. Davidson, arriving with his brigade, attempted to re-form Scott's men; but the impetus of the Lightning Brigade's attack carried the entire division back in continued retreat. Col. Hodge later reported: "For five and one half hours over seven miles of country the unequal contest continued; my gallant brigade was cut to pieces and slaughtered."[16]

After chasing the mounted Rebels for three miles on foot, the Lightning Brigade finally halted to catch their breath and bring up the horses so they could remount. The road along which the running battle had taken place was covered with dead and wounded, and with knapsacks, guns and other accoutrements. Many of the dead, wounded and prisoners were dressed in Federal uniforms taken from the supply center at McMinnville and in civilian clothes looted from the store in Shelbyville. These were stripped off of them by the men of the Brigade along with gold watches, money, hats and boots—anything that the Union sol-

diers thought had been taken during the raid and probably a lot
that wasn't. Captured horses were loaded down with bundles of
plunder taken at Shelbyville. The Brigade, now mounted, continued its pursuit of the retreating Rebel force.

It was customary during the Civil War that when a sizeable
troop movement was being made in a combat area, the positions
in the column would be rotated on a daily basis. On this day,
October 7, it had been the 123rd Illinois' turn to be at the rear
of the Brigade. Shortly after noon Col. Monroe of the 123rd
complained to Capt. Rice, the Brigade adjutant, that he didn't
think Col. Miller was being fair to him. He remarked that the
other regiments were getting to do all the fighting and that his
regiment was not being given a fair chance. After a heated dis-
cussion Col. Monroe told Capt. Rice that he was going to re-
sign. Capt. Rice then rode to the head of the column and told
Col. Miller what Monroe had said, Col. Miller answering, "At
the next engagement bring the 123rd to the front."[17]

Gen. Wheeler, on learning of Davidson's situation, ordered
Martin's and Wharton's Divisions to move between Davidson
and Farmington. By the time the Lightning Brigade had traveled
to within one mile of Farmington, Wheeler had gotten his
scattered forces together and had set up a line of battle with
his entire force. Wheeler's line lay in a dense woods across the
Farmington Pike with four artillery pieces, two positioned on
either side of the road. To face this huge Confederate Cavalry
force, Gen. Crook had only the Lightning Brigade. Long's Brigade was still some distance to the rear.

Capt. Rice rode back to the 123rd Illinois, saluted Col. Monroe, and said, "Colonel, the brigade commander directs me to
have you bring your regiment to the front." Col. Monroe, with
a big smile on his face, sang out, "Attention! Forward, quick
trot, march!"[18]

The 123rd was formed immediately to the left of the road
and the 17th Indiana to the right. The 72nd Indiana was then
placed to the left of the 123rd and 98th to the right of the
17th. The skirmishing fire gradually turned into a full scale battle. At this moment the Brigade sustained one of its greatest
losses of the war—the brave and gallant Col. Monroe was
killed while posting one of his companies in the line. The Rebel
artillery, with rapid fire grape and canister, had part of the Brigade pinned down in the dense undergrowth, but the staggering
fire from the seven shooters and the return of artillery fire by

Lilly's Battery soon began taking its toll in the Rebel ranks.

While Gen. Wharton was moving his troops up to rendezvous with Martin and Davidson, his rear guard, the 4th Tennessee and the 1st Kentucky of Harrison's Brigade, got cut off by the Union advance. After a hasty conference, Col. Anderson of the 4th and Col. Chenoweth of the 1st Kentucky decided to cut their way through to the rest of Wharton's command. The Tennesseans and Kentuckians quickly removed their captured Federal uniforms and donned their worn, faded gray, and Col. Chenoweth, waving his sword over his head, shouted, "Follow me, my brave Kentuckians!"[19]

These two regiments were closer to the battle than they thought, and after moving only a few yards through the woods, bullets from the Spencer rifles were zipping all around them. After a short distance they came upon a narrow lane that led out to the main road where they could see their Confederate comrades and the order was given, "Left into column!" The lane was sunken and a rail fence paralleled it between the Rebels and the Lightning Brigade; it offered a certain amount of protection from the flying bullets. Although the two regiments reached the line with few casualties, the rail fence and trees along the lane were riddled with lead. A member of the 4th Tenn. said that later, when members of the regiment reminisced about the incident they would always ask, "Did you ever see as much kindling wood flying in the air as at that time?"[20]

After two hours of desperate fighting in the woods along the Farmington Pike, an officer delivered Col. Miller a message from Gen. Crook:

Colonel—From what information I get from you, and what I get from other sources, I am convinced the enemy's forces have made a junction at Farmington. His forces are much larger than yours. I have no word from Gen. Mitchell's Division (McCook's). Minty is 10 miles in the rear. Cannot you keep off an engagement? In less than an hour it will be dark. I am confident an action will be certain defeat with so unequal forces.

George Crook, Commanding Cavalry.[21]

After reading the message, Col. Miller told the officer to tell Gen. Crook, "It is impossible!" He immediately gave the order to charge, and the Brigade rose up along the line as if one and advanced through the brush and briars with their Spencers spurting a solid stream of lead. The 72nd Indiana found an artillery battery in their front. Col. Kirkpatrick shouted, "Come on, Seventy-Second, let's take that battery!" His men charged at the double-quick and captured it.[22]

All along the line the Lightning Brigade soon had the Rebels on the run, and within 15 minutes after the word to charge had been passed, Wheeler's men were streaming through the town of Farmington, throwing down blankets, guns and anything else that might slow them down. By the time the Brigade, with the help of Long's Brigade which had recently arrived, had chased the Rebels a half mile on the other side of town it became too dark to continue the pursuit and Col. Miller ordered his men to make camp for the night.

Immediately after the battle, Col. Miller sent the following dispatch to Gen. Crook:

General—At the time of receiving your order, to prevent an engagement was impossible; the enemy would have attacked me had I not him. I have whipped him and stampeded all his troops; have taken all four of his cannon and 300 prisoners, but not without loss to my command. Col. Monroe 123rd Illinois, with two other officers, are among the killed. Send forward medical aid as soon as possible.

> A. O. Miller
> Col., Commanding Brigade[23]

The Lightning Brigade had given another demonstration of its battle effectiveness. In addition to the 300 Rebel prisoners, Wheeler lost 100 killed and 150 wounded, while Wilder's Brigade lost only 13 killed and 79 wounded. One of Wheeler's severest losses in the battle was the death of Major McDonald of General Forrest's old regiment, the 7th Tennessee Cavalry.

After the battle of Chickamauga, General-in-Chief Halleck in Washington had ordered the XI and XII Corps from the Army of the Potomac under Gen. Joseph Hooker to reinforce Rosecrans in Chattanooga. However, when Wheeler's raid on the supply lines became imminent, these troops were strung out along the railroad from Nashville to Chattanooga to protect the transportation of supplies moving to the besieged army in Chattanooga. Hooker's headquarters was in Bridgeport, Alabama, but his Chief-of-Staff, Gen. Butterfield was in the Shelbyville area to personally effect Hooker's orders. General Butterfield, who wrote the army bugle call, "Taps," was senior officer present, and Gen. Crook was now responsible to him since coming into the area of Hooker's command.

Through a mix up of orders, Col. Minty had remained at Shelbyville while the battle was in progress. At 5 P.M. one of Gen. Butterfield's aides rode up and ordered him to the front. Minty and his brigade arrived just as the battle was over. Gen. Butterfield had Minty relieved of command and placed under arrest for disobedience of orders and tardiness of movement in the face of the enemy. However, a short time later Minty was tried and found innocent of the charges and reinstated to his command.

On Oct. 8, the day after the Battle of Farmington, the 5th Iowa Cavalry was attached to Minty's Brigade and Col. Low of that regiment was placed in command of the brigade. At daylight Wilder's and Minty's brigades moved out in pursuit of Wheeler's retreating force with the cavalry brigade in advance and Col. Low in command of the combined force. Wheeler was moving south toward the Alabama line, and although he had taken a terrible beating at Farmington, he still had the wagon train that Wharton had captured on the 6th. The Union troops passed through Cornersville at noon, and without stopping to feed the horses pushed on through a series of beautiful and fertile valleys. One of Lilly's men noted, "The valleys were covered with fine plantations, good corn fields, large residences and plenty of sweet potatoes, our main staff of life right now. Every potato patch generally has half a regiment of cavalry in it and the battery boys ain't far behind. Before we reached camp our extra wagon was loaded down with them."[24]

At dark the force moved through Pulaski, Tennessee, county seat of Giles County, and camped at 9 P.M. just across a small river. The command moved out at daylight on the 9th on the Lamb's Ferry Road pushing as hard as they could so as to catch Wheeler before he could reach the Tennessee River. At 3 P.M. the 5th Iowa in advance of the column came on to the Rebel rear guard posted across Sugar Creek. This large and freshly mounted regiment formed in column by companies, drew their sabers and charged right over the barricade, capturing several of the enemy and scattering the remaining Rebels all over the woods.

The column then quickened its pace, chasing the Rebels toward the river with the cavalry brigade in front, killing and capturing any of the Confederates that had been left to retard their advance. At 5 P.M. the Federals reached the Tennessee River at Muscle Shoals only to find that Wheeler, by marching all night, had managed to get across the river with most of his force.

The Union command then pulled back from the river to near Rogersville, Alabama, where they went into camp and remained there through the 10th, resting and rounding up Rebel prisoners from the woods where they had scattered during the chase.

Wheeler had crossed the Tennessee River on the night of September 30 with seven brigades of cavalry 50 miles north and east of Chattanooga. Nine days later he recrossed the Tennessee 150 miles west and south with less than half his command, the remainder having been killed, captured or having deserted during the raid. Wheeler had traveled over 300 miles, and although he managed to capture a few wagons and some supplies and destroy a couple of bridges, his raid was considered a failure.

In his report to Washington, Major-General Thomas, who replaced Rosecrans as commander of the Army of the Cumberland, stated:

On the night of September 30 the enemy's cavalry, under Wheeler crossed the Tennessee River near Washington, Tennessee and moved thence against Gen. Rosecrans' communications. Wilder's Brigade pursued him through middle Tennessee and drove him back across the Tennessee River without his having materially interfered with Gen. Rosecrans' communications. The brigade had several brisk skirmishes with the enemy, and at Farmington a severe battle was fought with Wheeler's forces, driving them from the field with heavy losses.[25]

The pursuit of Wheeler through middle Tennessee could not be termed a major battle because of the numbers involved, but for the men of the Lightning Brigade it was probably the most strenuous campaign of the war. In only nine days they had traveled three hundred miles over rugged terrain on two days' rations, fought three skirmishes and one pitched battle. But they had accomplished their mission; they had kept open the supply lines to the besieged troops in Chattanooga.

7

"Wait for the Wagon"

THE ENTIRE DAY OF OCTOBER 10 THE BRIGADE REMAINED IN camp near Rodgersville, Alabama. It had just completed a long tiresome expedition over rugged terrain, and both the men and their horses showed the strain of going without sleep for days on end and the everpresent shortage of food and fodder. The day was spent resting and foraging. Fortunately, the surrounding countryside yielded a bountiful supply of food for both the men and their horses. The Brigade had been picking up loose horses all the way from McMinnville to the Tennessee River and there were now 1,000 more horses than men with the Brigade.

In the process of procuring food and feed, the foragers raided a large number of applejack stills, and on the evening of the 10th, with the horses curried and fed, the men of the Lightning Brigade ate and drank and in general, "raised hell,"—a welcome respite from the tensions of war.

During the Battle of Chickamauga, a riderless Rebel horse, excited by the noise of battle, had come galloping into the lines held by the Lightning Brigade. The horse belonged to a Confederate officer and was fully rigged—saddle, bridle, saddlebags and all. Taking the runaway horse into custody, were three officers of the 72nd Indiana, and the prize was divided three ways. One officer took the horse, another a bottle of brandy from the saddlebags. Capt. Robinson took possession of the remaining contents of the bags—two sets of rebel underwear. Not having any way of carrying his prize, Capt. Robinson donned both sets, wriggling and tugging to get them over the two pairs of 1863 model "G. I. scivvies" he was already wearing.

Through the rest of the battle, on the trip to Friar's Island and during the pressing and exhausting pursuit of Gen. Wheeler's cavalry force, Capt. Robinson had suffered the bulging and sweaty agony of four sets of "hog hair" underwear. The captain's men noticed that he had grown pale and dejected.

On this Saturday holiday, Capt. Robinson, who hadn't been out of his clothes for over three weeks, proceeded to the nearest stream to bathe. When he removed the first pair of underclothes, he discovered that he was crawling with body lice and as each succeeding layer was removed the number quadrupled. By the time he got down to bare skin, he was a writhing, crawling mass of vermin.

Up to this time the company record for gray-backs per soldier, killed and counted, was 120; however, when Capt. Robinson's men saw the enormous, uncountable number that were living on his person, they conceded the championship without verification.

Captain Robinson soon returned to vigorous health, but for the rest of his days he always believed that the Rebels had intentionally infested him with lice in a sinister act of sabotage.[1]

The following day, Sunday October 11, the Brigade left at daylight on the Huntsville road and after travelling 20 miles camped east of Athens, Alabama, near a beautiful little stream. A short distance from camp was a water—powered, grist mill, its paddles turned by the current of the stream. Col. Miller took possession of the mill and, with a detail of men from the Brigade, set it to making flour. The flour from the mill, together with the pork and sweet potatoes that the countryside yielded, provided the finest Sunday meal that the Brigade had eaten in weeks.

On the 12th the Brigade moved on east to Huntsville, Alabama. Huntsville in 1863 was a beautiful and impressive sight to the Union soldiers who passed through it. The streets, paved with stone and lighted by gas lights, were lined with beautiful homes, many of them the summer homes of wealthy planters. The white residents of the town kept indoors, peeking through windows and from behind curtains as the Lightning Brigade passed through town. The Brigade camped on the east edge of town at dark.

Next morning, after a torrential rain that washed away many of the tents, the Brigade sloshed through the mud to Maysville where they got word that Roddey's Rebel Cavalry had crossed the Tennessee River.

The 43 year old Gen. Roddey, a former Tennessee riverboat crewman, knew this part of the country like the back of his hand. He could move his cavalry force rapidly. The Lightning Brigade, on the other hand, was loaded down with a large amount of superflous equipment as well as the 1,000 extra horses that they had accumulated. Col. Miller, to correct the situation, detailed a detachment of men to take the artillery, wagons, sick men and surplus horses to Decherd, Tennessee, while the remainder of the Brigade moved after Roddey.

Capt. Kilbourn, 72nd Indiana, was placed in charge of the convalescents, Capt. Lilly in charge of the wagons and artillery and Capt. Stokes of the Chicago Board of Trade Battery was placed in charge of the entire Decherd expedition. The expedition camped the first night near New Market, Alabama, and the following day moved on toward Decherd. The trip to Decherd in the rain and mud took two and a half days, twice the normal time.

When the detachment from the Lightning Brigade arrived at Decherd, they were so covered with mud that the newly arrived troops from the Army of the Potomac on picket duty nearly mistook them for Rebels. This was the first time that any of Wilder's men had come in contact with the eastern soldiers. General Hooker and parts of the XI and XII Corps, Army of the Potomac were in the area on their way to the relief of Chattanooga. On picket at Decherd were the 154th New York Infantry and the 33rd New Jersey Infantry.

That evening after the men of the Lightning Brigade had made camp, some of the men from New Jersey went into lengthy descriptions of the terrible hardships they had been forced to endure since their departure from the East. They complained that they had not had a single bite of butter in a week. The men from the Army of the Cumberland could hardly hold their tempers. They had been forced to live off the land for the most part, and never since they had come into the army had they ever been issued butter.

When the detachment left New Market on the preceding day, Capt. Stokes had ordered Capt. Kilbourn to remain behind briefly to parole a Rebel prisoner, a captain who was too sick to travel. Kilbourn detailed Sgt. Witherel, Co. K., 98th Illinois, two privates, and Capt. Kilbourn's colored servant, Aleck, to remain behind with him to help with the situation.

This part of the country was full of southern bushwackers— local partisans who preyed on isolated groups of Union soldiers. In January of 1862, Brig. Gen. Robert L. McCook, one of the famous "fighting McCooks of Ohio," was wounded in the leg at the Battle of Mill Springs in Kentucky. Disregarding this wound, he led the charge that routed the Confederates and won the day for Gen. Thomas. McCook refused hospitalization or sick leave, choosing to stay with his brigade, directing his command from his horse-drawn ambulance. Before his wound healed, however, and while his escort was reconnoitering, a band of bushwhackers led by a man named Frank Gurley turned over McCook's wagon and killed him in cold blood in this area of middle Tennessee.

While Capt. Kilbourn and his men were taking care of the details of paroling the Rebel captain, one of the old colored ladies of the neighborhood gave them a friendly warning, "You'd bettah get out o' heah, lots o' bushwhackah's round!"[2] As soon as Kilbourn had finished his business, he took the old lady's advice and moved out to catch up with the rest of the command. Just as the party was leaving town, however, Kilbourn noticed one of the brigade wagons stuck in the mud and abandoned. Inspection revealed that the wagon was loaded with two saddles, several Spencer Rifles, and 4,000 rounds of Spencer ammunition. Capt. Kilbourn couldn't stand the thought of losing these valuable supplies; he sent one of the privates ahead to send a colored teamster and to continue on to the command for help.

When the teamster arrived he, Capt. Kilbourn, Sgt. Witherel, the private and Aleck set about extricating the wagon. Mud was half knee deep and the rain was pouring down, but they soon got the wagon out and headed on toward Decherd. Three miles down the road they had to pass by a strip of woods. Kilbourn rode ahead to survey the situation and seeing nothing out of the ordinary he returned and ordered his detail to move ahead. Shortly after entering the woods eight men, jumped out into the middle of the rain-drenched road, each with a cocked pistol in his hand.

Kilbourn and his men had their guns under their rubber ponchos. The guerillas had the drop on them. There was nothing for Kilbourn to do but surrender, which he did. The disgust of being taken soon fell on him, however, and he wheeled his horse in an attempt to escape. The barrel end of a cocked pistol pressed against his chest and the Reb behind it dared him to try again.

The prisoners were taken to the home of the father of Lt. Col. Hambrick of the 4th Alabama Cavalry who was home on leave. A few minutes later three more union prisoners were brought in, including the private that Capt. Kilbourn had sent ahead for help. They were given a good supper but were closely guarded.

The next morning Sgt. Witherel, the two privates and the two colored men were turned loose, but Kilbourn, guarded by two very young Alabamans was headed south toward the Tennessee River on his way to Andersonville Prison. On the way to the river they passed the pile of ashes that had once been the home of Frank Gurley, the man who had shot Gen. McCook in '62.

Kilbourn's guards were young, maybe only 16 or 17 years old. The fact that the recent heavy rains had swollen the streams that they had to cross before they could get to the river ferry and the fact that large numbers of Union troops were reported to be in the area, helped the young men to lose their willingness to continue the trip. This caused them to become highly susceptible to bribery, and two evenings later they traded coats with Kilbourn, took his watch and let him escape.

At one o'clock the next morning, after walking 23 miles in seven hours through the rain and darkness, Capt. Kilbourn reached the pickets of the 23rd Kentucky Union Cavalry. After spending the night with Capt. Barth of that regiment, he traveled on to Stevenson, Alabama, where he reported to Gen. Hooker. Two days later Capt. Kilbourn rejoined his brigade at Brownsville.

On the 22nd, Capt. Kilbourn, with a squad of men detailed by Col. Miller, captured Frank Gurley whose whereabouts he had learned from his young captors.

While the artillery and the horse detail was making its trip to Decherd and back and for six days thereafter, the remainder of the Brigade was scouting the country in search of Roddey's Rebel Cavalry. In nine days of chase the Brigade traveled 202 miles, and although they prevented the Confederate cavalry from causing any damage, they were unable to bring them to battle.

On October 23 General Ulysees S. Grant took over command of all Union forces in the west, and Gen. Thomas replaced Rosecrans as commander of the Army of the Cumberland. Grant found the Union forces in Chattanooga destitute. Between 40,000 and 50,000 starving soldiers and several thousand horses and mules, beseiged in Chattanooga since their defeat at Chickamauga, were in desperate condition. Disease was rampant and the morale of the Army of the Cumberland was on the verge of disintegration. Over ten thousand animals had already starved to death. Grant found the men in Chattanooga on nothing but half-rations of hard bread. The only relief for the bread diet, during this month of near starvation, had been an occasional ration of beef. But the cattle, after being driven over the barren trail through the mountains, were in such poor condition that the beseiged men of Chattanooga referred to the resulting meal as, "half-ration of hard bread and beef dried on the hoof."[3]

The Lightning Brigade at Maysville, Alabama, although worked to the point of exhaustion and in almost continuous combat with the enemy, was spared the suffering that most of the Army of the Cumberland had been forced to endure.

On October 30, while Grant was effecting his plan for the relief of Chattanooga, Gen. Thomas sent the following message to Col. Miller at the Brigade's winter headquarters at Maysville:

Colonel: I have just telegraphed the authorities at Washington that I would hold Chattanooga or starve. When doing that I allowed you to protect the right of my line and guard the river from Bridgeport to Decatur, Alabama. I know your lines will be over a hundred miles long, and that your horses and men are much fatigued and have been separated from your wagon train for over a month all of which I take into notice. Knowing your former zeal and integrity,

I remain yours,

Geo. H. Thomas, Maj. Gen.
Commanding, Army of Cumberland[4]

Confederate General Bragg controlled the Tennessee River from Chattanooga west to Bridgeport, Alabama. Now the Lightning Brigade was to hold the river for the Union from that point west to Decatur. Across the river from them were three of the most able cavalry leaders in the Confederate Army—Roddey, Forrest and Wheeler.

It appeared that the Brigade would be headquartered at Maysville for some time so the men set about building permanent shelter for the cold weather that winter would bring. The long expected wagon train arrived on the evening of the 29th with the Brigade's tents, clothing, knapsacks and cooking utensils. The huts and barracks built by the men took on a wide variety of shapes and sizes. Rails, felled trees, and mud were used for sidewalls. Roofs were made from straw or tents from the newly arrived wagons. Some of them had chimneys for inside fireplaces. They were crude but comfortable and the men of Wilder's Brigade, who hadn't been in one place long enough to pitch a tent since they left Murfreesboro in June, took to the task of construction like children with new toys. William Hammer, 123rd Illinois, wrote home, "Putting me up a little shanty —fixed me up a kind of bed stid and got me a lot of cotton to lay on and it makes me think of home—the roof of my shanty is made out of a tent and the sides and ends is weathered bord with plank."[5]

The nearest railroad station was 15 miles to the east at Paint Rock Station on the Paint Rock River. On the 31st the brigade wagons and an armed escort were sent to Paint Rock to pick up supplies for the Brigade. They returned on the evening of November 1st and the next day the regiments drew the first government issue rations they had received in several weeks.

One of Wilder's men described the feast that he enjoyed on November 4th:

. . . Our men indulged in a grand dinner today. Had everything the country afforded served up in Sam's best style. Bill of fare consisted of fresh pork, sow belly, fried chicken, potatoes, pumpkins, corn bread, hardtack, molasses and a great big pot pie, baked a la Dutch oven. Such dinners are seldom met with in the army, and we all appreciated it by eating a sufficient quantity to last three days. Our mess contains the Quartermaster sergeant, Jack Johnson, Orderly Sergeant Martin Miller, Wagonmaster Jim Binford and myself. Our cook, Sam, is one of the best of his profession now following the Army. A little short chunky darky, black as midnight, with a continual grin on his sable countenance and a joke for everybody.[6]

The Confederates were continually attempting raids to the north side of the river. The land north of the river was excellent farming country, and the purposes of their raids were to round up all the hogs and cattle, grains, vegetables and horses possible, both to deprive the Union Army of them and to supply their own army positioned on Missionary Ridge and Lookout Mountain.

Col. Miller dispatched details daily to thwart these threats along the long stretch of the Tennessee River that he was responsible for protecting. One detachment from the 72nd Indiana traveled over 100 miles on one patrol to destroy all the small boats on the river as far west as Decatur. Near Whitesburg they caught a Rebel flat boat in the middle of the river loaded with hogs and after a short fire fight both hogs and Rebels succumbed to the Spencer Rifles.

Through the first half of the month of November, the Lightning Brigade performed the boring task of patroling the river. Pay day, the first in four months, came on November 16, and this temporarily brightened the men's spirits.

November 18, however, brought a dark and dismal cloud over the Lightning Brigade. After marching, riding, eating, sleeping and fighting together for 11 months through four battles and many skirmishes, the Lightning Brigade received orders that would split it up. Lilly's Battery received orders to report to Gen. Elliott of the 1st Cavalry Division near Murfreesboro. The 17th Indiana and the 98th Illinois were assigned to Col. Eli Long's Brigade of Cavalry that had been stationed near Woodville, Alabama, this brigade having orders to move with Sherman during the forthcoming Battle of Chattanooga. Col. Miller, with the 72nd Indiana and the 123rd Illinois, remained in Alabama near Huntsville.

The Lightning Brigade would not be together again until April, 1864. From November 18, 1863, until the beginning of Sherman's Atlanta campaign, the regimental members of the Lightning Brigade were engaged in separate campaigns.

The 72nd Indiana and the 123rd Illinois operated together in Alabama and Mississippi. The 98th Illinois and 17th Indiana participated in the Battle of Chattanooga and the Knoxville Campaign, and from January, 1864 until April, while the 17th was on furlough and veteranizing, the 98th took part in the cavalry operations in northwest Georgia.

8

"Johnny Is My Darling"

Part I (17th Ind. and 98th Ill.)

BY NOVEMBER 1 THE UNION FORCES HAD OPENED WHAT THE soldiers called the "cracker line." By taking possession of Raccoon Mountain west of Chattanooga, Brown's Ferry and Wauhatchie, the supply units were able to bring rations and forage by water to within 7 or 8 miles of Chattanooga. The Confederate seige was lifted and General Grant began his military plans for driving Bragg and his Rebel forces off Missionary Ridge and Lookout Mountain.

General Bragg felt his positions to be impregnable. He held all the higher ground to landward of Chattanooga and the Federals had their backs to the Tennessee River. He knew that the Union forces in Chattanooga were in a depleted state because of the shortage of food, and that disease had taken a considerable toll in the northern ranks. Confederate leadership, in fact, felt so secure that in early November Gen. Longstreet was dispatched with 20,000 men to move northeast and attack Knoxville which was held by Union General Burnside and 12,000 men of the IX and XXIII Corps. Actually, the weakening of his force at Chattanooga was not Bragg's idea. He had done this at the insistence of Confederate President Jefferson Davis who, knowing that Bragg and Longstreet were at odds, thought that this would solve his personnel problems.

Bragg had thought all the time that the Union Army would, in the face of his commanding position, withdraw from Chattanooga back into middle Tennessee. But the Union had General Grant in command now and this wasn't the way Grant played the game. Grant was a firm believer that you couldn't win a bat-

121

tle by going backward. He was determined to fight his way out of Chattanooga and on the 18th of November he issued his orders for battle.

Gen. Hooker with one division each from the Armies of Tennessee, Potomac and Cumberland was to attack the Rebel positions on Lookout Mountain, drive them off and then cross Chattanooga Valley and attack the south end of Missionary Ridge. Gen. Sherman with his Army of the Tennessee plus Howard's Corps, Army of the Potomac, and Davis' Division of the Army of the Cumberland was to cross the Tennessee River north of Chattanooga and attack the north end of Missionary Ridge. Gen. Thomas with the remainder of the Army of the Cumberland was to attack the center of Missionary Ridge in direct assault after Bragg had become engaged on his flanks. In connection with this three-pronged attack, Col. Eli Long's cavalry brigade was to move around the north end of Missionary Ridge and destroy the railroad and telegraph lines behind Bragg's lines so as to cut off his communications with Longstreet. On the 18th Gen. Grant sent the following message to Sherman:

Chattanooga, November 18, 1863
Major-General W. T. Sherman:

Enclosed herewith I send you copy of instructions to Major-General Thomas. You having been over the ground in person, and having heard the whole matter discussed, further instructions will not be necessary for you. It is particularly desirable that a force should be got through to the railroad between Cleveland and Dalton, and Longstreet thus cut off from communication with the South; but being confronted by a large force here, strongly located, it is not easy to tell how this is to be effected until the result of our first effort is known.

I will add, however, what is not shown in my instructions to Thomas, that a brigade of cavalry has been ordered here which, if it arrives in time, will be thrown across the Tennessee above the Chickamauga, and may be able to make the trip to Cleveland or thereabouts.

U. S. Grant
Maj.-Gen'l[1]

On the evening of Nov. 17, Col. Eli Long received orders at his headquarters at Woodville, Alabama, to proceed to Chattanooga with his Cavalry brigade plus the best mounted men of the 98th Illinois and 17th Indiana Mounted Infantry regiments, and a detachment of the 4th Michigan Cavalry of Minty's Brigade. The strenuous pursuit of Wheeler through Tennessee in

October and the shortage of horse shoes had taken its toll among the mounts of Minty, Long and Wilder. This necessitated leaving the poorly mounted men in Alabama, and when Col. Long amassed his force of seven regiments, he had an effective force of only about 1,500 men. This was the only cavalry brigade involved in the Battle of Chattanooga and consisted of the 98th Ill. and 17th Ind. regiments and the 1st, 3rd, 4th (battalion) and 10th Ohio Cavalry regiments, 2nd Kentucky (Union) Cavalry and the 4th Michigan Cavalry.

The Brigade reached Brown's Ferry on the evening of the 22nd, and crossed to the north side of the Tennessee River, then moved along the river opposite Chattanooga to the place where South Chickamauga Creek empties into the Tennessee, north and east of the city.

Early in the morning of the 24th, Sherman's infantry was ferried across the river on pontoons; as soon as they were over, a pontoon bridge was laid across so as to bring over his artillery and cavalry. By 3:30 in the afternoon Col. Long's Cavalry Brigade was across the bridge and on its way to the rear of the Confederate lines.

That same morning Gen. Hooker and his command began the assault of Lookout Mountain at the other end of the line. As Long's men waited on the north side of the river for the bridge to be completed, they could see Hooker's men, four miles to the south, moving up the steep slopes of the mountain. A Sgt. of the 17th Indiana said, "We could plainly see the outlines of Hooker's gallant men as they charged up over craggy slopes till they were hidden from our view by the rain-cloud that intervened. Still, we could plainly hear the crack of the small arms, as well as the cheering of our noble boys as they would drive the Johnnies from point to point."[2]

While Sherman's troops attacked the north end of Missionary Ridge, Col. Long and his brigade moved rapidly through Rebel artillery fire between Missionary Ridge and the Tennessee River. Eight miles from Chattanooga, behind Bragg's lines, they struck Tyner's Station on the Dalton R. R., captured the telegraph operator and tore down the telegraph lines. They moved on east destroying sections of the railroad tracks and burned two Rebel caissons. The Brigade went into camp about midnight, Col. Long sending a party on to Cotewah where they captured and destroyed 4,000 lbs. of flour. At two o'clock in the morning a Rebel wagon train, not having any idea that Yankee cavalry could be in the area, stumbled into Long's camp. The Yankees remained quiet until the train was well into the camp, and then they pounced on them, capturing the teamsters and mules and destroying the wagons.

On the morning of the 25th the Brigade moved south, parallel to Missionary Ridge. After going a short distance, they came to a road down which a Rebel wagon train had passed a short time before. Col. Long immediately led his brigade in pursuit. When the teamsters discovered that they were being followed, they pushed their teams at a gallop. The chase continued for several miles with the wagon train driving their teams west toward Missionary Ridge as fast as they could go with Long and his men on their heels. By the time the train reached the eastern base of the Ridge, the teamsters realized that they were going to be overtaken. They unhitched their teams and left the wagons for Long's men to plunder and destroy. Many of the wagons contained ammunition and one of them contained the personal baggage of Confederate General Marcus Wright who at the time was busy with Cheatham's Division fighting Sherman's infantry at the north end of the Ridge. While Long's men were ransacking the wagon train, they could see the Rebel flags floating in the breeze at the top of Missionary Ridge and could hear the sound of musketry and artillery fire from the battle that was raging there. One of the Wilder men with the Brigade commented later that he presumed, "This was about the time the old Fourteenth Corps was charging to victory."[3] And he may have been right. Parts of the 4th Corps and the 14th Corps of which Wilder's Brigade had been a part at Chickamauga, launched an attack that afternoon that drove the Confederates from Missionary Ridge and caused Bragg to withdraw his army south to Dalton, Georgia. After capturing the wagon train of 60 wagons, the Brigade moved north to Cleveland, Tennessee, where they went into camp that night.

On the 26th Col. Long sent detachments out on a railroad-destroying expedition. One group under Col. Seidel of the 3rd Ohio moved toward Charleston on the East Tennessee and Georgia Railroad. Major Patten, 1st Ohio, and his men went south on the Dalton road and Major Dobb of the 4th Ohio took a detachment back toward Chattanooga on the Chattanooga-Cleveland road. The remainder of the command moved into Cleveland and destroyed all the Rebel property that could not be used by the Brigade. They confiscated a large quantity of corn and several bales of new grain sacks for their own use, burned several railroad cars and razed a copper rolling mill. The Brigade, back together by nightfall, camped again outside Cleveland.

Early on the morning of the 27th the Brigade camp was attacked by Kelly's Confederate Cavalry Brigade. Just before daylight the pickets, a detail of the 17th Indiana, heard the sounds of horses and wagons in their front. They immediately reported to Col. Long's headquarters that a Rebel force was approaching. Either Long's staff member didn't believe the report or maybe he ignored it, but in any case for some reason the Brigade was not ordered into line of battle and at daylight the Rebel cavalry caught them by surprise. Col. Long ordered the Brigade to evacuate on the Harrison road. The 4th Michigan which was guarding the prisoners that had been accumulated during the raid, got on the wrong road and the 17th Indiana was ordered to hold off the Rebels until they could get back on the road to Harrison. The 98th Illinois and the men of the 17th kept their Spencer rifles busy holding off the Rebels during the retreat, and although the withdrawal was accomplished with very small losses, it was a bitter pill for the men from Wilder's Brigade to swallow. They weren't used to retreating. One of the 17th Indiana men complained bitterly,

The consequence was a disgraceful stampede took place, and I will here say the only stampede that any of Wilder's men was ever a party to; this all on account of the lack of diligence on the part of the officers in camp, as they had ample warning hours before of the approach of the enemy. . . . Well, we got out of that scrape by the skin of our teeth, but we have always since believed that . . . we could have cleaned out that rebel force, consisting only, as we afterward learned, of a small brigade under command of General Kelly.[4]

The Brigade arrived back at Chattanooga that night.

On arrival at Chattanooga Col. Long received orders to accompany Gen. Sherman's force to Knoxville to relieve Gen. Burnside who was being held under seige by Longstreet. Sherman's men were tired and hungry. They had had a stubborn uphill fight at the north end of the Ridge during the Battle of Chattanooga, and the two divisions of Granger's Corps attached to Sherman for the march to Knoxville had led the glorious charge that broke the center of Bragg's line on the Ridge. But President Lincoln and Gen. Halleck in Washington had constantly reminded Grant of Burnside's plight even during the heat of the Battle of Chattanooga, and even though Sherman and his men had just gone through a fierce three-day battle, it was imperative that they be sent to Knoxville. Burnside reported on the 27th that he had beaten off one attack but that he had only enough rations to last until the 3rd of December.

On the 29th Long's Brigade moved back to Cleveland and then east to Benton. Between Cleveland and Benton the Brigade captured eight hundred head of hogs belonging to the Confederate government. On the 1st of December the Brigade moved to Columbus, on the Hiwassee River and returned to Benton where the 4th Michigan and 4th Ohio were detached to escort the captured hogs and some prisoners back to Cleveland. The remainder of the command proceeded to Charleston but orders soon arrived from Gen. Sherman to move immediately to Athens and the Brigade reached there at midnight. The weather was cold and there was snow on the ground. Long's men were extremely tired from the long movement that day and they bivouacked in the middle of town. J. K. Wallace of the 98th Illinois remembered that his company slept on the brick pavement at an intersection in the heart of the city.[5]

On the December 2 Long sent Capt. Wade of the 98th Illinois in charge of a detachment of 150 men back to Calhoun to guard the railroad bridge across the Hiwassee River. The remainder of the Brigade then moved in advance of Sherman's infantry north toward Loudon, the 3rd Ohio in advance. Loudon, thirty miles southwest of Knoxville, was held by Confederate General Vaughn and an infantry brigade, artillery and a cavalry detachment. Vaughn had the city well fortified with elaborate and formidable earthworks. Col. Long's lead regiment ran into Vaughn's cavalry pickets a short distance from Loudon and routed them, taking thirty prisoners. As the column approached closer to Loudon, the Confederate artillery opened up with heavy shelling. Long immediately dismounted his brigade and moved forward in line of battle. After advancing a short distance Long realized that Vaughn's fortifications and numbers were stronger than he had anticipated and he withdrew. Col. Long reported Vaughn's strength to Gen. Sherman and Howard's infantry division was dispatched to reinforce the cavalry brigade. However, darkness arrived before Howard could reach the scene and Long's men bivouacked a mile from town. During the night Gen. Vaughn evacuated Loudon after running three locomotives and forty-eight freight cars into the Tennessee River and destroying the pontoon bridge.

That night Gen. Sherman sent an aide, Major Audenried, forward with orders to Col. Long that he must make contact with Burnside at Knoxville within twenty-four hours. Burnside had told Gen. Grant that if he wasn't relieved by the 3rd of December he would be forced to surrender because of the shortage of rations. Sherman's orders to Long were to "push into Knoxville at whatever cost of life and horse-flesh."[6] The Brigade moved out before daylight the next morning (3rd) with forty miles to travel over what Sherman described as "villainous" roads. The Brigade travelled east to Maryville and then north towards Knoxville, pushing their already overtaxed horses to the limit. At 2 o'clock the next morning, the advance regiment, the 98th Illinois, struck the pickets of Col. Wofford's Georgia infantry, driving them aside. At 3 o'clock Col. Long and his brigade camped two miles from Knoxville inside the Confederate lines. Soon after daylight the next morning, Col. Long reported to General Burnside and notified him that Sherman and his force was on its way from Loudon to attack Longstreet and lift the seige.

Long's forced march from Loudon had been torturous. A lieutenant of the 98th Illinois recalled that they reached Knoxville "with worn out horses and badly done up men, as we were poorly clad, and Longstreet's men had cleared the country of about everything but old men, women and children."[7]

That night (4th) Longstreet, having been notified of the nearness of Sherman's large infantry force, abandoned the seige and withdrew to the east where he went into winter camp at Greenville, Tennessee. When Sherman learned that Longstreet had pulled out, he halted his exhausted column at Maryville. On the morning of the 6th Gen. Sherman went into Knoxville to meet with Burnside.

When Sherman sat down to dinner at Burnside's headquarters he was shocked. On a beautiful dining table with a clean white tablecloth was spread a huge roast turkey dinner. Each place was set with silverware. Sherman could not help exclaiming that he thought "they were starving."[8] Burnsides explained that at no time had Longstreet had him completely surrounded, and that he had been able to keep a line of supply open on the south side of the river through which he had received a good supply of beef, bacon, and corn meal. Had the enlisted men of Burnside's command heard this remark, they would have been furious. Burnside's personal food supply may have been in good shape but the men themselves were hungry. In fact they were desperate as described by a member of the 17th Michigan:

Each day our rations grew less and less, and the probability of holding out much longer became smaller in proportion. . . . Whenever any of us could get off duty we would stroll over to where the teamsters were feeding mules; should the teamsters be gone the mules invariably lost their ration. Frequently the kernels of corn that the mules and horses could not help losing were picked up out of the dirt and eaten by the nearly famished troops. I shall never forget the expression of reproach I fancied an old blind mule once gave me. He may have gone to sleep supperless that night for all I know. I have never stopped to consider for my thoughts have never reverted to that incident without reviving the old unsettled question of which, conscientiously, was the worst—stealing from a blind mule that couldn't protect itself, or starving to death?[9]

Much to the relief of General Grant and the officials in Washington, Knoxville was now safe. Longstreet was now cut off from Bragg and in the early spring he would return to Virginia never to fight in the west again. Longstreet had a sizeable wagon train of nearly three hundred wagons that had been cut off from his troops. After the Union forces occupied Knoxville, the train attempted to escape to the southeast through North Carolina. Col. Long and his brigade were dispatched on the evening of the 6th in an attempt to catch the fleeing wagon train. They headed south through Maryville where they were joined by the 4th Michigan and the 4th Ohio who had just returned from Cleveland. The Brigade crossed the Unaka Mountains and followed the Hiwassee River to Murphy, North Carolina. They drove a small detachment of Morgan's Rebel Cavalry from Murphy and camped six miles on the other side of town. The men had hardly tied their horses when a band of Cherokee Indians appeared at their camp, but the soldiers soon discovered that they were loyal to the Union. At least they claimed to be and they seemed to be friendly enough. Col. Long set a detachment ten miles on east to pick up information about the wagon train. When they returned they reported that according to what they could learn from the residents of the area, Longstreet's wagon train was five or six days march ahead of them. Knowing that catching the train would be impossible, Col. Long rested his horses for a day and then retraced his route northwest to

Watering Horses. (From *Battles and Leaders of the Civil War*, Thomas Yoseloff Publisher)

Union Cavalryman—The Water-Call. (From *Battles and Leaders of the Civil War*, Thomas Yoseloff Publisher)

The sink-hole near Widow Glenn's House. Colonel Wilder's Brigade of mounted infantry at one time gained the pool after a hard contest and quenched their thirst. In the water were lying dead men and horses that had been wounded and had died while drinking. (From *Battles and Leaders of the Civil War,* Thomas Yoseloff Publisher)

Alexander's Bridge from the Confederate Side of Chickamauga Creek. (From *Battles and Leaders of the Civil War.* Thomas Yoseloff Publisher)

Uphill Work. (From *Battles and Leaders of the Civil War*, Thomas
Yoseloff Publisher)

Confederate Cavalry attacking a Union wagon train. (From *Battles
and Leaders of the Civil War*, Thomas Yoseloff Publisher)

A typical member of Wilder's Brigade—Private Wilson Henderson, Co. A 98th Illinois Mounted Infantry.

Captain Eli Lilly.

General William H. Jackson, C.S.A. (U.S. Signal Corps Photo)

General Braxton Bragg, C.S.A. (U.S. Signal Corps Photo)

General William S. Rosecrans. (U.S. Signal Corps Photo)

General George Crook. (U.S. Signal Corps Photo)

General James B. McPherson. (U.S. Signal Corps Photo)

General George H. Thomas. (U.S. Signal Corps Photo)

General William T. Sherman. (U.S. Signal Corps Photo)

General Joseph E. Johnston, C.S.A. (U.S. Signal Corps Photo)

General Kenner Garrard. (U.S. Signal Corps Photo)

General Nathan Bedford Forrest, C.S.A. (U.S. Signal Corps Photo)

John T. Wilder. (U.S. Signal Corps Photo)

General John B. Hood, C.S.A. (U.S. Signal Corps Photo)

General Joseph Wheeler, C.S.A. (U.S. Signal Corps Photo)

General James H. Wilson. (U.S. Signal Corps Photo)

General John H. Morgan, C.S.A. (U.S. Signal Corps Photo)

General Frank C. Armstrong, C.S.A. (U.S. Signal Corps Photo)

General Bushrod R. Johnson, C.S.A. (U.S. Signal Corps Photo)

Spencer Carbine. (The West Point Museum Collection, U.S. Army Signal Corps)

Tellico Plains, Tennessee, where the Brigade remained until the 14th of December.

On the 15th the Brigade moved west to Calhoun on the Hiwassee River. The 98th Illinois, 17th Indiana and the 1st Ohio Cavalry went into camp at Calhoun. The other Ohio regiments and the 4th Michigan were sent in various directions to set up courier lines, and the 2nd Kentucky returned to Alabama.

The troops at Calhoun had to live off the country since there were no government supplies at hand. Five miles from town was a plantation and a grist mill owned by a man named Getty. Getty, who was residing in Athens, was a Union man and supposedly was the son of the founder of Gettysburg, Pennsylvania. A detail of ten men each from the 98th Illinois and the 17th Indiana was sent to his mill to grind meal for the Brigade. Some of men foraged in the area for wheat and corn while the others operated the mill. The foragers soon discovered a still house a few miles from the mill, and since it was almost Christmas, the grist-mill detail traded a load of corn for a ten-gallon keg of whiskey— "And oh, what a merry Christmas our little band of Seventeenth and Ninety-eighth boys did have in that old Getty mansion."[10] They decided to have a dance on Christmas Eve. Invitations were sent out to some local young ladies and men, including some paroled Rebel prisoners who had been captured at Vicksburg. A big supper of turkey and chicken was served and according to the forage-master, a sergeant of the 17th Indiana, "After supper the dining-room was cleared up, and the dance set in in dead earnest. We had enough girls to run two sets, and we paid a darkey $5.00 to play the fiddle. Well, we danced all night till broad daylight and went home with the girls in the morning."[11] The party was such a success that they planned another one for New Year's Eve, but on the 31st orders arrived from Col. Long to return immediately to their command at Calhoun.

In the meantime, while the boys on the milling detail were living it up at the Getty mansion, the remainder of their regiments had had a brush with Wheeler's Rebel Cavalry. On the morning of the 28th, a wagon train under escort of a portion of Sheridan's infantry division arrived at Charleston across the river from Calhoun where it was attacked by Wheeler and 1,500 cavalrymen. Col. Long mounted his men who were not on duty which he said "was less than 150 men," and crossed the bridge to where the train escort was engaged with the enemy. Long ordered his men to charge, the Ohio men with sabers drawn and

the Illinois and Indiana men with their Spencer rifles. The Rebels
retreated down the Dalton road losing 121 prisoners, the 98th
Illinois capturing the Inspector General of Kelly's Division.[12]

Soon after the first of the year, the 17th Indiana veteranized
and returnd to Indiana on veteran's furlough. The Ohio Cavalry
Regiments also veteranized and the members who re-enlisted
went to Ohio on furlough. The 98th Illinois and the remaining
cavalry stayed at Calhoun until early February. On February
4 Col. Funkhouser, having recovered from his wounds received
at Chickamauga, rejoined his regiment with the balance of the
98th that had been left in Alabama, bringing the regimental
strength to 350 men.

The East Tennessee Campaign was a bitter one for the men
of the 17th and 98th. It wasn't that there was so much fighting,
but that their equipment, clothing and horses were in a badly
depleted state when the campaign began. They had chased
Wheeler's cavalry all over middle Tennessee, campaigned in
northern Alabama, and participated in the Battle of Chattanooga. Then without time or opportunity to get new shoes,
clothing, horses or horseshoes, they had set out on their hurried
relief of Knoxville in the dead of winter. It was such a disagreeable time, in fact, that a great many of the veterans of the 17th
Indiana who suffered through it did not re-enlist. But then the
duty in east Tennessee had its bright spots, too. No doubt the
detachments from the two regiments that were detailed to the
grist mill on the Getty plantation left with fond memories. And
Capt. Funkhouser of Co. A., 98th Illinois met a young Tennessee girl, Hattie McGaughey, whom he returned for and married
at Athens two years after the war. Although the young bride
lived only two years after their marriage, Capt. Funkhouser
must have maintained a deep feeling for her, for he named his
first born of his second marriage Hattie, in her remembrance.

The 98th Illinois, now near full strength, and the non-veterans
of the Ohio Cavalry regiments, along with those veterans who
did not re-enlist, remained at Calhoun until the 22nd of February. But as one of Col. Long's men said, "He never allowed
his command to remain idle very long,"[13] and he moved his
detachment south toward Dalton, Georgia. Col. Long's command now numbered about six hundred, and in the last week of
February he had a three-day fight with the enemy.

On the 23rd the Brigade, 98th Illinois 350 strong, and 250
Ohio cavalrymen struck a Mississippi infantry regiment three

miles from Dalton, driving them from their camp and capturing twelve prisoners. The enemy reformed and brought up reinforcements while Col. Long withdrew to the northeast and encamped.

At 6 A.M. on the 24th, the Brigade moved to Varnell's Station, nine miles north of Dalton. At 10 A.M. Col. Long sent scouting parties out on the various roads leading from Varnell's. Detecting no enemy in the immediate vicinity, he moved his force south toward Dalton. Five miles from Dalton his advance, Co. A. of the 98th Illinois, ran into Rebal cavalry dismounted and waiting behind rocks and trees. The Rebels surprised the Union men with their first fusilade and caught them mounted. Several of them were wounded and captured.

When the 98th Illinois was organized in August of 1862, the three Henderson brothers of Clay County, Illinois joined up together. Joseph, the oldest, was discharged for disability in April of 1863, but on February 24, 1864, the other two brothers, Calvin and Wilson, were with Col. Long's advance scouts. When the Rebel cavalry opened up on them, Wilson was hit by a musket ball in the side. He managed to stay on his horse, however, and got back for medical aid. He discovered later that the bullet had gone through his cartridge box which slowed the impact of the ball enough that it imbedded itself only one inch in his side. Calvin was captured in the engagement and sent to Andersonville Prison. Although neither of the Henderson brothers was severely wounded in the affair, it did cause considerable suffering to both of them. Suffering not from enemy bullets, but from the dreaded disease of the time—small pox. Wilson was sent to a hospital in Nashville, and although his wound was not serious, he contracted small pox. He recovered just in time to participate in the Atlanta Campaign in May. Calvin was involved in the wholesale, mishandled small pox vaccinations at Andersonville which resulted in gangrene. Although he avoided amputation, he spent the rest of his life with a withered arm.

After the initial encounter by Long's advance scouts, the remainder of his force moved up and drove the enemy cavalry to within three miles of Dalton where they fell back on their infantry support, Stewart's Division. Col. Grose then brought up his Union infantry brigade to support Long, and a lively fight took place near Buzzard's Roost Gap in Rocky Face Ridge. Darkness soon fell and Col. Grose withdrew his brigade, leaving the 98th Illinois in his front.

On the 25th Long's Brigade was enlarged by the addition of 100 men from the 4th Michigan Cavalry. Moving on the left of the infantry, they attacked the enemy, advancing some distance where they held their ground the remainder of the day.

General Bragg's entire Confederate Army was in the Dalton area and this movement against him was primarily a reconnaissance mission to feel out the Confederate strength. A report by Brig. Gen. Cruft, temporarily in command of the 1st Div., 4th Army Corps included the following:

Feb. 24 Colonel Long took the advance about 3:30 P.M. supported by Colonel Grose, and they drove the enemy's cavalry two miles before them, when they came upon a large infantry force of the enemy near Glaze's house in position on the railroad below Buzzard Roost Gap, and about three miles from Dalton. After considerable musketry and the use of the section of artillery, the enemy, with quite a spirited skirmish, were driven back under cover of their rifle pits, and held at the railway until nightfall, when our troops fell back, say two miles, and bivouacked.

In this engagement the casualties fell principally on Colonel Long's command, who is reported to have charged the enemy in splendid style.

Colonel Eli Long, commanding Second Brigade, Second Division of Cavalry, with his command, covered the exposed flank of the division during the entire march, and conformed his movements to those of the division. Though acting under independent orders from department headquarters, he at all times co-operated with me, and by the bravery with which he rushed his column and the care which he took to communicate all the intelligence which he could obtain, contributed largely to attaining the objects of the reconnaissance.[14]

One of Col. Grose's infantrymen described the fight on the 25th:

After a brisk fight of about 25 minutes, cannonading become quite lively and shell flew through the tree tops keeping time with minnies who was hunting their cousins (when the boys hear a minnie ball going by, they (yell) hallo cousin, their sound imitates that word.) We laid in line until midnight when we fell back about 8 miles. The 59th boys come out all safe. Some 8 or 10 of the 75th were wounded, among them was our Major who was wounded by a limb that was shot off by our battery.[15]

Long's Brigade spent the month of March picketing, first at Cleveland, Tennessee, and then around Ringgold. In early April they were ordered to Columbia, Tennessee, south of Nashville, for re-equipping.

Part II
(72nd Indiana and the 123rd Illinois)

Colonel Miller, in command of the Lightning Brigade during Colonel Wilder's absence, maintained his headquarters at Maysville where the Brigade members had built quite comfortable winter quarters. For the remainder of November, through December and during the first part of January, Colonel Miller kept the 72nd and the 123rd busy rounding up livestock, fighting guerillas and scouting for Rebel cavalry detachments. Most of these combined scouting expeditions were led in the field by Col. Biggs who had succeeded to the command of the 123rd Illinois after the death of Col. Monroe at Farmington.

On the 1st of December, a few days after their base camp had been moved to Huntsville, Capt. Thomson and five men of the 72nd Ind. left for Chattanooga with prisoners. They traveled by rail from Brownsburg to Bridgeport, and then took a steamboat on the Tennessee River on to Chattanooga. After turning over their prisoners at Army Headquarters, Capt. Thomson asked permission to go to the Chickamauga battlefield to find and bury two of their comrades who had fallen on the night of Sept. 19th. Permission was granted but Thomson was warned that the enemy was camped close by.

Captain Thomson and his men reached the battlefield at dark. Ten weeks had passed since the ill-fated battle on Chickamauga Creek, but the woods, hills and ravines were still covered with unburied Union dead. The heat of the September days and the freezing and thawing of the November nights had left them a ghastly sight. The small detachment spent the night in a log house that had been used during the battle as a surgeons' amputation station. The men didn't sleep much that night, nor did they talk much. They spent the night mostly in deep thought, enveloped by the somberness of the dark, still night and the piles of decaying limbs piled outside the house. And they thought of the contrast of this night as compared to the night of Sept. 19, when they had tried to rest in the cold, smoke-laden woods, haunted by the cries and moans of their wounded comrades between the lines.

The next morning Capt. Thomson and his men found the bodies of their fallen friends. They gave them as fitting a burial as possible under the circumstances and returned to Chattanooga.

On December 22 the 72nd Ind. and 123rd Ill. received orders to move north as part of Gen. Crook's cavalry division. They pulled out on the 24th, moved 22 miles and camped that night near Athens, Alabama. The next day, Christmas, the division moved out on the road to Pulaski, Tennessee. The entire division wagon train was along and the 72nd Indiana was the rear guard.

Christmas of 1863 was warm and bright, but by mid-morning the roads thawed out and became a soft, miry mess. The division wagon train, strung out for 10 miles, crawled through the quagmire at a snail's pace. When darkness came that night, they hadn't moved a dozen miles since early morning. The men of the 72nd Indiana had spent more time waiting than they had riding. They were getting plenty disgusted with the wagon train. Their brigade buddies in the advance regiments were already camped 15 miles ahead of them. But most military units in the Civil War, as in all other wars, had at least one "sharpie"—the guy that always has the solution no matter how ridiculous. As the men of the 72nd cursed the slowness of the train that night, the "sharpie" of the regiment came up with an idea for getting the wagon train to move faster.

The greatest fear that teamsters had during the war was that of being captured by Rebel guerillas. Tennessee and northern Alabama were full of them and the teamsters on General Crook's wagon train knew it. The 72nd men set the leaves on fire in the woods behind the wagon train and threw handfuls of Spencer cartridges into the fire. The exploding cartridges sounded like a full scale skirmish. The teamsters, convinced that the rear guard was being attacked by guerillas, made more progress in the next hour than they had in the past five. But the train finally became completely bogged down in the mud and even the prodding of the 72nd couldn't move them.

On January 2nd, Col. Wilder, who had been home on sick leave since the Battle of Chickamauga returned to Brigade Headquarters at Huntsville. After a brief stay he went to east Tennessee to veteranize the 17th Indiana. Gen. Crook was transferred to Chattanooga and Col. Miller became senior officer and commander of the post at Huntsville.

In late January General Sherman, having returned to Vicksburg from Knoxville, arranged an expedition into Mississippi. He left Vicksburg with 20,000 men and moved toward Meridian, around Feb. 10, destroying the railroad south from Okolona as he went. The 72nd Indiana and the 123rd Illinois joined Sooy

Smith's command for this campaign. Gen. Smith was inexcusably tardy in getting his force underway from Tennessee. Sherman arrived at Meridian on the 14th, waited until the 20th, moved over to Canton and remained until the 28th, and then, giving up on Smith, he returned to Vicksburg. When Smith and his expedition finally arrived at Okolona and proceeded south, they met only token opposition. On the afternoon of the 20th, however, when Smith and his troops reached West Point thirty miles south of Okolona, they ran into Forrest's Cavalry. Forrest had only two regiments with him, the 2nd Tenn. and 7th Tenn. Cavalry. On the morning of the 21st, for some mysterious and unexplainable reason, General Smith ordered a retreat after only a little minor skirmishing. Smith's forces, pushed from behind by Forrest's Tennesseans, pulled back to division camp three miles from Okolona.

Early the next morning one of Smtih's three brigades was ordered into line of battle, but before an engagement could begin Smith again ordered a retreat with the 7th Ind. Cavalry and a battalion of the 4th U. S. Cavalry as rear guard. Smith had Forrest outnumbered three to one. The men in the ranks knew that they could handle Forrest's force and they couldn't understand why they were continually being ordered to retreat. Shortly after the withdrawal got underway, Forrest attacked the 7th Indiana and the 4th U. S. Regulars. Smith's rear brigade, the Third, was ordered back to support them. This brigade had lost all confidence in the leadership of the expedition and possibly they had decided that the enemy force outnumbered them after all. In any case, discipline completely broke down and they fled at the first charge of the enemy. The panic was contagious and Smith's panic-stricken troops retreated nine miles in six hours. Finally, at 5 o'clock in the evening some of the regiments, acting without orders, stopped and set a line of battle, determined to stop the advance of the enemy. The 4th Missouri Cavalry charged the Confederates, and although the charge was repulsed, it ended the battle. Forrest who stated later that his force "did not exceed 2,500 men," captured six artillery pieces and 33 stands of colors.

The 72nd Indiana and the 123rd Illinois, accustomed to the excellent leadership of such officers as Wilder, Reynolds, and Thomas were filled with shame by the fate of the Sooy Smith expedition. But they could hold their heads up high for they were among the regiments who stayed to fight. They were not accustomed to defeat; in fact since the organization of Wilder's Brigade they had never been whipped.

The 72nd Indiana especially did itself proud. It was a member of McCrillis' Brigade that had initiated the stampede, and although the other four regiments of that brigade broke and ran over them, they remained with their Spencer Rifles to defend the rear, some of them joining in the final charge with the 4th Missouri.

Gen. Smith, in a letter to the Commanding Officer of the 72nd on March 19, said, ". . . You were run over by four regiments of your brigade in the morning, in a perfect stampede; yet, nothing abashed, you waited to fight rather than follow those who were retreating."[16]

On April 3, the 72nd Indiana and 123rd Illinois left their camp near Mooresville, Alabama, and proceeded to Columbia, Tennessee, to prepare for the Atlanta Campaign. They had been picketing, foraging, scouting and fighting for three months in northern Alabama and Mississippi, but they had spent enough time at their base camp that some of them had made fast friendships with the local citizenry, especially the ladies. The departure of some of the Union boys caused tears to flow as described by William Hammer, 123rd Illinois, in a letter to his sister:

Well Emily I feel sort of sleepy to day I was out to bid my Ala Girl good Bie and you better believe that I gave her a good hugin and Kissen I huged her from sun down till 3 oclock it was pirty near day lite when I got in camp EE Shuey was with me he huged Marthey and I Mary Emily you dont know how sweet Mary is she is a nice girl and she is good looking as well as sweet you had ought to seen how she laid up to me and the best of it is the old woman and old man goes to bed but when Eny of the rest of the boys goes there the old folks sets up as long as they stay but there hant bin a soldier but me and shuey that huged them for the girls wont let eny body talk with them only me and Shuey and always when we go there the old folks allways go to bed emily you don't know how bad I felt when I left there last night for the girls like to cried there eyes out they hated to see us go away poore thing I felt so sorry for them after we had got on our horses they came out to the fence and cried like good fellows and told us that they never expected to see any solders that has bin eny kinder to them than we have it has been 3 months tomorrow since I have got Accuainted with them and ever since I have been ere they would send me in buter and pies and sweet cakes and pound cakes and a thousand thing that to tegious to mention they allways send the things . . . in by a darkey they dont send eny body eny thing but me and E. E. Shuey[17]

The 72nd and 123rd, along with the Chicago Board of Trade artillery battery, arrived at Columbia on April 8.

Part III
"Back Together"

At Columbia Wilder's Lightning Brigade was reunited, back together for the first time since November 18. The 17th Indiana was back from its veteran's furlough, the 98th Illinois arrived from Ringgold, and the 72nd Indiana and 123rd Illinois had come in from Alabama. And Col. Wilder, having recovered from his illness, was back in command. The Brigade drew new horses, had their good horses shod, replaced worn out equipment and trained their new recruits that had recently been brought into camp. This was the big buildup for the Atlanta Campaign that would begin in early May.

Several leadership changes had taken place in recent months. Gen. Grant had, by special act of Congress, been made a Lt. Gen., and placed in command of all Union forces. He had gone east and established his headquarters with the Army of the Potomac. Gen. Sherman was a man whom Grant knew he could trust. A hard driver and aggressive fighter much like Grant, he was put in command of all Union forces in the West. Under Sherman, poised for the move toward Atlanta, were Gen. Thomas with his Army of the Cumberland, Gen. McPherson with the Army of the Tennessee, and Gen. Schofield and his Army of the Ohio. On the Confederate side President Davis had found it necessary to replace Gen. Bragg. Gen. Joe Johnston, a capable soldier and excellent strategist, although at odds with Davis personally, was the logical choice and he assumed command of the Army of Tennessee.

Until the spring of 1864 the Federal forces had never launched a large, coordinated, well-planned attack involving the huge armies in both the east and west. But with General Grant in command of all the armies things were different now. He planned his spring campaign carefully. He brought Gen. Sheridan east to command the cavalry of the Army of the Potomac which had never been really effective. He had Sherman in control in the west. Now Grant was ready. His plan was basically simple. The bulk of the Northern military force was divided into two armies. One in the east under Gen. Meade, with whom Grant had his headquarters, and the one in the west under Gen.

Sherman. The South's military might was largely in two armies also—the Army of Northern Virginia in the east under Gen. Robert E. Lee and in the west the Army of Tennessee under Gen. Joe Johnston. Lee was south of the Rapidan River in Virginia facing Grant and Meade, and Johnston was at Dalton, Georgia, facing Sherman. Meade's primary objective was to destroy Lee's army and his secondary objective was Richmond, the southern capitol. Sherman's primary mission was to whip Johnston's army and secondarily to take Atlanta. In the past much of the fighting in the war was to gain control of principal cities. Grant knew that the only way he could end the war was to decisively defeat the Southern armies. Meade and Sherman were to launch their offensives in early May in one grand, dedicated, united effort to end the rebellion.

Johnston's Confederate Army consisted of approximately 70,-000 men. Sherman, including a large cavalry corps, had a few over 100,000 men at the beginning of the campaign. The Atlanta campaign would be neither easy nor short. It lasted four months and each side sustained in the vicinity of 40,000 casualties.

9

"We'll Fight for Uncle Abe"

BY THE END OF THE FIRST WEEK IN MAY, SHERMAN'S HUGE military force was in position, poised for the attack. Gen. Thomas' Army of the Cumberland was the largest, being made up of Howard's 4th Corps, Palmer's 14th Corps and the 20th Corps under Gen. Hooker. Thomas' army contained 50,000 men. The next largest, McPherson's Army of the Tennessee, 35,000 strong, consisted of the 15th Corps under Gen. Logan, the 16th Corps under Gen. Dodge and the 17th Corps under Gen. Blair. Gen. Scholfield's Army of the Ohio, the smallest with 15,000 men, was the 23rd Corps with a small division of cavalry under Gen. Stoneman. Also attached to the Army of the Cumberland was Gen. Washington Elliot's Cavalry Corps made up of the divisions of McCook, Garrard and Kilpatrick. The Lightning Brigade was assigned to Garrard's Cavalry.

Although Gen. Garrard's 2nd Cavalry Division was a part of the Army of the Cumberland, the greater part of its movements during the Atlanta Campaign was in conjunction with the movements of the Army of the Tennessee, since McPherson had no cavalry force of his own assigned to his command.

Brig. Gen. Kenner Garrard was a West Pointer, and as Col. of the 146th New York, he had fought at Fredericksburg, Chancellorsville and Gettysburg. After having been in charge of the Cavalry Bureau in Washington during the winter of 1863-64, he had been transferred to the west to command a cavalry division.

139

Garrard's command for the campaign was as follows:

1st BRIGADE	2nd BRIGADE	3rd BRIGADE
Col. R. H. G. Minty	*Col. Eli Long*	*Col. J. T. Wilder*
4th Michigan Cavalry	1st Ohio Cavalry	98th Ill. Mtd. Inf.
7th Penn. Cavalry	3rd Ohio Cavalry	123rd Ill. Mtd. Inf.
4th U.S. Reg. Cavalry	4th Ohio Cavalry	17th Ind. Mtd. Inf.
		72nd Ind. Mtd. Inf.

Division Artillery: Chicago Board of Trade Battery (Lt Robinson)

On May 11, Minty's and Wilder's brigades arrived at Villanow at the west end of Snake Creek Gap, southwest of Dalton, Georgia. Col. Long's brigade had not yet returned from Nashville where they had gone for new horses. After crossing the Tennessee River on their trip from Columbia, Minty and Wilder had had a tiresome and laborious journey. They had crossed Lookout Mountain and the Sand and Pigeon Mountains on their way to LaFayette and then Taylor's Ridge to Villanow. The scaling of Lookout Mountain had been an especially trying ordeal, but once they got to the top, the men enjoyed it. They had fought within sight of this mountain at Chickamauga and Wilder's boys had fought in its shadows at Chattanooga, but none of these men had ever before been on it. When they beheld the scenery from the crest of Lookout, they were astonished at the tremendous expanse of country that was visible to them. A man with the 4th Michigan was so impressed with the sight that he exclaimed, "Oh, Lord, boys, I can see the Atlantic ocean, the city of Richmond, and the army of the Potomac fighting its way to the city!"[1]

Sherman had launched his offensive on May 7 with Thomas moving from Ringgold, McPherson from Villanow and Schofield from south of Red Clay. Sherman's strategy was to attack Johnston at Dalton with Thomas' and Schofield's Corps while McPherson moved around to the south and came in on the rear of the Rebel army. Thomas began his attack at Tunnel Hill on the 7th. Stanley's and Newton's divisions of Howard's Corps soon took the ridge at Tunnel Hill which was only lightly defended, but when Thomas moved on against Rocky Face Ridge, he ran into strong Confederate resistance. Thomas continued his attack at Rocky Face until the 9th. In the meantime McPherson had moved south from Villanow through Snake Creek Gap and on the 9th appeared before Resaca, thirteen miles south of Dalton. The appearance of McPherson at Resaca completely surprised Johnston, but McPherson did not attack, mistakingly thinking that it was defended by a superior force. He pulled back and set up defensive positions. Although outflanked by McPherson's entire corps, Johnston remained at Dalton until the 11th when he withdrew and moved down the railroad to Resaca with his entire army. When Sherman discovered that Johnston had begun his movement, he left Howard's Corps at Dalton and moved with the remainder of Thomas' army and Schofield's through Snake Creek Gap to join McPherson in front of Resaca. By the morning of the 14th, both Sherman and Johnston were deployed in line of battle.

On the 14th Sherman ordered Gen. Garrard to move his cavalry force along the Oostenaula River toward Rome, Georgia, thirty miles to the south, and to cross over the river, if possible, and threaten the railroad north of Kingston and south of the Confederate Army. The division got underway at two o'clock in the afternoon with Wilder in advance. They made half the distance by ten P.M. and went into camp. Early on the 15th the division, with Minty's Brigade in advance, continued their movement toward Rome. A few miles from Rome Gen. Garrard decided to attempt a crossing of the river. He sent Minty's Brigade on to demonstrate against the city while Col. Wilder's Lightning Brigade tried to effect a crossing. When Minty reached Armuchee Creek his advance, the 4th Michigan, found the bridge strongly defended by Rebel cavalry. Minty sent two companies of the 4th Michigan to cross the creek below the bride and six companies above while the other battalion of the 4th Michigan, followed by the 7th Pennsylvania, attacked the bridge itself. Minty drove the Rebels within three miles of Rome when he discovered enemy reinforcement flanking him on both left and right and four pieces of artillery emplaced in strong postion. On learning that a large enemy infantry force was approaching Rome, Minty deemed it advisable to withdraw and join the balance of the division. While Minty had been skirmishing with the Rebel cavalry, Col. Wilder had been unable to find a suitable crossing place on the Oostenaula. The next evening, after grazing their horses most of the day, the division moved back north to make a crossing at Lay's Ferry, four miles south of Resaca.

While the men grazed their horses on the morning of the 16th, scouting parties were sent out in all directions. A detachment from the 72nd Indiana stopped at a farmhouse. The war thus far had not reached this deep into Georgia and Yankee soldiers were something new. The lady of the house and her daughter came outside to see them. When they found out that these soldiers really were Yankees, the lady exclaimed, "I say, Cap'n our folks has not told us the truth about you'uns; they told us you'uns was painted savages, and that you all had horns; but you'uns is just like our folks, but I believe you'uns is the best lookin'."[2] Late in the evening the division started for Lay's Ferry.

On the 14th and 15th a battle had been fought at Resaca. The Confederate Army was behind strong works and Sherman suffered 4,000 casualties in his assaults during the two days. But when Sweeny's Division of McPherson's Army got a pontoon bridge across the river south of Resaca, Johnston's position became perilous. On the night of the 15th he crossed the river and withdrew south along the railroad toward Adairsville. On the 16th Sherman began his pursuit with Thomas' Army of the Cumberland moving in the center pushing Johnston's rear guard, Schofield's Army moving parallel to Thomas to the east and McPherson's column, having crossed the river at Lay's Ferry, moved on the west toward Rome. Sherman detached Gen. Jefferson C. Davis' Division from Thomas and sent him south on the west side of the Oostanaula toward Rome to reinforce Garrard and his cavalry division.

Evidently neither Garrard nor Davis knew what the other was doing. Garrard did not know that Davis was coming to support him and Davis did not know that Garrard was moving back north to make a crossing of the river. During the night of the 16th the two columns met each other on the road. The road was soft and muddy and lined on both sides with thick brush; since foot soldiers always had the right of way when passing mounted troops, the Lightning Brigade had trouble getting past Davis' men. As Wilder's men attempted to move through the thickets on the side of the road, they occasionally crowded the infantry. There was never any love lost between infantry and cavalry anyway, and Davis' men began cursing the mounted men and making some of the disparaging remarks that infantry usually made to cavalrymen—"Johnnies ahead, eh? That's right, skin out for the rear; that's the safest place." Wilder's men, thinking that some of the regiments had been with Sheridan at Chickamauga, answered by yelling, "Make way for Sheri-

dan! make way for Sheridan!" Although none of Davis' infantry regiments had been with Sheridan, a detachment of
Davis' artillery (2nd Minnesota) had fought along side Wilder
and Sheridan with Davis' old division. Evidently the word had
spread through Davis' entire division about the incident at
Chickamauga because all along the line they began shouting to
their buddies. "Hush! hush! that's Wilders Brigade."[3] The infantry boys didn't have much respect for ordinary cavalry, but
they did have a lot of respect for the Lightning Brigade. They
knew about their Spencer Rifles and they knew that Col. Wilder
and his men had dismounted and fought in the line with infantry
at Chickamauga. The Brigade moved on toward Lay's Ferry
without any more trouble, arriving there close to midnight.

On the afternoon of May 17, Gen. Garrard and his division
again moved south toward Rome in advance of McPherson's
Army of the Tennessee.

Gen. Jefferson C. Davis, in the meantime, had arrived at
Rome and found himself confronted by Confederate Gen.
French with Ector's Brigade of Infantry and Morgan's and
Ross' Cavalry Brigades. An hour before sunset he received an
order from Gen. Thomas directing him to move north, cross
the Ooostenaula at Lay's Ferry and rejoin his command. However, while reading the message, Davis was attacked by the Confederate defenders of Rome. Davis soon drove his attackers
back to their fortifications, but found them too strong to attack
and pulled back for the night. During the night, the Rebels withdrew and abandoned Rome, burned the bridge across the river,
and moved east toward Kingston in order to join Johnston's
main force which had stopped near Adairsville that evening.
The next morning, Davis, having only four days' rations, requested that Thomas send him pontoons so that he could cross
the Oostenaula at Rome and join the main army without the
forty mile detour around Lay's Ferry. Rome being an important
industrial town, Davis was ordered to remain there until relieved by a brigade of Blair's Corps, which was on its way to
join McPherson's Army; but Davis was cut off from Sherman's
army and he requested a cavalry force to fight its way through
to him.

During the night of the 17th, Johnston pulled out of Adairsville and moved south through Kingston, then southeast to near
Cassville.

The Lightning Brigade and Minty's brigade, a few miles in

advance of McPherson's Army, changed their course of march
at Hermitage and moved southeast toward Kingston. At noon
of the 18th they reached a small community named Woodland,
five miles north and west of Kingston. From Woodland Gen.
Garrard ordered Col. Wilder to cut the railroad and telegraph
lines leading to Kingston from both the north and west. Wilder
sent six companies of the 17th Indiana west to cut communications between Kingston and Rome, and the other four companies of the 17th east to do the same job between Kingston
and Adairsville. The 72nd Indiana was split up and sent out on
picket duty on the roads leading east, north and west from Woodland.

A short distance south of Woodland Minty's Brigade, in the
advance, ran into the pickets of Ferguson's Confederate cavalry.
The 4th Michigan was dispatched to drive in the Rebels pickets
and the remainder of the division was deployed in line of battle.
The 4th Michigan drove the pickets to within a mile of Kingston when they come upon a large enemy force of infantry and
cavalry, at least part of which were the troops under Gen.
French who had evacuated Rome during the previous night.
The Rebels counterattacked with a large cavalry force and rapidly drove the 4th Michigan back to the division line, Minty's regiment losing thirteen killed and eighteen wounded, ten of whom
fell into enemy hands. Minty's men now had Spencer Carbines
and as the 4th Michigan rode back through Garrard's lines the
remainder of Minty's command along with the 98th Illinois and
123rd Illinois of Wilder's Brigade stopped the Rebel advance
cold with a fusilade from their Spencers. Colonel Earle of the
2nd Alabama Cavalry, in leading his command in the charge
of the Federal line, fell dead only 10 feet from Wilder's position,
shot from his horse by Pvt. Thomas Bonner of Co. A, 98th
Illinois.[4] The Rebel attackers withdrew toward Kingston but
picket firing was soon heard in all directions from Woodland.
Gen. Garrard became concerned about his position, but shortly
before dark the van of McPherson's infantry reached Woodland
and relieved him. Late that night the 123rd Illinois was sent to
Rome to check on the security of Davis' force and render any
assistance that might be needed.

Reveille for the Lightning Brigade was called at daylight on
the 19th and, on orders from General Sherman, Garrard's Division moved south and east of Kingston, destroyed the saltpeter
works a few miles from town, and then took possession of Gil-

lem's Bridge on the Etowah River. After having constructed barricades for the defense of the bridge they were relieved by the 15th corps of McPherson's Army. The division then moved on down the river and took possession of another bridge where they were joined by the 123rd Illinois which had returned from Rome.

Sherman's forces passed through Kingston at noon in their pursuit of Johnston and then moved east toward Cassville. On the morning of the 20th, Sherman discovered that Johnston and his army had withdrawn from the Cassville area and taken strong positions in the mountains near Allatoona. Sherman's supply trains had not yet caught up with him, and he decided to give his army a three day rest. The Lightning Brigade spent this time bathing, washing clothes, shoeing horses, foraging for food and in general getting everything in shape for the continuation of the campaign. On the 22nd they had an inspection and that night they had preaching by the chaplain. As one of the men said, "We were never better fixed for moving."[5]

Sherman's Union Army was dispersed almost east and west, north of the Etowah River. Davis' Division anchored the west end of the line at Rome and Schofield's Army and Hooker's Corps were on the east near Cartersville. Halfway between, near Kingston, was McPherson's two corps (Blair's 17th Corps had not yet joined him) and the remainder of Thomas' Army of the Cumberland. The Confederate Army held the territory south of the Etowah. Johnston's Army was positioned from Allatoona Pass to the southwest along Allatoona Creek with his skirmish line forward along Pumpkin Vine Creek.

Early on the 24th the Union Army crossed the Etowah River and resumed its advance. McPherson moved his Army of the Tennessee south and slightly to the west toward Van Wert, led by Garrard's Cavalry. Davis moved down to Van Wert from Rome. Thomas' Army crossed the river near Kingston and moved south to the east of McPherson.

Gen. Garrard, with the Lightning Brigade and Minty's Brigade, moved through Van Wert and then turned southeast toward Dallas, being six miles in advance of McPherson's Army. Late in the evening, Minty's advanced brigade ran into Rebel cavalry two miles from Dallas. Minty dismounted the 4th Michigan and drove the cavalry pickets to within a half mile of town. There, however, the Rebel cavalry, reinforced by part of Bate's Infantry Division, charged Minty and drove him back on the

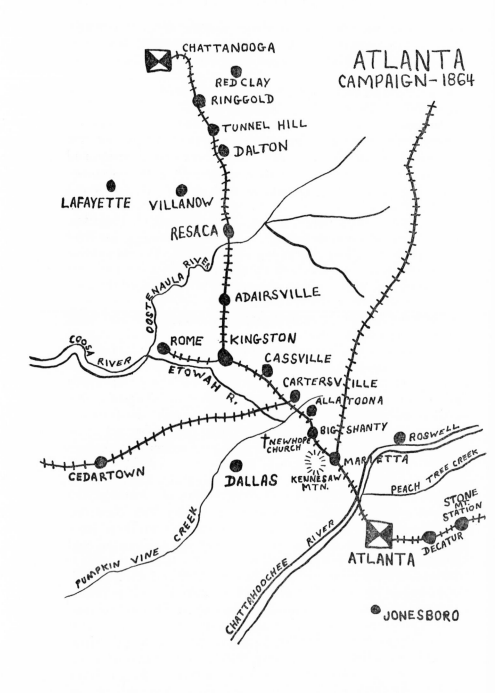

ATLANTA
CAMPAIGN—1864

CHATTANOOGA
RED CLAY
RINGGOLD
TUNNEL HILL
DALTON
LAFAYETTE
VILLANOW
RESACA
OOSTENAULA RIVER
ADAIRSVILLE
COOSA RIVER
ROME
KINGSTON
CASSVILLE
ETOWAH R.
CARTERSVILLE
ALLATOONA
BIG SHANTY
NEW HOPE CHURCH
CEDARTOWN
DALLAS
KENNESAW MTN.
ROSWELL
MARIETTA
PEACH TREE CREEK
PUMPKIN VINE CREEK
CHATTAHOOCHEE RIVER
STONE MT. STATION
DECATUR
ATLANTA
JONESBORO

remainder of the division. Wilder's Brigade and the Chicago
Board of Trade Battery were brought up and they drove the
Confederate attacking force back to Dallas. Darkness prevented any further action on the 24th and the division pulled back
a short distance and camped for the night. Gen. Garrard reported the presence of Rebel infantry to Gen. McPherson, but
McPherson did not believe it. Sherman's strategy had been to
move the Army of the Tennessee around the Confederate left
flank, but Gen. Johnston had not been fooled by the maneuver.
He had slid his forces to the west to cover the Union movement. General McPherson made some casual remark to Gen.
Garrard about the enemy force he had encountered being "only
pickets", and walked away. In the next few days McPherson
found out how accurate Garrard's report had been. Sporadic
picket firing kept up all through the night along Pumpkin Vine
Creek.

Next morning Rebel infantry attacked Wilder's pickets, driving them across the creek. The entire Brigade was ordered into
line and the Confederate movement was contained, the line being
held until relieved by the arrival of Gen. Logan's 15th Corps.
Garrard then ordered Wilder to move his Brigade around the
left of the Confederate line to Powder Springs, twelve miles
southeast of Dallas and behind the center of the Rebel lines.
The Brigade made the trip to Powder Springs and back safely
and provided McPherson with a considerable amount of intelligent information.

While the Brigade was on its scouting expedition to Powder
Springs, things had gotten hot in the center of the Union line.
Geary's Division of Hooker's Corps had run into Hood's Confederate Corps northeast of Dallas at New Hope Church. After driving in the pickets of Stewart's Division, Hooker was
stopped cold by Stewart's main force. By the time Hooker could
get his other two divisions under Butterfield and Williams in the
line, Hood had Hindman's and Stevenson's Divisions up and the
two forces fought savagely for the rest of the day amid a severe
thunderstorm. In fact, Hooker and Hood fought head-on at this
place for a week. This field near New Hope Church soon became
known as the "Hell Hole" by the soldiers.

On the 26th the 4th U.S. Regulars of Minty's Brigade was
detached on special duty for Gen. McPherson. Minty with his
other two regiments picketted to the Union front and right, having a sharp skirmish with Ferguson's Rebel Cavalry. While

Minty was on picket, the Lightning Brigade remained in camp. The Brigade was out of corn and the horses were suffering considerably.

The Atlanta Campaign took a cruel and sickening toll of horseflesh. The mounted troops were on the move almost continuously and forage in Georgia was very poor. Even the devoted and dedicated grooming and care of the horses rendered by the men could not overcome the inhumane suffering caused by overwork and lack of feed. Major Jennings of the 7th Pennsylvania Cavalry reported on the condition of the horses in his regiment:

May 5, we marched twenty-three miles without feed. At Mound City received twenty-eight pounds of corn for three days, to be carried upon the horses, in addition to five day's rations, and traveled thirty-three miles, crossing the Raccoon, Sand, and spur of Lookout Mountains. The young horses commenced a fag; a few were abandoned, and the hearty and strong horses were fatigued. . . . From the 16th of May to the 19th, the horses were without feed, except the leaves and short grass to be found on the hill around Adairsville, Ga. During this time we traveled thirty-five miles; the last five, from Kingston to the Free Bridge, was traveled at a gallop, causing the horses to give out by the dozens. . . . On the morning of May 22 the commanding officers of companies reported a loss of 76 horses, which had died of starvation and abandon. Upon investigation, the veterinary surgeon corroborated the statement, and pronounced forty-three more unserviceable and unfit to travel. . . . From May 26 to June 2 (seven days) the horses were without feed, and actually starved.

On September 13, Major Jennings reported that from the beginning of the Atlanta Campaign to that time his regiment lost 401 horses out of a total of 961. "The majority of horses died and abandoned were literally starved."[6]

Early on the 27th the 72nd Indiana was ordered to join Minty behind the left of the Confederate lines on the west side of the Dallas-Villa Rica road. As the 72nd approached Minty's position, his pickets were being attacked by Ferguson's Cavalry. The 72nd immediately dismounted and with the 4th Michigan and 7th Penn. on each flank mounted, moved to the attack. Armstrong's Rebel Cavalry soon came up to join Ferguson and a lively fight got underway, but the Yankees and their Spencers soon overpowered the enemy cavalry and they withdrew toward the Confederate lines near Dallas. During this time Lt. Col. Kitchell of the 98th Illinois arrived with a portion of that regiment and joined in the engagement. Col. Minty then ordered breastworks of logs and rails thrown up. Col. Kitchell and the 98th were placed behind the breastworks in support. Minty moved closer to Dallas with the other three regiments and one section of his artillery. The artillery section had no sooner started shelling the Rebel lines from the rear when four regiments of enemy infantry were dispatched to meet the threat. The Rebel infantry turned the left flank of Minty's line and furiously attacked the 72nd Indiana and 7th Penn. The artillery section being in danger of capture Minty withdrew back to the barricades where, with the help of the 98th Illinois, he halted the enemy advance. The Rebel infantry made several assaults on the Union position without success and before nightfall the Confederates abandoned their attack and withdrew. At dark Minty and his four regiments returned to their camp where they joined the remainder of the division. By this time vigorous fighting was underway along most of the battle line. Howard's Corps had attacked the Confederates on the left end of the line near Pickett's Mill, but without success.

Although Gen. Davis had moved in on McPherson's left, Sherman still had a gap of almost three miles between Davis and Hooker. On the morning of the 28th McPherson was ordered to pull out and move to the left and take position on Hooker's right. But before McPherson could move, he was furiously assailed by Hardee's Corps and Jackson's Rebel Cavalry. The Lightning Brigade and a portion of Minty's Brigade were dismounted and placed in the line with the infantry next to Logan's Corps, anchoring McPherson's extreme right flank.

Hardee attacked McPherson in column of deployed regiments and a violent fight ensued. Bate's division assaulted the 1st and 2nd divisions of Logan's Corps and Jackson's dismounted cavalry assailed Logan's 4th division on the immediate left of Wilder's Brigade. The 53rd Ohio of Gen. M. L. Smith's 2nd division ran out of ammunition while beating off a furious charge of Finley's Brigade of Floridians, but they got replenished before the next advance. Hardee's attack was beaten off all along the line. Jackson's cavalry, after being repulsed by Walcutt's brigade of the 4th division, carried its next attack to the Lightning Brigade on the end of the Union refused right. The Brigade had thrown up temporary earthworks and the Rebels were attacking over open ground. When the Brigade opened up with their seven shooters the Rebel attack disintegrated. Their loss was severe, but their failure was as much due to surprise as anything else. Dr. Cole, surgeon for the 72nd Indiana, was told by a captured Rebel, whose wound he was dressing, that before the assault on the Lightning Brigade they had been told that that section of the Union line was "held by colored troops, who would be easily driven back."[7] What a shock it must have been, charging with this false sense of security, to plunge headlong into the Lightning Brigade and their Spencer Rifles. Fighting and skirmishing continued along this line until June 1.

Sherman's strategy of feinting, hooking and sidestepping had taken him deep into Georgia; but with all his cleverness, he hadn't been able to fake Johnston out of position. Each time Sherman would make a lateral move Johnston, like a shadow, would always be in front of him. The pressure maintained by Johnston's Army at New Hope Church, Pickett's Mill and Dallas kept Sherman from sliding his entire army to the east as he had planned. So on June 1, leaving Garrard's Cavalry to protect his right, he withdrew McPherson's Army of the Tennessee from Dallas and headed it around the rear of the rest of his army toward a new position on the Union left. After McPherson was on his way and Garrard's men had been relieved by infantry pickets, the cavalry division moved north and camped for the night at Burnt Hickory on Pumpkin Vine Creek. Next day they moved to the Etowah River near Cartersville where the Union Pioneers were rebuilding a railroad bridge which had been burned by the Confederates.

Before Sherman had launched his big offensive early in May, he had, on orders from General Grant, built a duplicate of every railroad bridge that he expected to need during the Georgia campaign. As the Army moved south these bridge timbers, already sawed to size, were moved along the railroad. When the Transportation Corps would come upon a burned out bridge, they merely unloaded the pre-cut timbers and erected a new one. Garrard stayed in this area to protect the bridge from Rebel cavalry raids until June 7. That evening the division moved south along the Western and Atlantic Railroad to Ackworth.

Sherman's movement to the east had not gone unnoticed. On the 4th of June, Johnston had also moved his lines to the east and taken position from Lost Mountain on the west to Brush Mountain on the east, with his forward troops on the right extended up the railroad to Big Shanty. By the 8th McPherson, joined by Blair's 17th Corps, was near Ackworth and Sherman ordered a general movement of the army for the morning of the 9th. However, the advance was delayed a day because Sherman, not being sure of the disposition of the enemy army, wanted to spend that day probing the enemy lines. For this operation, he called on Garrard's cavalry. The division's mission was to ascertain whether the enemy line extended across the railroad.

The Lightning Brigade, being a mounted unit, had made many of these reconnaissances and the purpose of many of them, like this one, was to locate the enemy for the infantry and determine its strength. This type mission, especially in new country, was extremely hazardous, but the men expected it as part of their duty. What they did object to, however, was that in many cases the generals in command did not always believe their reports after they returned. At Chickamauga General Crittenden had not believed Col. Wilder's report that the Rebels had crossed the creek until 10,000 of them were across. On the 24th of May in this year, when Garrard's cavalry had run into General Bate's entire Confederate infantry division at Pumpkin Vine Creek, General McPherson had ignored the report, saying that it was "probably only pickets." And now the crowning blow of all —Sherman, who had specialized in artillery at West Point and who had a special dislike for cavalry, sent one of his staff officers along with Garrard and his men to make sure that they got the information he wanted.

Col. Wilder's health was failing again and once more Col. Miller took command of the Lightning Brigade. At seven A.M. they moved down the Marietta Road toward Big Shanty preceded by Minty's Brigade. A mile from Big Shanty the division came upon the enemy behind rail barricades. The Rebels had four lines of log and rail breastworks from 200 to 400 yards apart in front of their main line of entrenchments at the base of Kenesaw Mountain. These four lines of works were manned by Martin's cavalry division and Walthall's brigade of infantry. Gen. Garrard immediately deployed his force in line of battle. Wilder's Brigade was dismounted and positioned with the 123rd Illinois on the left, the 98th Illinois in the center and the 17th Indiana on the right with the 72nd Indiana in reserve. The dismounted 7th Pennsylvania was moved to the extreme right to protect Col. Miller's right flank, and the 4th U.S. and the 4th Michigan were dismounted and moved to protect the extreme left flank. The line advanced and drove the enemy skirmishers through a skirt of woods and into their first line of works. At this time Col. Miller felt it necessary to prolong his right and he moved up the 72nd Indiana to the right of the 17th Indiana. The Brigade charged the enemy and drove him from his barricade, whereby he fell back 400 yards to his second line. A few prisoners were taken on this first assault and they were brought to Gen. Sherman's aide for interrogation. The staff officer made some remark about "cavalry pickets" and walked away. The Brigade was ordered again to advance, this time to move forward to a certain point, fire four rounds and lie down. The Confederate force, now strengthened by the troops in the second line of works, put out such a heavy fire, however, that the men of the Lightning Brigade felt it more dangerous to stop than to go ahead, and they charged into the breastworks, driving the enemy back across the railroad into his third line of works. Prisoners from this charge were brought before the staff officer to see if he was satisfied. Col. Miller pointed out the main Rebel line at the base of Kenesaw and told him that advancing further might necessitate fighting the whole of Johnston's Army. Sherman's aide said that he was satisfied himself, but that since all the prisoners and enemy dead seemed to be cavalry, Sherman would say that he had not gone far enough to be positive about the disposition of Johnston's army. The enemy, now enlarged again by the troops manning the third line of fortifications, outnumbered the Union force two to one. Garrard then moved up two sections of the Chicago Board of Trade Battery and began shelling the enemy position. After a half hour of shelling, the Brigade charged the Rebels again, and again they drove them from their barricades. They took position in their fourth line of works. This fourth line was a much stronger position than the others had been. The barricades were more elaborate, made largely of logs and earthworks. Col. Miller handed Sherman's staff officer his glass through which he could see enemy infantry throwing dirt up to strengthen their works. General Garrard then told the officer, "Col. Miller can bring you in some infantry the next drive he makes, if that is what you want, for you can certainly see that the Johnnies behind the works are infantry."[8] This fourth line of breastworks, in addition to being stronger than the others, had telegraph wires strung across in front of it about two feet above the ground to hamper the Union advance. The word soon got around through the ranks of the Brigade that they had to produce an infantry prisoner on the next charge and, since the men were aware of the purpose of their mission, they no doubt reasoned that if they got that job done they could go back to camp. Col. Miller then ordered the advance. They held their fire until they had covered half the 200 yards to the Rebel works, and then with a yell they charged the enemy, firing their Spencer Rifles as fast as they could work their levers. The Rebel fire was terrific, but they couldn't hold their position and the Lightning Brigade charged over the barricades, killing a lieutenant of the 29th Mississippi "Tigers" and capturing almost a whole company. The Rebels retreated rapidly to their main entrenchments at the base of Kenesaw, leaving their dead and wounded on the field. Sherman's staff officer then turned to Gen. Garrard and said, "Well, if that does not convince Sherman where Johnston's army is, he will find out when he occupies the ground we are now on with his infantry."[9] The division, having accomplished its mission, then returned to its camp near Ackworth. It took Sherman five full days of fighting before he could get his infantry as close to Kenesaw Mountain as the Lightning Brigade had been on June 9.

On the 10th, while the Lighting Brigade moved east through a thunderstorm on a scouting expedition, the entire Union Army moved forward. The Army of the Tennessee moved to Big Shanty. Next day the railroad bridge across the Etowah was finished and a train load of supplies reached the army at Big Shanty station. This 100 yard-long railroad bridge had miraculously been completed in only nine days.

On Saturday the 11th, the 1st and 3rd Ohio of Long's brigade, which had joined the division during the week, had a brief fight with enemy cavalry but being heavily outnumbered they withdrew to division camp. Late in the afternoon Minty's men also had a short fight with Rebel cavalry. Wilder's Brigade was dispatched to assist Minty, but by the time they got there the Rebels had pulled back.

It had rained every day of the month and on Sunday the rain came down in torrents making troop movements virtually impossible. The men of the Lightning Brigade pitched their tents for the first time since leaving Columbia, Tennessee on the last of April. The weather was no better on the 13th but foragers were sent out to bring in corn for the horses. On the 14th the rain slackened somewhat and a vicious artillery duel commenced which resulted in the death of Confederate General "Bishop" Polk.

Next day the Union army edged forward in a general ad-

vance hoping to find a weak spot in the Rebel lines between
Kenesaw and Pine Mountains. Sherman soon discovered, however, that Johnston had abandoned Pine Mt., consolidated his
forces and was in a very strong position from Kenesaw to Lost
Mountain. McPherson was lapped around the north side of Kenesaw, and Thomas and Schofield held the lines to the west and
south. Col. Wilder having left the Brigade to retire from service on account of his health, Col. Miller took permanent command of the Brigade. On orders from Gen. Garrard Col. Miller
moved the Lightning Brigade to the right to take position, dismounted, in the line between Long's brigade and the infantry.
The men threw up a line of breastworks and joined it to that of
the infantry. They maintained this position until the 19th, during which time they were continuously shelled by the Rebel
artillery both day and night. Union artillery was busy, too, and
the thundering duel between the gunners continued for three
days. The story went around the lines that someone had told
Sherman that he would never take Kenesaw Mountain. He supposedly answered that he would "take it or shoot it damn full
of old iron."

By the 19th Johnston had further consolidated his position
by abandoning Lost Mountain. He now had Kenesaw Mountain
as his primary position with his flanks protected by strong fortifications and by Noonday Creek on the east and Noses Creek on
the west. In shortening his lines on the night of the 18th, Johnston had pulled back his flanks and moved back from his forward entrenchments. On the morning of the 19th Sherman, mistakingly thinking that the enemy had retreated, ordered a
general movement along the line. The infantry soon discovered,
however, that the enemy hadn't gone and the advance was stalled.
Wilder's mounted infantry Brigade, having been ordered to
cross Noonday Creek, woefully discovered the same thing.

At 8:00 A.M. the Lightning Brigade dismounted and approached Noonday Creek with the two cavalry brigades of Long
and Minty to their right and left rear, mounted to protect the
flanks. When less than a half mile from the creek, they struck
enemy skirmishers and at the same time came under fire of a
three-gun Rebel battery from a lunette downstream. The Brigade pushed the enemy skirmishers across the creek only to dis-
cover strong enemy fortifications on the opposite bank, manned
by Confederate infantry. In the meantime a violent thunderstorm had suddenly cut loose making visibility so bad that be-

fore they realized what was happening, the Brigade found itself on the bank of this narrow deep creek, not fifty yards from the Rebels with their dirt and rock barricades. Finding themselves in this "damned if you do, damned if you don't" situation, there was nothing to do but hit the mud and open fire. The enemy opened up a terrific fire from across the creek, wounding several men of the 72nd Indiana who at the right of the line were not a hundred feet from the enemy works. The Rebel side of the creek was higher and the Confederates had the angle on Wilder's men, firing down on them as they lay in the mud on the opposite side. The Rebel battery downstream opened an enfilading fire of shell on the Brigade, but their opening rounds overshot their target. Fortunately for the Union men the smoke produced by thousands of rounds of small arms ammunition and the heavy downpour of rain soon cut visibility to almost zero. Both sides could only fire at the gun flashes of their opponents. This gave the Lightning Brigade a brief advantage since they could outfire the Rebels at least seven to one with their Spencer Rifles. General Garrard brought up the Chicago Board of Trade Artillery which in a short time silenced the enemy battery. They then moved to a position to the right rear of the 72nd Indiana so as to be in position to rake the Confederate works across the creek. The extremely high moisture content of the air induced by the heavy rains for the last several days had damaged some of the Board of Trade Battery's ammunition, however, and the first few rounds they expelled from this position fell short into the lines of the 72nd Indiana, showering them with canister. The fight on the creek lasted until two o'clock in the afternoon when the enemy, in danger of being flanked on their left by some of McPherson's Infantry who had managed to cross the creek, pulled back leaving only skirmishers to hold their works on the creek bank. By this time, the torrential rain had raised the creek to flood stage and, being unable to cross it, the Brigade withdrew a short distance and laid in the mud all night without fires.

General Sherman, frustrated by his failures along most of his line on the 19th, and questioning Garrard's aggressiveness, issued peremptory orders to Garrard to cross Noonday Creek on the 20th.

Shortly after noon Garrard sent Col. Minty and his brigade two miles downstream to cross the creek at a ford and move south on reconnaissance to determine the position and strength of General Wheeler's cavalry which had been assigned by General Johnston to protect the right flank of the Confederate battle line. By the time he had reached at point due east and a mile across the creek from Wilder's Brigade, he had run into a hornet's nest of Rebel cavalry. The 7th Pennsylvania was savagely attacked by William's Kentucky brigade and when the 4th Michigan and two battalions of the 4th Regulars moved to their assistance they were hit by two more Confederate brigades. A gallant charge by a battalion of the 7th Pennsylvania momentarily stayed the Rebel charge, but the impact of two whole Rebel cavalry divisions under Kelly and Martin plus the independent brigades of Williams and Dibrell soon put Minty in complete rout. Minty was cut off from the route he had taken from the creek crossing downstream and now he was being pushed west toward the creek at a point where it was unfordable, the vicious Confederate attack hitting him from three sides.

In the meantime, Col. Miller, who had been ordered to follow the cavalry brigade saw Minty's trouble. Not having time to move two miles to the ford, he received permission from Gen. Garrard to dismount and cross the Lightning Brigade on foot across a rickety wooden bridge nearby. Col. Miller crossed the bridge with the 17th Indiana, the 98th Illinois and the 123rd Illinois. Four companies of the 72nd Indiana were on picket duty and the remainder of that regiment was left on the west side of the creek to hold the horses. Miller formed his three regiments on a ridge between Minty and the creek. Col. Minty soon sent back word that he was being flanked on both the left and right and Col. Miller sent the 98th forward on the left and the 17th forward on the right, holding the 123rd in reserve on the ridge. Before these two regiments were halfway to Minty's position, which was still a half mile from the creek, Col. Miller realized that Minty would not be able to stop and set up a line of battle. His force was falling back rapidly with the Rebels close on his heels yelling and slashing—Anderson's four Confederate Regular regiments charging with their sabers drawn, supported by the Fifth Georgia Cavalry with pistols. Miller immediately called back his two regiments and placed the 17th Indiana to the left of the 123rd Illinois and the 98th Illinois to the left of the 17th Indiana. Before Miller could get his regiments in line Minty's cavalry came pouring back through his lines with the Rebels in close pursuit. The Rebel force hit the Lightning Brigade with the full force of eight brigades. The Confederates began pouring through a gap between the 17th Indiana and the 123rd Illinois, but Col. Biggs and his 123rd fought its way back to the left and closed up on the 17th. Minty in the meantime, got his command organized and placed the 7th Pennsylvania and part of the 4th Michigan in the gaps between Miller's regiments. The remainder of the 4th Michigan and the 4th U.S. along with his artillery section were positioned back on the west side of the creek to the left. Gen. Wheeler had his forces ready for another attack on the Union line with, from his right to left, Williams' Brigade then Kelly's Division and then Martin's Division, supported by Dibrell's Brigade. It had been raining since early morning, and while Minty had been having his initial fight, the rain had turned to a cloudburst. It was coming down in torrents as Wheeler launched his next attack. Williams' Brigade of Kentuckians and Anderson's Brigade of Kelly's Division attacked the Union left as Wheeler's entire force moved to the attack all along the line.

The 5th Georgia Cavalry of Anderson's Brigade was a relatively green outfit, full 800 strong. "They were brave enough but lacked the training and steadiness necessary to stand up to Sherman's veterans."[10] The Kentuckians of Williams' Brigade called them the "Five Georgia." As the Rebels moved to the attack the "Five Georgia" went in with the Kentucky brigade against the 98th Illinois. The 1st Kentucky Cavalry, though badly depleted in numbers, was a tough veteran outfit. Wilder's men had fought them several times in the summer of '63. Although the Rebels hit that end of the line with a furious assault, the 98th repelled them with the enormous firepower of their Spencers and they rapidly withdrew. One of Williams' Kentuckians said that "the Five Georgia went in as game as any fellows you ever saw; but pretty soon they got confused and a lot of them were thrown from their horses. As I recollect, none of them were shot, but every man as he came back declared that he was the only one left."[11]

While Williams and Anderson were being beaten off on the left Martin's Division and Dibrell's Brigade were attacking the Union right. They were repelled by the 123rd Illinois and 17th Indiana but they got in close enough to the 123rd before they withdrew that Col. Biggs' men captured some of them inside their lines.

Wheeler launched another assault just as the Board of Trade Battery opened up and as a part of the 72nd Indiana was heard yelling as they crossed the creek to support the remainder of the brigade. This attack was repulsed at night fall and Wheeler withdrew his force.

Garrard ordered his command to withdraw to the west side of the creek. They had to wade the flooded bottom land waist deep in getting back. The heavily clouded skies and torrential rain had caused nightfall to come on so suddenly that many men of both sides, along with most of the dead and wounded, were mixed up together on the east side of the creek. Andrew Bryant of the 72nd Indiana, cut off across the creek by the Rebel skirmish line, got back to his outfit by calling out the name of a Confederate regiment. It was so dark that the Rebels couldn't recognize him as a Union soldier. Private Joseph Butler of the 98th Illinois lay in the rain all night across the creek with a broken thigh. When brought back the next morning, he said that he could hear the Rebels all around him during the night looking for their wounded and stripping clothing from the Union dead. Butler's leg was amputated but he died on the 23rd.

It had been a bitter fight but neither side really gained much. General Garrard, however, did have control of Noonday Creek and that was what Sherman had wanted. Garrard lost 67 men killed, wounded, and missing while Wheeler's loss was 94 killed and 351 wounded.

June 21 was the nineteenth consecutive day of rain. Garrard had to bring back his dead and wounded on pack mules because of the mud and water. Sherman sent a message to Gen. Halleck in Washington telling him that he had possession of both creeks on the Rebel flanks and that as soon as the weather settled so that he could move his troops and artillery, he would launch a general attack on Kenesaw Mountain.

The brigade picketed in the vicinity of Noonday Creek until the 26th when they moved their camp a mile or two across the creek to the immediate left of the left wing of the Union infantry. They went to sleep that night with orders to be ready to move at six o'clock in the morning.

On the 27th Sherman made his ill-fated assault on Kenesaw Mountain. The rain had stopped on the 25th and the sun came out hot and steaming. Dismounted, the Lightning Brigade along with the rest of the division moved out at 6 A.M., and closed up on the infantry where they held their position for the day. Sherman's main assault forces were Logan Corps on Garrard's right and Howard's 4th Corps and Palmer's 14th Corps of the Army of the Cumberland. The Confederates were firmly entrenched behind heavily constructed fortifications. The slopes of Kenesaw were steep. Some of the Union infantrymen reached the crest of the mountain only to be slaughtered by the Rebels firing from behind their works. But the Yankee assault troops were determined. They kept hammering away at the Rebel positions in the 110 degree heat. The fight was so hot and bloody that one of the Tennesseeans of Cheatham's Confederate Division exclaimed "Hell has broke loose in Georgia, sho' 'nough!"[12] There was no doubt about that. Gallant as the Union attack was, it was a complete failure. The Rebels were too strongly entrenched to be taken by direct assault. From 9 A.M. to 11:30 A.M. when the attack ended, Sherman lost 3,000 men. Confederate casualties were only 600. Sherman spent until July 2 planning his next move.

Sherman had driven the Confederate Army of Tennessee over 100 miles of Georgia soil since the beginning of the big push. It had been two months of continuous fighting and a chain of strategic masterpieces on the parts of both Sherman and Johnston. Although Sherman had made a considerable advance into Rebel territory he had not, with his numerically superior force, been able to get Johnston cornered for an all-out "show down" battle where he could bring all his forces into play. Johnston, on the other hand, had given up ground from Dalton to Marietta, but he had kept his army in constant contact with that of Sherman's and had inflicted heavy casualties on the Union Army.

The Union Army of the Potomac in the east had become bogged down in front of Petersburg, Virginia. Grant and Meade had made progress since the campaign started but at a terrible cost. They lost 17,000 in the Virginia Wilderness in the first week of the campaign and later at Cold Harbor lost 7,000 men in one assault that lasted only eight minutes. The Army of the Potomac lost 50,000 men in the first month. Grant's incessant hammering of Lee's Army of Northern Virginia had taken him as far as Petersburg by early June. Here, through some brilliant maneuvering, Grant got in a position to take Petersburg and the Rebel army in one grand stroke; but the blundering of some of Grant' subordinates, especially the pompous political general Ben Butler, caused the opportunity to be missed. So Grant had been forced to bring Petersburg under seige and he would lose another 42,000 men before it would fall in the spring of '65.

On July 1 General Sherman notified Gen. Halleck in Washington of his movement plans. He had decided to slide his army south around Johnston's left flank toward the Chattahoochee River and threaten the railroad south of Marietta, thereby forcing the Confederate Army to withdraw from their strong positions on Kenesaw Mountain.[13]

During the night of July 2nd McPherson's Army of the Tennessee was pulled out of line on the left and moved behind Thomas, taking position south of Schofield on the extreme Union right. The Lightning Brigade and parts of Garrard's other two brigades were dismounted and placed in McPherson's works to cover the withdrawal of his Army. But Johnston was not caught napping. When Sherman awoke on the morning of the 3rd he discovered that the Rebel army had also pulled out of their works and moved south toward the Chattahoochee. Garrard's Cavalry and the 15th Corps of McPherson's Army, which had been left behind to help hold the Union left, were immediately dispatched to pursue the retreating Confederate Army. The Lightning Brigade and the cavalry moved around the north end of Kenesaw and entered Marietta at noon where they met the advance of the 15th Corps which had passed around the south end of Kenesaw and entered Marietta from the west.

As the Lightning Brigade approached Marietta, they came upon a sign nailed up on a tree that had been left by the retreating Rebels. On it was painted a picture of Gen. Sherman hugging a Negro woman and under it the caption, "Come on, and we'll give you a warm reception on the 4th."[14]

The Rebels lived up to their word. At Smyrna, six miles below Marietta, they celebrated the 4th by giving General Thomas' Army of the Cumberland a short but hot fight from their entrenchments at Smyrna campground. That night Johnston withdrew his entire army on south where they took position behind fortifications on the north bank of the Chattahoochee River. These previously prepared works were a surprise to Sherman. He had no idea that while he had been holding Johnston under seige at Kenesaw, thousands of slaves had been constructing these elaborate works along the Chattahoochee which Sherman himself described as "the strongest pieces of field-fortifications I ever saw."[15]

Sherman immediately ordered Garrard's division to move up the Chattahoochee eighteen miles to the northeast to Roswell. Johnston's works on the Chattahoochee were too strong to take by direct assault. Sherman had learned the futility of this type of attack at Kenesaw. He was going to have to move around Johnston's flanks again. There was a bridge and also a ford across the river at Roswell and Garrard's mission was to take and hold Roswell so as to have possession of these crossings. The division, after two lively skirmishes with Wheeler's cavalry, arrived at Roswell on the 5th. The 7th Pennsylvania of Minty's Brigade, in advance, drove the Rebel pickets out of Roswell and across the bridge to the south side of the Chattahoochee but were unable to prevent the Rebels from burning the bridge after they had crossed.

Roswell, located on high ground overlooking the Chattahoochee River, was a manufacturing town, full of plants manufacturing cotton goods, woolen cloth, flour, paper and machine parts. The city had been founded by the King family in the early 1800's. Roswell King, from Connecticut, had travelled in this part of Georgia in the 1820's and on returning east had induced some of his friends and relatives to join him in settling the area. His son, Barrington King, took over his father's interests and he and five other families founded the town of Roswell in 1839. Barrington King founded the Roswell Mfg. Co. and was the community industrial and cultural leader. The gigantic King mansion in Greek architecture which he built still stands. King brought Dr. Pratt from Darien to found the Presbyterian Church. Several members of the first congregation were slaves and two of them, Chas. Pratt and John Hall, later became missionaries in Africa. Dr. Pratt's home was across the road from his church and some of General Garrard's men camped on his property.

Much to the surprise of the Union officers the factories had not been evacuated and were operating at full capacity. They continued to do so even after the arrival of Garrard's cavalry, humming along as if the war was a thousand miles away. The owners of the plants swore that they were not manufacturing goods of war. The large textile factory with a capacity of 30,000 yards of cloth per month had a French flag flying over it, the owner claiming that its ownership was held by a neutral country and could not be confiscated as an enemy plant. On the morning of the 6th Gen. Garrard and Col. Miller of the Lightning Brigade entered the factories only to find that most of the cloth being made in the plants was stamped "C. S. A." There was no doubt that the products being made in Roswell were destined for use by the Confederate Army. The employees were then removed from the plants, the records and papers taken into custody, and the factories burned to the ground. That evening Garrard sent a message to General Sherman telling him of what he had done. Sherman replied on the 7th:

Your report is received and is most acceptable. I had no idea that the factories at Roswell remained in operation, but supposed the machinery had all been removed. Their utter destruction is right and meets my entire approval, and to make the matter complete you will arrest the owners and employees and send them, under guard, charged with treason, to Marietta, and I will see to any man in America hoisting the French flag and then devoting his labor and capital in supplying armies in open hostility to our government, and claiming the benefit of his neutral flag. Should you, under the impulse of anger, natural at contemplating such perfidy, hang the wretch, I approve the act beforehand.[16]

On the 8th Sherman moved Schofield's Army of the Ohio from between Thomas and McPherson around to the left in a position to cross the Chattahoochee near the mouth of Soap Creek a few miles to Garrard's right. Garrard had located a ford near Roswell and he received orders to cross it on the 9th and to secure a lodgement on the other side. The river was wide but shallow and ran approximately east and west about a mile south of Roswell. The enemy had constructed a sizeable line of works on the far bank in order to stop the expected crossing of Federal troops. Long's Brigade was held in reserve with part of his force on picket duty. Wilder's and Minty's Brigades moved just after dark on the evening of the 8th and camped near Roswell at a point only one mile from the river. No fires were allowed since they did not want to tip-off the Rebels as to their exact point of crossing. At 3 A.M. these two brigades were aroused, fell into ranks, and moved silently toward the river.

The Lightning Brigade was to cross first and its skirmishers, two companies each from the 17th and 72nd Indiana, formed a line 300 yards long along the edge of the river. It was cloudy with no moonlight and a thin layer of fog lay over the water. Preparations for the crossing were easily concealed from the enemy as the men silently moved through the early morning darkness without their horses. The Chicago Board of Trade Battery was positioned on a high hill overlooking the river while one company of the 72nd along with two companies of the 17th were placed on bluffs along the river as sharpshooters. At the first crack of dawn the Board of Trade Battery opened up

on the opposite bank and the Brigade moved out. The Chattahoochee River at that point was extremely wide but the men had
no idea how deep they would find it; however they had the utmost confidence in Col. Miller and they knew that he would not
ask them to attempt the crossing unless it had a good chance of
success. As soon as the artillery opened fire, the skirmish line
jumped into the water followed close behind by the remainder
of the Brigade. The water was near shoulder deep and the men
waded with their rifles held above their heads. In the meantime
the Rebel cavalry pickets on the opposite bank had been alerted
by the artillery fire and had rushed to the edge of the water to
see what was going on. The skirmish line was half way across the
river before the enemy could see through the thin fog the heads
and shoulders of the Yankee invaders and no doubt they beheld
an eerie sight. It seemed like an entire Union brigade had suddenly arisen from the bottom of the river. Wheeler's cavalrymen immediately opened fire on the men in the water. The
Lightning Brigade returned their fire from the river as they
waded up to their armpits along the soapstone bottom. Wilder's
men soon found that they could work the levers of their Spencer
rifles under water and since the cartridges were metallic it didn't
bother their effectiveness a bit. So they began walking in a
crouch, keeping only their head above water so as to make a
smaller target for the Rebels. Then they would raise up and
fire their Spencer and duck down again to throw another cartridge into the breech. The fight was a lively one with a solid
sheet of fire erupting from the river. The Rebels, armed with
muzzle loaders using paper cartridges, could not believe their
eyes, and as the Brigade approached the far side they could
hear the Rebs yelling, "Look at them Yankee sons of bitches,
loading their guns under water! What sort of critters be they,
any how? It's no use trying to fight agin' fellas that'll dive down
to the bottom of the rivah an get that powdah and ball!"[17]
The enemy pickets pulled back from the water's edge as the
heavy fire from the river took its toll. Gen. Garrard, riding
along the river bank, shouted out to his men, "Bully boys! bully
boys! Whiskey in the morning!"[18] As the skirmishers reached
shallow water near the opposite bank, a race began to see who
would be the first man ashore. The main body quickened its pace
and when the Brigade reached the far bank the Rebels turned
and ran, losing three or four prisoners.

Martin's Confederate Cavalry division was camped a short

distance from the river and the defenders had been his pickets. When he received a report of the crossing, he was told that the entire brigade was already across. He thought it best not to engage the Union force. The Lightning Brigade then moved to a ridge about 300 yards from the edge of the river and deployed in line of battle and threw up earthworks. Minty then crossed the river and took position on the left along the ridge. These two brigades held the position until late in the evening when they were relieved by Newton's Division of the 4th Corps, which was sent to hold the position temporarily until relieved in turn by Gen. Dodge's 16th Corps which had been sent back to the left by Gen. McPherson. Wilder's Lightning Brigade was the first Union force across the Chattahoochee River. Later in the day Schofield's 23rd Corps crossed further down on boats near Soap Creek. As night fell Sherman had troops across the river in two places on the right flank of the Confederate Army. Wilder's and Minty's Brigades, after being relieved, moved back across the river and camped in town at Roswell.

Next morning after breakfast Gen. Garrard kept good his word and issued a gill of whiskey for each man. Some of the men who didn't drink gave away their ration and several of them lost their gill in card games. As a result a good number of the men wound up with much more than their allotment and got roaringly drunk. But the whiskey wasn't the sole source of the trouble. Most of the factory workers in Roswell were women. This being Sunday and because most of the factories had been burned, the women and whiskey soon got mixed together. By afternoon Garrard found it necessary to move his division out of town to a new camp. Before they got moved out some men of G Company, 72nd Indiana, noticed a newly constructed vault in a cemetery, and as they passed by it one of the men claimed he could smell meat. The others concurred and after finding a flat rock close by that showed signs of having had meat laid on it, they knocked a hole in the wall of the vault. It was full of bacon, hams and molasses. Some local Rebel had certainly concocted an ingenious hiding place for his stores, but he hadn't taken into account the keen sense of smell of these men of the Lightning Brigade, sharpened by the recent shortage of bacon in their ration issue.[19]

When General Garrard and his troops had arrived at Roswell, they had taken over the Presbyterian Church for use as a hospital. Dr. Pratt, fearing that the church's silver communion service was in danger of confiscation, gave it to a mill superintendent who in turn sent it a piece at a time to Miss Fanny Whitmire who kept it hidden in a barrel for the rest of the war. The sick and wounded soldiers that were treated in the church took a door off a cabinet and made a checkerboard on it. Both the silver communion service and the checkerboard door are still in the church today as is the official church Bible, the front page of which still carries the message, "Run Johnny Run, the Yanks will get you," written by one of Garrard's men at the time.

General Johnston crossed the Chattahoochee with his Confederate Army on the night of the 9th after discovering that the Federals had made two crossings above him. Things were relatively quiet for the next few days. Wilder's Brigade along with Long and Minty spent until the 17th picketing and scouting in a large area on the left flank of the Union Line. On the 14th they moved their camp eight miles northeast of Roswell to a placed called McAfee's Bridge. On the 15th the 72nd Indiana and the 123rd Illinois went in reconnaissance to Crosskeys thirteen miles northeast of Atlanta. Wheat, oats and early apples were ripe and the men enjoyed their brief period of relative quiet. A raiding party captured some Confederate medical stores one day in which were a thousand pounds of corn starch. The corn starch used as a thickening for stewed blackberries made excellent pudding.

During this time the Union army had been building dozens of pontoon bridges across the river, and on the 17th the entire Union army crossed the Chattahoochee in a general advance. The Lightning Brigade crossed at McAfee's and moved to Crosskeys on the left of McPherson's Army of the Tennessee.

That evening General Johnston was replaced by Gen. Hood as commander of the Confederate Army of Tennessee. When notified of this command change in the Rebel army Gen. Sherman immediately called in Generals Schofield and McPherson, both of whom had been classmates of Hood at West Point. They agreed that this leadership change meant "fight." Schofield told Sherman that Hood was "bold even to rashness, and courageous in the extreme."[20] Confederate President Jefferson Davis had asked Gen. Robert E. Lee's advice on the matter and Lee had replied, that "Hood was a bold fighter"; he later added that "General Hardee had more experience in managing an army."[21]

General Johnston was an excellent military strategist. He had cleverly withdrawn his army from Dalton to Atlanta, forcing the

Union troops to assault well constructed breastworks, and taken a huge toll of casualties in the numerically superior Union ranks. As Sherman's supply lines grew increasingly longer he had to leave more and more troops behind to guard them. Johnston's plan had been to pull Sherman deep into southern territory to the point where there would not be such a great difference in numbers and then, after cutting Sherman's lines in the rear with cavalry raids, attack him. But Jeff Davis was feeling political pressure because of the Rebel retreat and he demanded a Confederate offensive. Gen. Hood had a good reputation as an offensive tactician at the brigade and division level. Consequently, Davis made his decision to replace Johnston with Hood with instructions to attack the Union Army. This was exactly what Sherman wanted and it no doubt hurried the downfall of the Confederacy.

On the 18th Minty's and the Lightning Brigades, followed by a brigade of McPherson's infantry, struck the railroad between Decatur and Stone Mountain and destroyed three miles of track. Col. Miller and his men used the heat system. They built fires on the railroad at the ends of the rails and in a short time there were fires going all up and down the tracks. When the rails got hot enough, the expansion from the heat would cause them to pop up, twisting themselves into weird designs and throwing the ties in all directions. That evening the force pulled back three miles and camped near the extreme left of McPherson's army.

Next day Sherman continued his advance on Atlanta with Thomas and his Army of the Cumberland approaching from the north, Schofield's Army of the Ohio on Thomas' left and McPherson on the extreme left coming in from the east. Wilder's Brigade was sent back toward Stone Mountain again east of McPherson's left flank. The Brigade hit the Rebel pickets two miles from the railroad they had destroyed on the previous day. They soon came on the main Rebel force consisting of two whole brigades. The Lightning Brigade dismounted and drove the Rebels into Stone Mountain Station. Here the Rebels took refuge in and behind houses and fired at the Brigade from the windows, an extremely heavy fire coming from a big two story house. Col. Miller brought up an artillery piece and fired into the house, blowing a chair out from under the owner and causing the Confederates to abandon it in a hurry. Col. Miller and his men then drove the Rebels out of town, but not before they burned the depot containing southern commissary stores and 200 bales of cotton in order to prevent its capture by the Union troops. The Brigade, having accomplished its mission, then returned to its camp north of Decatur.

Wednesday the 20th Gen. Hood made his promise good—he furiously assailed Thomas' Army of the Cumberland along Peach Tree Creek less than five miles north of Atlanta. Thomas' men had crossed the creek and were deployed in line of battle, but Hood's assault hit them while they were taking a break at noon mealtime. The attack caught them more or less by surprise but they quickly recovered and soon drove the Rebels back into their entrenched lines, but not before both sides had suffered many casualties. Hooker's XX Corps, the hardest hit of Thomas' three suffered 1500 casualties. While Thomas was beating off Hood's attack on the Union right, the Lightning Brigade was moving south to Decatur, guarding McPherson's left and his wagon trains.

At 1:30 A.M. on July 21 Gen. Garrard received a message from Gen. Sherman ordering him to move with his division on a three day raid to Covington, forty miles east and south of Atlanta. This turned out to be one of the most successful mounted raids of the campaign but Sherman's decision to send his largest cavalry unit away, leaving McPherson's flank exposed and unguarded in the face of as aggressive an adversary as Hood, was a disastrous decision.

Garrard's three brigades, Wilder's, Minty's and Long's, were scattered from Decatur to Roswell some twenty miles to the north. During the day Garrard notified Sherman that it would take some time to get his scattered forces together but that he would travel at night to make up the lost time.[22] The division got underway at 4 P.M., passed around the north side of Stone Mountain and then headed southeast, travelling 25 miles before bivouacking on the Yellow River at midnight.

The division was aroused at 3 A.M. on the 22nd and by daylight it was on its way toward Covington. As soon as they crossed the river two companies of the 98th Illinois were sent down the river to the railroad where they found a wooden railroad bridge guarded by a company of Rebels. The men of the 98th soon drove the Rebels from the bridge, killing a Confederate whose hair was white as snow. One of the men said that he "must have been 80 years old."[23] The Union detachment fired the bridge and while it was burning they heard a train approaching from the west. They moved west a short distance and hid while the train passed them and travelled up to the bridge. When the train stopped they came up from behind and captured it along with the Rebel colonel, a captain and 15 enlisted men who were passengers. The 15 cars containing a large quantity of cotton and molasses were burned and the two 98th companies then rejoined the balance of the command and moved on toward Covington. At 11 o'clock, five miles from Covington, the division closed up and Long's brigade was sent to burn the bridge across the Ulcofauhatchee River east of town while Minty's and Wilder's moved on the town, reaching there at 2 o'clock in the afternoon. After destroying railroad property and burning a large warehouse and a mill containing a huge inventory of corn and flour, the division moved north to the small town of Oxford. Here they burned 2000 bales of cotton and three of four warehouses. The fourth warehouse was filled with shoes and tobacco which the men soon confiscated, filling their haversacks, saddle bags and pockets with tobacco first and then taking what shoes they could hang on the horses. The division worked its way back toward Decatur, burning bridges and destroying Rebel property along the way, and reached that place on the 24th shortly before noon. To their surprise they found Decatur in the possession of the Confederate Army and their wagon train was nowhere in sight.

Garrard and his command hadn't got half way to Covington on this raid before Wheeler and his Rebel cavalry had spotted their movement. Wheeler had reported this fact to General Hood early on the 22nd. But Hood did not order Wheeler to pursue Garrard. This was a pleasant surprise for him. He had already moved Hardee's Corps on the night of the 21st to his extreme right so as to launch a flank attack on McPherson. Without Garrard and his men guarding his flank McPherson was taken by surprise by Hardee's assault on the 22nd. This battle went down in history as the Battle of Atlanta and, although the Confederates were finally stopped, General McPherson was killed during the battle and heavy casualties were suffered by both sides.

On arriving back at Decatur the Lightning Brigade drove the Rebel pickets through town and then moved two miles to the north where they found their pack mules and wagons. Their guard, Sprague's brigade of infantry, had been driven from Decatur by Wheeler earlier that day. The division camped that night immediately to the rear of the left of the Union Army. But they didn't get much sleep. The word had gotten around that Wilder's men were loaded down with tobacco and all during the night the infantrymen from the Army of the Tennessee came into the Lightning Brigade area calling out, "Is this Wilder's Brigade? Give me a chew of tobacco."[24]

On the 25th Garrard moved his division forward and joined it to the left of the infantry line. The men spent the 25th and 26th shoeing up their horses, repairing equipment and getting ready for the continuance of the Campaign. On the 27th Sherman merged Minty's and Wilder's brigades commanded by Gen. Garrard with Stoneman's Cavalry Division, the combined force under the command of Gen. Stoneman, for a raid on the Macon Railroad below Atlanta. At the same time he sent Gen. McCook and his cavalry around the Confederate left on a railroad raid toward Lovejoy's Station. Sherman's thinking was that if he could cut Hood's supply lines by cutting the Macon Railroad he would force Hood to abandon Atlanta. Stoneman moved out before sunup on the 27th on the road to Decatur. Before leaving he had requested permission from General Sherman to liberate the Union prisoners at Andersonville Prison, forty miles south of Macon. Sherman authorized this move providing Stoneman first accomplished his primary mission of destroying the Macon Railroad and that he also send Garrard back to the main army after this was accomplished. Stoneman, however, did not obey orders. Instead of moving on the railroad with his entire force, he posted Garrard and his two brigades southwest of Decatur at Flat Shoals as a decoy for Wheeler's Rebel Cavalry and moved with his own small force directly to Macon. Garrard's men arrived at Flat Shoals shortly after noon and bivouacked, leaving their horses saddled. Col. Miller, in command of the Lightning Brigade noted, "Stoneman is on our left. We are to do the fighting and he is to do the raiding and tear up the railroad."[25] It didn't take Wheeler long to find Garrard. At 10 P.M. that night Minty's pickets, the 4th Michigan, were driven in by Wheeler's Cavalry and the entire division moved into line of battle where they remained throughout the night. Daylight of the 28th found them entirely surrounded by General Wheeler and three divisions of Rebel cavalry—and Atlanta between Garrard and the main Union army. By 8 o'clock Wheeler was attacking the Union force around its entire perimeter and then after a severe shelling by his artillery, he sent in a demand for surrender. This was refused, and after consultation with his staff Gen. Garrard decided to cut his way out. As usual when a crucial dismounted attack was to be made he called on the Lightning Brigade. This was only natural. The Lightning Brigade had more experience at dismounted infantry type fighting. They had taken Hoover's Gap over a year before with their Spencer Rifles; they had saved the Union Army from complete annihilation at Chickamauga, had routed the Rebels between Big Shanty and Kenesaw and had fought in the line with the 15th Corps at Dallas. The Brigade formed for attack shortly before noon with a battalion of the 4th U.S. Regulars on each flank, mounted. When Col. Miller ordered the attack, the Brigade moved out with a yell and hit the Confederates along the Lithonia Road. The Rebels resisted for only a short time and then the force of the attack broke the Rebel line wide open. After advancing 600 yards the Brigade remounted and the entire division moved toward Lithonia with the 7th Pennsylvania of Minty's Brigade as rear guard, skirmishing with Wheeler's small pursuing force.

By this time Gen. Wheeler had discovered that Stoneman was moving on Macon, and he had been notified that McCook had moved around the other end of the Confederates' lines. He immediately sent Gen. Iverson with his own brigade and those of Allen and Breckinridge after Stoneman, and leaving Gen. Kelly with Dibrell's brigade to harass Garrard, he moved with Ashby's and Anderson's brigades to the southwest of Atlanta to aid Gen. Jackson in blocking McCook. Garrard, after spending the 29th at Lithonia, moved northwest to Buckhead near Sherman's headquarters where he arrived on the 31st, having lost only 12 killed and 78 wounded and missing in fighting his way out of an encirclement by six brigades of enemy cavalry. Stoneman in the meantime moved on Macon without destroying the railroad as ordered. Finding Macon defended only by militia he began shelling it from across the river. However, before he could take Macon and move on to Andersonville, he was overtaken by Gen. Iverson and his three cavalry brigades. Stoneman was surrounded and although remnants of his force escaped and returned to the Union lines Gen. Stoneman and 700 of his men were captured.

Gen. Stoneman's disobedience of orders combined with his tactical blunders caused Sherman's plan to result in complete failure. McCook's force had also been surrounded by Wheeler and Jackson's cavalry and his part in the plan crumbled with a loss of 600 men killed, wounded and captured. Garrard's mission had been to stall Wheeler so that Stoneman could get a two day start toward Macon and then he was to return to the left of the main army. This he did. And although his men had a feeling of failure, his was the only force that accomplished what it had been ordered to do.

General Sherman, displeased with the performance of Stoneman and McCook, then pulled Schofield's 23rd Corps from the left of the Union line and moved it around to the right to move on Hood's communications south of Atlanta. Minty's and Wilder's Brigades dismounted and took Schofield's place in the trenches. A day or two later Sherman pulled Palmer's 14th Corps out of line also and moved it to the right with Schofield. The 4th and 20th Corps spread their lines to fill the gap left by Palmer. Minty's Brigade was on the right next to the infantry, Grose's division of the 4th Corps being on their immediate right. Col. Miller and the Lightning Brigade joined Minty on the left, thereby being the extreme left of the Union line. Long's Brigade picketed to the left and rear of the Lightning Brigade's position, mounted.

The Brigade remained in the rifle trenches until the 15th, the longest period of time they had remained in one place since they had been mounted in the early spring of '63. Sherman's supply system was working well and they had ample food; their horses and pack mules were in the rear where they could get sufficient feed. During this period they were under daily fire from the Rebel artillery and the skirmish line exchanged rifle fire with the enemy constantly throughout the two weeks. A captain of Minty's Brigade wrote to his wife:

> In the trenches, Atlanta,
> Aug. 13, 1864

My Dear Wife:

. . . . . I have very little to communicate. Our lines are drawing around Atlanta closer daily. Our regiment is on the advanced skirmish line every third day. Our horses are in the rear, and we are playing infantry. We teach the rebs, as the boys say, a new game of seven-up with our seven shooting carbines. Yesterday an advance, or demonstration, was made, and our regiment took part. We penetrated the suburbs of the city, and took the rebel rifle-pits. The main works were found too strong so we did not assault them. The rebels fired heavily, but the company, being sheltered by a rising ground, sustained no loss. I think we went further than any other troops heretofore. All seemed pleased, except the rebs . . . . .

_____ _____26

Captain,
Seventh Pennsylvania Cavalry

Soon after the Lightning Brigade entered the trenches, the weather turned wet and the dampness along with the intense August heat created a considerable amount of minor illnesses among the men. They were used to moving around, and although each regiment got its turn on the skirmish line and the exchange of both rifle fire and artillery was lively, the men soon got tired of the monotony of staying in one place. But the enemy wasn't exactly happy with its lot either as evidenced by a letter written by a Confederate infantryman to his wife. It was picked up by a member of the 72nd Indiana after the writer had succumbed to a round from a Spencer rifle:

In the trenches before Atlanta,
Aug. 15, 1864

My dear wife,
    Your war-worn husband takes his pen in hand, in a strange land, on a foreign strand. My ink is pale, I have no ale. My paper is poor; so is my grub. Our quarters in camp are passable, but quarters in my pocket are not. Last night I had a wagon bolster for a "piller" while I was covered with a sheet of water. . . . So that you may know how we work in spite of the cussed Yanks, I send you a diary of daily labor. 5 o'clock, called up by a roll of the drum, from a roll in the mud; no rolls of bread. 6 to 7, shoulder spades. Throw up the earth, also yesterday's rations. 7:30, another roll of the drum, and we roll logs. Filing off into line, as well as defiling my breeches with the sacred soil of Georgia; drawing ramrods but no pay; no shelling out by the government, but a cussed sight by the Yanks. . . . My eyes are sunk so far into my head that I can look down my windpipe into my restaurant department. . . .27

The letter was not completed—interrupted by either another roll of the Rebel drums or by the crack of a Spencer rifle. The Rebel troops were getting haggard by this time. No doubt about that. Rations were poor, clothing badly worn and they hadn't been paid for months. Georgia troops especially were noted for a fondness for peanuts and no doubt at this time, with rations short, the Confederates consumed more than a normal amount of them and quite possibly the inspiration for the civil war song

"Goober Peas" was born here. But this had not taken the fight out of them. In fact it was said that the Army of the Tennessee would "charge Hell with a cornstalk."[28] And the Union army was to have a lot of fighting to do and would suffer many more casualties before the Confederates would give up Atlanta.

On the 15th of August the Lightning Brigade and Minty's Brigade were ordered out of the trenches. They picked up their horses in the rear, moved out with their pack train and headed for Decatur.

Decatur was again found to be in possession of the Rebels and after skirmishing with their pickets, the two brigades went into camp a short distance from town. The Brigade picketed and scouted in the Decatur area on the 16th and 17th. Toward evening on the 17th the Lightning Brigade received orders to relieve Col. Long's Brigade which had been picketing from the left of the main Union line to Roswell on the Chattahoochee. Long's and Minty's brigades were ordered to join Gen. Kilpatrick and his 3rd Cavalry division at Sandtown, southwest of Atlanta, for a raid on the railroad south of Atlanta. Kilpatrick and his force completely circled the Confederate Army and Atlanta, destroying the railroad, and returned on the 22nd. This force had severe fights near Jonesboro and Lovejoy's Station, both Minty and Long suffering heavy casualties. While Long and Minty were on the Kilpatrick Raid, the Lightning Brigade foraged and skirmished in the Decatur area. By the 23rd the tracks that Kilpatrick had destroyed south of Atlanta were repaired and Rebel trains were running again; consequently, the Lightning Brigade moved out between Decatur and Stone Mountain and tore up four miles of the Augusta railroad on the 24th.

On the 25th Sherman decided to move his entire army to the southwest around Atlanta. That evening the 4th and 20th Corps pulled out of their entrenchments after the brigades of Wilder, Long and Minty had dismounted and joined them in their works. These two infantry corps slipped out without the enemy realizing they had gone. Near midnight Garrard's men also left the trenches and followed the infantry back to the Chattahoochee where they crossed at Vining's Station. Sherman left the 20th Corps to guard the crossing and moved the 4th Corps south. The next evening the 15th and 17th Corps were pulled out of line and moved on south of the 4th and 14th Corps. This sudden disappearance of the Union troops in his front caused Hood to think that they were retreating. He sent Wheeler's cavalry in a wide circuitous route around the Union Army on a raid on the northern supply lines. Wheeler had successfully damaged the railroads behind the Federal lines and Hood had the false impression that this had caused Sherman enough of a supply problem that he had been forced to lift his siege of Atlanta and withdraw. Actually Sherman was flanking Hood on the left and moving his whole gigantic army to the rear of Atlanta. In fact the word soon spread through the entire South that Atlanta had been saved and great celebrations were commenced.

General W. H. Jackson, one of Hood's most dependable cavalry leaders, had followed the "retreating" Union troops for some distance after it had been discovered that they had pulled out. Jackson knew that the Northerners were not actually retreating and he reported this fact to Gen. Hood. But Hood did not believe him, or maybe he just didn't want to believe him. In any case it was the 28th before Hood even became suspicious of Sherman's movements and it was not until the 30th that General Hardee, commanding the Confederate left, was able to convince Hood that almost the entire Union army was concentrated below Atlanta. Hood hurriedly ordered Hardee with his corps and that of Gen. Stephen D. Lee south to Jonesboro, keeping Stewart's Corps and Smith's Georgia State Militia in Atlanta. Hardee attacked the Union army at Jonesboro late in the evening on the 31st and, although he inflicted severe casualties on Sherman's army, he was forced to fall back into his breastworks at night. During the night Hardee received orders to send Lee's corps back toward Atlanta. The next morning Gen. Lee moved out and left Gen. Hardee with one army corps at Jonesboro facing six of Sherman's corps. Evidently Hood still did not realize the true situation. Later in the day, in an attempt to surround Hardee, Sherman moved on him with his entire force and attacked. But Hardee, a former commandant at West Point and one of the South's most reliable generals, held off all day against overwhelming odds and that night withdrew south to Lovejoy's, escaping from Sherman's noose. Hood, suddenly realizing what was going on, immediately dispatched the remainder of his army, the corps of Stewart, Lee and Smith, from Atlanta to join Hardee at Lovejoy.

In the meantime Gen. Slocum, now in command of the Union 20th corps, had been slowly moving south from the Chattahoochee, feeling his way toward Atlanta from the north. On September 2, with Atlanta evacuated, the 20th corps entered the city unopposed and accepted its surrender from the mayor. Atlanta had at last fallen. It had been 118 days of continuous battle since the campaign had begun with the 4th corps attack on Tunnel Hill over 100 miles to the north. Each side had lost in the neighborhood of 40,000 men, but Sherman finally had Atlanta.

Sherman followed Hood to Lovejoy's Station where he found him strongly entrenched. Union forces at this time numbered 81,000 effectives, battle-worn but keyed up by the capture of Atlanta. Hood's Army of less than 40,000, though tough and still full of fight, were short of provisions and somewhat dejected by the loss of the city. In any case, Sherman had them outnumbered more than two to one and had the impetus of victory going for him. But for some unexplainable reason, instead of delivering the final crushing blow to Hood's Army, which in the beginning of the campaign had been Sherman's primary objective, he suddenly withdrew his huge army from Lovejoy's on the 4th of September and marched back north to Atlanta to "enjoy a short period of rest, and to think well over the next step required in the progress of events."[29] The Lightning Brigade, which had been busy protecting the Federal wagon trains during the maneuvering south of Atlanta, guarded the rear of the infantry columns as they moved north. They went into camp near the 23rd Corps which was camped at Decatur, east of Atlanta.

The Brigade remained in camp until September 21. Each day three men from each company were allowed to travel into Atlanta to see the fortifications left by the enemy.

Atlanta was not its original name. In 1837 it was just a place where the railroads from the east would join the railroads going to the north and west. As the construction of these railroads got underway, this community of shacks, known as Terminus, became a boom town, filled with saloons, gamblers and adventurous women. The railroads were finished by 1845 and the name of the town was changed to Atlanta. The flourish of commerce brought on by the railroads made Atlanta, in only 15 short years, one of the South's most wealthy and important cities. But the Gate City, as Atlanta had come to be known, no longer looked like the beautiful and exciting city pictured in *Gone with the Wind* by the time Sherman's army occupied it. The artillery bombardment during the campaign and the fighting in its outskirts had left Atlanta a pitiful sight. Sgt. McGee of the 72nd Indiana observed on a trip into the city that, "we passed by a house that stood a half mile outside the rebel works, that was

just literally honeycombed by bullets. It had been used by both
sides alternately as a skirmish post."[30]

Lt. Bleakley of the 98th Illinois wrote to his parents that Atlanta
is damaged a great deal by our artillery, houses burnt and riddled to pieces
and a great many citizens killed, but there would have been hundreds
more had they not made bombproofs by digging in the ground a room
something like a cellar covered over with earth and lived in it while the
shelling was going on. . . . They destroyed most of the public property
before they left. They burnt five trains of cars loaded with ammunition
and arms principally. And a large foundry. It is quite a reck where the
trains was burnt as there were many cars loaded with shell and when
they exploded they strewed the ground for hundreds of yards with the
pieces.[31]

Atlanta was a mess sure enough. Some years later a traveler,
looking at a shell-scarred lamp post on the city's Whitehall
Street, asked a policeman why a placque showed this ancient
lamp post as a Civil War Memorial. The policeman answered,
"Because that's about all we had left."

Sherman had the Army of the Cumberland at Atlanta, Schofield's 23rd Corps at Decatur and the Army of the Tennessee
a few miles southwest at East Point. Hood moved his Confederate army back up to Jonesboro. And the two great armies
took a few days rest and licked their wounds.

10

"Hard Times in Dixie"

THE NORTH WAS HIGHLY ELATED BY THE FALL OF ATLANTA. Sherman received congratulatory wires from President Lincoln and from General Grant, who had established his headquarters at City Point, Virginia. Grant's own offensive in the east was still bogged down in front of Petersburg, but since he was in command of all the northern armies and since the Atlanta campaign had been a part of his overall strategy, the fall of Atlanta had been welcome news. Lincoln was doubly pleased. Not only from a military standpoint, but especially because of the upcoming national election in which his opponent, Gen. Geo. B. McClellan, was running on a platform that claimed the war to be a failure.

The loss of Atlanta was a disheartening blow to the South. Morale in the civilian population dropped to a new low. Recruiting became next to impossible. Gov. Brown of Georgia withdrew his state militia from Hood's command, claiming that the fall of Atlanta had terminated his obligation to the Confederate States. There was even some talk among the heirarchy of the Georgia government of making a separate truce between the United States and the State of Georgia.

Hood's Army of Tennessee, depleted in numbers and short of provisions, was not out of fight yet. But they had lost most of what little respect they had ever had for Hood, which had never been much. Gen. Joe Johnston had been a great favorite of the men. They respected his military wisdom and they trusted him as a man. They had not been happy when Hood replaced Johnston and now, after Hood's failures at Peach Tree Creek, the Battle of Atlanta and in the defense of the city itself, the men of the Army of Tennessee took an "I told you so" attitude.

177

Hood, a courageous and aggressive fighter, had one extremely bad personal trait. He was never man enough to accept blame for anything that went wrong. He always placed the responsibilities for defeat on his subordinate officers and, worse yet, on the tough and loyal men of his Army of Tennessee. Confederate President Jefferson Davis came west late in September to give the Army of Tennessee a pep talk in order to boost morale. As he rode through camp he could not keep from hearing anonymous requests from the men for the return of Joe Johnston.

Sherman, in the meantime, had evacuated the entire civilian population of Atlanta and turned it into an armed camp. The Yankee army, expecting to remain idle for some time, began making themselves comfortable. Provisions were plentiful. They caught up on their letter writing, repaired equipment and built shelters. The campaign had been tough. The men of the Lightning Brigade especially were in need of recuperation. They had been constantly on the move and usually on short rations. Hard work on hardtack and bacon for an extended period of time was not conducive to good health and several of the men were suffering from scurvy. Shortly after making camp near Decatur, however, they received a most welcome present from the Christian Commission that not only spiced up their menu but cured the scurvy as well—a shipment of pickled onions. The men thoroughly enjoyed this change of pace and the vinegar took care of the scurvy. In only a day or two everyone was feeling better.

The men of the Brigade had not been paid in over ten months, but now they had been promised that their much needed money was forthcoming. This promise was broken, however, not by Col. Miller but by Gen. Hood. On the 21st Hood moved his army west to Palmetto Station, 35 miles southwest of Atlanta. Garrard's cavalry division was immediately dispatched to find out what the Rebel army was up to. Hood's move evidently surprised Sherman and it shook the Federal headquarters from its complacency.

The Brigade moved southwest to Sandtown on the 22nd, crossed the Chattahoochee on the 23rd and traveled 10 miles on south where they found that the Rebel infantry was in the process of crossing the river. Three brigades of Confederate cavalry had already crossed and were on their way north toward Marietta. Col. Miller moved his Lightning Brigade north in pursuit of this mounted Rebel force, camping near Sandtown on the night of the 23rd and at Powder Springs on the 24th. On Sunday the 25th the Brigade moved north thirty miles across Lost and Pine Mountains and at nightfall arrived at Ackworth, seven miles north of Kenesaw Mountain on the railroad. All during this chase the Rebels had managed to stay a day ahead of the Brigade, and when they arrived at Ackworth they found that the Southerners had torn up part of the railroad and captured a train bound for Atlanta. The next day part of the Brigade scouted southwest toward Dallas. Finding no Rebels there they moved northeast on the 27th to Hickory Flat, and on the 28th south through guerrilla country to Roswell where they crossed the Chattahoochee and camped for the night.

The three or four county area north of Marietta and east of the railroad was the sphere of operations for a group of local partisans known as "McCollum's Scouts," led by a young man named Ben McCollum. McCollum supposedly had enlisted in the "Cherokee Brown Riflemen" (Co. F, 2nd Georgia Infantry) when it first organized in 1861. He was soon discharged, however, for being under age. But in 1864, now three years older, McCollum and his band of 25 or 30 young men played havoc with the Union sympathizers of the area as well as the foragers of the Union Army. They were tough and deadly—they killed first and asked questions later. McCollum had quite a reputation in north Georgia, but on this last Wednesday of September Col. Miller moved his Brigade safely through McCollum's Territory.[1]

On the same day General Hood ordered his entire army across the Chattahoochee in a general movement north to cut Sherman's communications and supply lines. Next day the Lightning Brigade moved south to Crosskeys where they were joined by the remainder of the division.

When General Sherman received word that the entire Rebel army had moved north across the Chattahoochee, he seemed to be at a loss as to what to do. The Brigade spent the next two days in camp at Crosskeys waiting for definite orders. Orders were issued and countermanded several times a day as the Union command attempted to ascertain Hood's intentions. The movements and disposition of Hood's Army had Sherman completely baffled until he was notified on the 2nd of October that the entire Army of Tennessee was in line of battle near Lost Mountain west of Marietta, twenty-five miles north of him. Sherman then swung into action and, leaving the 20th Corps at Atlanta, he started the remainder of his army north in pursuit. Garrard's cavalry division moved to the Chattahoochee bridge between Atlanta and Marietta where they had to wait until morning to get a right of way to cross.

Before Gen. Garrard and his division crossed the river on the morning of the 3rd, he was joined by General Washington Elliott, Sherman's chief-of-cavalry. Although Elliott was Garrard's immediate superior he had never accompanied the division during the entire campaign. The men speculated on the significance of this incident at the time but later they got the story. The weather had been wet and disagreeable for three days. This, along with his concern over the actions of the Rebel army, made Gen. Sherman very out of humor. On this morning, October 3, Sherman lost patience with Elliott and, possibly thinking that Elliott was not showing enough concern of their predicament, turned to him and said something like this, "Elliott, why in the hell don't you do something? Damn it, get out and do something. If you can't do nothing else, get out and hunt up an old wagon that is stuck in the mud; get that and bring it in."[2] So Elliott moved with Garrard's division for the next few days. They moved to Powder Springs during the day and camped four miles north of town.

After having torn up several miles of railroad on the 3rd, Hood sent various parts of his army to attack stations along the railroad, all of which were guarded by Union garrisons. Stewart's Confederate corps took Big Shanty on the 4th and Gen. Loring's force took Ackworth. The next day Gen. French attacked the Union depot at Allatoona where Sherman had stored a huge number of supplies. Gen. French's attack was beaten off, however, by the heroic defense of Gen. Corse and his badly outnumbered force that were manning the defenses of Allatoona. Sherman observed this battle from Kenesaw Mountain, thirteen miles away, to which place he had arrived although most of the Union Army was still stuck in the mud along the Chattahoochee.

The men in the ranks were concerned about the state of affairs. The entire Confederate Army of Tennessee was between them and home, and they were tearing up the railroads upon which the Union army depended to keep itself supplied with food. Col. Miller's diary for this period summed up the feeling of the rank and file:

October 3rd. Moved to near Powder Springs. The enemy are moving for the railroad in force. At least two corps are over the Chattahoochee and camped at Lost Mountain last night. They are going for us certain. Our hardtack will be cut off for a fact.

October 4th. Marched to Kenesaw Mountain. The enemy are in force on the railroad at Big Shanty. Took prisoners from both Lee's and Stewart's Corps today. They are going for our grub.

October 5th. Moved out near Lost Mountain. We had some skirmishing with the enemy who occupy a line from Powder Springs to Allatoona Mountain. The scene looks dark.[3]

Captain Funkhouser, Co. A. 98th Illinois, returning from a furlough home, was stranded in Chattanooga because the Chattahoochee bridge was washed out and because the Rebels had destroyed part of the railroad to Atlanta. News of Hood's operations north of Atlanta had reached Chattanooga, and on the 7th Captain Funkhouser reflected the concern of the people there in a letter to his father:

"I think you had better ship your tobacco though you can tell best—you can see the papers every day and tell when it is going up or down. But I think there will be a decline in it. . . . Hood has split his army up in 7 or 8 parties and coming back up in this direction. They are stealing everything they come across."[4]

On the 6th Garrard's cavalry was ordered to move up the railroad to pick up the Rebel trail. After sending their pack mules back to Marietta for rations and forage they moved to Big Shanty, Ackworth and then to Allatoona where they found that Hood's army had moved southwest toward Dallas.

Early next morning the division moved south on the Allatoona-Dallas Road, and after riding only a few miles they came upon the enemy's rear guard, Armstrong's Rebel cavalry. A lively fight took place. Brigadier-General Young and Col. Camp of the 14th Texas dismounted cavalry had been wounded at Allatoona while fighting with French's Division and were traveling in the rear of the Rebel column in an ambulance. The 4th U. S. Regulars of Minty's brigade captured the ambulance and its passengers during the initial skirmishing. Wilder's Brigade was then brought up, dismounted, and they drove the Rebels from the works that they had hastily constructed. The division pursued the Confederates as far as New Hope Church where the "Hellhole" battle had been fought the last of May.

On the 8th most of the division remained in camp near New Hope Church while the 98th Illinois of Wilder's Brigade scouted to Dallas and the 7th Pennsylvania of Minty's Brigade went on reconnaissance toward Van Wert. The 98th reported that Hood's army had gone toward Rome and the next day, while most of the division observed Sunday in camp, the 4th Michigan verified this report by discovering the main Rebel army to be at Cedartown south of Rome.

Sherman, figuring that Hood's objective was Rome, started his armies in that direction on the 10th. Garrard's cavalry was ordered to move on Rome to reinforce Gen. Corse, who was holding Rome with a single division, and at the same time to verify the movements of Hood's army. By riding all night they got to within nine miles of the town by daylight when they ran into Rebel pickets. Unbeknown to the Union command, Hood had flanked Rome with his main army and moved north toward Resaca, leaving Brig. Gen. W. H. Jackson and his Rebel cavalry to demonstrate and detain the Federal army at Rome. The 72nd Indiana and 123rd Illinois were dismounted and charged two brigades of Jackson's cavalry, driving them for a mile. Gen. Garrard then ordered the two regiments to post pickets and return to the rest of the division to have breakfast. After eating and caring for the horses the pickets were withdrawn and the division moved down a road along the Etowah River. They reached Rome just before dark.

The division left camp at 8:30 the morning of the 12th with orders to move north to the bridge across Armuchee Creek which was supposed to be held by a part of Wheeler's Cavalry that had just returned from a raid into Tennessee.

Rome, Georgia is at the junction formed by the Etowah river coming from the east and the Oostenaula River coming in from the north. These two rivers form the Coosa River at Rome which then runs to the southwest. The countryside around Rome is hilly and heavily wooded. Before breakfast the Brigade pack mules were sent ahead into Rome to draw rations. Long's and Minty's brigades moved out first and crossed the Etowah. As these two brigades were crossing the river, Wilder's Brigade was passing over a high bluff three-quarters of a mile behind them. From this high ground they could see the Rebels forming their lines behind a ridge that ran north and south parallel to the Oostenaula on the west side of that river. By the time the Lightning Brigade had gotten across the Etowah Long's and Minty's brigades had passed through Rome and were crossing the Oostenaula. As Wilder's men passed through the edge of town they met their pack mules. Picket firing was heard west of the city so the Brigade could not stop; they drew their rations on the march as they rode past the pack train. By the time the Brigade reached the edge of the river west of town, Long and Minty, along with some of Gen. Corse's infantry, had begun skirmishing with the enemy. The Rebel skirmish line was a long one and they began driving the Union skirmishers back toward the river. When the Lightning Brigade got across the Oostenaula they found Federal infantry skirmishers retreating rapidly back to the river and hurrying along the river bank south toward the bridge. Long's and Minty's brigades, who had been up to the left of the infantry were holding their skirmish line fairly well, but they sent word back to General Garrard that they were badly outnumbered. Garrard, irritated by this message, replied that he would "send forward some who would fight."[5] The Lightning Brigade dismounted and moved up between Long who was on the left and Minty on the right and with two regiments on each side of the Coosaville Road, Wilder's Brigade moved to the attack. Jackson's skirmishers were driven almost a mile to the brow of the hill. The Brigade stopped and rested for a short time, but they found themselves within range of the Rebel artillery that was emplaced in the main enemy line on the ridge. While the Rebel artillery pot-shotted at them, Long's brigade took position on the left rear, mounted, and Minty's lined up on the right rear, dismounted, these two brigades to take advantage of any gain that the Lightning Brigade might make on their next attack. As soon as their lines were straightened, the Brigade moved to the attack on the enemy works 300 yards away. Their whirlwind attack shook the enemy out of his works so rapidly that his artillery had only enough time to fire one round before being forced to limber up and pull out with the infantry as they hurriedly retreated to the southwest. The Brigade made a left wheel in following the fleeing Rebels. During this maneuver the men, in their eagerness to pursue individual enemy soldiers, got so mixed up that almost none of them had a man from his own company next to him. Minty had moved his brigade straight west, and because of the wheeling maneuver they never made contact with the enemy. Long's men, mounted, chased Jackson's fleeing cavalrymen, but the Rebels got mounted and moved out before Long could take advantage of the situation. They came back without the Rebel battery which they had hoped to capture. The 7th Penn. and 4th Mich. of Minty's brigade were sent out on scout to relocate the enemy and found them posted behind rail barricades two and one-half miles away. Being late in the evening, Gen. Garrard decided not to renew the attack and the division pulled back a short distance and camped for the night.

While Garrard's division was fighting Jackson's Cavalry on the 12th, Hood appeared at Resaca. From there he tore up the railroad all the way north to Tunnel Hill, taking Dalton and 1000 prisoners on the way. Sherman, on learning that Hood had moved north, marched his army from Kingston toward Resaca, arriving there a day after Hood had left. The Confederate army felled large trees in Snake Creek Gap, and after reaching Tunnel Hill they moved west and went into camp near LaFayette on the other side of Taylor's Ridge and south of the old Chickamauga battlefield. Sherman, on reaching Rocky Face Ridge, found himself five and one half months and 40,000 casualties later exactly where he had started his campaign in early May.

Early on the morning of the 13th Garrard's Division made ready to contact its adversaries of the previous day. Long's men moved out first followed by the Lightning Brigade with Minty's bringing up the rear. After making the two miles to where the Union pickets had been keeping an eye on the enemy, Long's and Wilder's brigades dismounted and went into line of battle with Long on the left and Col. Miller and his men on the right. Minty's Mounted Brigade was held in reserve. As Garrard's division approached the enemy position, the Rebel skirmishers moved out to attack them, but the attack soon turned into a withdrawal with Long and Miller pursuing Gen. Jackson and his dismounted cavalry through a dense woods. Firing was sporadic as the men fought their way through the thick undergrowth of pine and hazelbrush. After advancing a couple of miles, however, the Brigade came out into an open area only to find that the Confederates had set up positions on a bluff with an open field in its front. The Rebel artillery opened up on the men as they crossed the field and they spent a considerable amount of time lying flat on their bellies as their advance was hampered by the heavy shells. Their forward movement continued in spite of the cannon fire, but when they got closer to the enemy lines Jackson's field pieces switched their charges to canister and the air seemed "fairly blue and thick with the devilish missiles."[6] The assaulting force finally got to the base of the bluff, and the Rebel artillerists could not depress their guns enough to get to them. Long and Miller then ordered a charge and the two brigades completely overran the Confederate position. As soon as they had the Rebels on the run, Minty and his mounted men made a picture book saber charge—galloping between Long and Miller in column of fours. They delivered the final crushing blow to the demoralized Rebel force, chasing them for eight miles before they became so widely scattered that Minty recalled his men and they returned to division headquarters.

Sherman, with his usual distrust of mounted troops, had ordered Gen. Cox with two infantry divisions of the 23rd Corps to assist Garrard in attacking Jackson's cavalry and to assure the destruction of a bridge over the Coosa River 12 miles west of Rome. Sherman told Cox to "send the cavalry off to the right flank and push ahead with your infantry; cavalry are too slow."[7] At 8 A.M. of the 13th Cox wrote to Sherman, "Garrard fills the road in front of me and is pushing on. My infantry is close on his heels." At 12:45 P.M. Cox again sent a message to Sherman, "The cavalry advance is now four miles beyond here. . . . I cannot now get as far as the advance of the cavalry is and get back to Rome to-nite." An hour later Cox notified Sherman that Hood had taken the Coosa bridge with him and that "a brigade of cavalry went two miles beyond it. I am returning with my infantry."[8]

Gen. Cox and the advance of his infantry had come within view of the battle scene just in time to see the final assault by Long's and Wilder's brigades and the saber charge by Minty's men. General Cox was very impressed with the agressiveness and effectiveness of Garrard's men and he made a short speech to the men of the division. He told them that during the entire war he had never seen such a spendid charge. The men gave him three cheers and then proceeded to march back to camp where they had left their horses.

Next day the division was assigned the task of protecting the rear of Sherman's wagon train which was moving north in order to try and catch up with the main army. They moved east toward Kingston and then north to Adairsville. From there they moved to Resaca and then, after seeing the train to the entrance of Snake Creek Gap, the division moved back south again toward Rome. On the 19th they moved west toward Gaylesville, Alabama, and on the 20th came upon the rear guard of Hood's main army barricaded across the Little Chattooga River on the other side of Gaylesville. Garrard's division skirmished across the river with Hardee's Corps of veteran infantry until dark.

Garrard and his men were acting as Sherman's eyes, leading his pursuit of Hood and keeping in almost constant contact with Hood's rear guard. A prisoner picked up on the 20th said that Hood intended to make a stand near Blue Pond, a small community to the southwest of their present position. Early on the 21st they found that Hood's Army had pulled out of their works and Garrard's division, reinforced by Watkins' Brigade of Kilpatrick's Cavalary, moved toward Blue Pond in search of the enemy. A few miles on the other side of Blue Pond, they ran into two divisions of Wheeler's cavalry supported by infantry in line of battle behind strong works. Minty's Brigade, which had the advance, pushed the Rebel skirmishers back to the main line of works, but the evidence of a greatly superior force made Minty hold up. The Lightning Brigade was brought up, dismounted, and moved to the attack with the cavalry brigades moving on their right. Col. Miller led his brigade up and over the enemy works. Here Col. Miller held up his advance and the Brigade dug in behind the vacated Confederate works. Although they had driven Wheeler's dismounted Cavalry from their works, they were still confronted by heavy masses of infantry, and to make matters worse Minty's and Long's Brigades on their right began giving way. Since the cavalry was unable to hold its position, the Brigade was in danger of being flanked and Col. Miller gave orders to gather up the dead and wounded and fall back a short distance to go into camp. The brigade lost 12 killed and wounded in the encounter. Before dark the 15th Corps of Sherman's infantry moved up and camped nearby.

The Lightning Brigade skirmished and fought the Rebel cavalry for the rest of the month in the area east and north of Gadsen, Alabama. On the 22nd Hood moved his main army west, travelling almost entirely across the state to Tuscumbia where he planned to cross the Tennessee River and make an invasion of middle Tennessee. Sherman, at Gaylesville, was in a quandary as to what to do while Hood was near Gadsen. When he finally discovered that the Rebel army had pulled out and moved west he made his decision. Ever since the fall of Atlanta, Sherman had been nurturing the idea of moving his army east across the state of Georgia to the sea and then fighting his way north to join Grant in his fight against Robert E. Lee. The disappearance of Hood's army gave Sherman his opportunity to initiate his plan.

11

"Here's Your Mule"

OCTOBER HAD BEEN A BAD MONTH FOR THE NORTH. HOOD HAD moved northward from Atlanta, and eluded Sherman for the entire month in north Georgia, and after having taken Dalton and Tunnel Hill, moved southwest to Gasden, Alabama, where he arrived on the 22nd. Grant and Meade in the east weren't faring any better. They were still around Petersburg, having accomplished very little more than enlarging their casualty list since June. In fact as late as the 27th of October they had lost 1800 men at Hatcher's Run in an unsuccessful assault by 43,000 men against Confederate defenses manned by only 28,000 of Lee's southerners.

In the middle of this Union mess Sherman decided to "march to the sea." He guessed wrong as to Hood's intentions. As early as October 9th he had written Grant, "I think Hood's movements indicate a diversion to . . . about sixty miles southwest of Rome from which he will threaten Kingston, Bridgeport and Decatur, Alabama. . . . Until we can repopulate Georgia it is useless to occupy it. . . . I can make the march and make Georgia howl" Grant, from his long distance vantage point in Virginia, had a better insight as to Hood's intentions, than did Sherman He was not in favor of the "march to the sea." On the morning of the 11th he answered Sherman, "Does it not look as if Hood was going to attempt the invasion of Middle Tennessee. . . . If there is any way of getting at Hood's army, I would prefer that. . . ." But Sherman insisted and finally Grant gave his consent, though very possibly he only did so because he realized that Sherman was going to do it anyway.[1]

Sherman decided to take Kilpatrick's cavalry division on his march to the sea and since Kilpatrick was short of horses and equipment, he ordered the Lightning Brigade, along wtih Long's and most of Minty's, to turn over their horses and equipment to him and go to Louisville, Kentucky for new mounts. The Lightning Brigade gave up their mounts on Nov. 1.

Sherman left the 4th and 23rd Corps with Gen. Thomas who had his headquarters at Chattanooga. With the 14th, 15th, 17th and 20th Corps he turned his back on Hood's Army, burned Atlanta, and departed on his famous "march to the sea." Most of history has recorded his march as a strategic masterpiece. In looking back it proved to be brilliant, but no doubt at the time there were many who felt it to be militarily ridiculous. Maybe Sherman was just lucky. But more likely it was because he left the fate of Hood and his Rebel army to General George "Pap" Thomas, who was very possibly the steadiest, most dependable and most capable general in the Union Army.

The Lightning Brigade, along with Long's Brigade and the 7th Penn. and 4th Mich. of Minty's, boarded a train for Louisville, where they arrived on the morning of November 15. The trip to Louisville was plagued by delays and a shortage of food, but the thing that made the ride the most miserable was that they rode most of the way on top of the cars, and packed on like sardines at that. In reference to this trip, Col. Miller recorded, "Arrived at Louisville and went into camp once more; I am tired of moving on the railroad; I would much rather be at the front and on a campaign than go to the rear."[2]

The Brigade camped on a beautiful grassy knoll near the railroad track at the edge of town, but looks was the only pleasant thing about it. The men had not been issued any new clothing for five months and what they had with them was ragged and worn; too much so in fact with winter coming on. But the worst was the shortage of wood. Every since they had left Louisville over two years earlier they had been in Rebel country and when they saw something they needed they took it. Louisville, however, was now considered to be Union territory, and they were given strict orders not to confiscate property or supplies from the local inhabitants. The third day in camp a freezing rain set in followed by subfreezing temperatures. The men had not been able to build winter sleeping quarters which normally consisted of wood sidewalls covered by a pup tent or gum blanket and consequently the morale of the Brigade began to suffer immensely. Col. Miller was trying his best to alleviate the situation. He wrote: "November 16. Tried hard all day to get things for the brigade. . . . Hope to get the men fixed up soon. November 18. Still raining; have a great deal of trouble in getting the command in living order."[3]

On the 21st the weather turned extremely cold again but on that day a shipment of clothing arrived which eased that problem. But there was still no wood to be had. The only wood that they were issued was barely enough to cook their meals, with none left over to build warming fires. The men finally got enough of it. They had been riding and fighting and suffering in the face of the enemy for over two years, and they weren't about to suffer within sight of their homeland which some of them could see across the river. They finally took things into their own hands and, regulations to the contrary, whole regiments at a time began taking fences, small sheds and any other stray boards that they could find in order to make themselves comfortable. So many men were involved that punishment would have been impractical and the Brigade and regimental officers merely turned their heads.

Another factor that contributed to the bad morale situation at the time was the fact that all the men of the Brigade were from Illinois and Indiana and some of their homes were but a short train ride from Louisville. No furloughs were granted. A few of the men went "over the hill" to see their families but most of them stayed. Not necessarily because they didn't think of going, but mostly because they hadn't been paid for 13 months and none of them had any money.

November 23, however, was pay day and they had money in their pockets. The members of the Lightning Brigade were properly oriented to army discipline and although a trip home was quite a temptation the incidence of A. W. O. L.'s was minimal. Many of the men's families came to Louisville to visit them and the sight of their loved ones and the jingle of silver in their pockets elevated the morale to new heights.

Forrest Farley of the 123rd Illinois wrote to his wife after arriving in Louisville and she came down to visit him. On the 16th of December he recorded in his diary, very unemotionally, of her departure: "Today is a very disagreeable day. My wife and myself started at 4 o'clock for New Albany. Went to the ferry boat crossed the river to New Albany side and at 10 o'clock my wife took the train for home. . . ."[4] Although he wrote very matter of factly in his diary, her visit must have brought back fond memories, because he wrote two letters to her within 24 hours after her departure.

On the 18th the Brigade began to receive their new horses, pack mules and equipment and the men began getting things in order for the commencement of their next campaign which they knew would soon be forthcoming. New saddles, bridles, spurs, blankets, picket ropes, cooking utensils were issued. Forrest Farley took care of some of his last minute chores on the 24th and 25th: "Got a likeness taken today ($100) to send to sister maryann. Branded horses to day . . . and . . . I went to church in Louisville, Ky. Herd a good Sermon. Returned to camp. Drew a cartridge box and spurs and curry comb. . . ."[5] Farley had gone to church on Christmas day, which was also a Sunday, not because he was hypocritical in his faith, or that this was his once-a-year duty to the Lord. He was a deeply religious man, devout in his faith. In fact on the last day of each month he recorded in his diary his thanks to God. On the 31st of December, 1864 he wrote: "I have been preserved through many dangers seen and unseen and I feel truly thankful to the Lord for His mercies to us all. O may I love and serve the good Lord in the year of 1865 better than I did in the year 1864. O may the Lord help me to watch myself that I may not go astray and the Lord give me grace sufficient for all the trials that I am called to pass through."[6]

While the Brigade was in Louisville, General Hood moved into Tennessee in hopes of destroying some of Thomas' somewhat scattered forces. He managed to get his Army of Tennessee into a position between Schofield's 23rd Corps and Nashville where Thomas was concentrating his army. Schofield managed to slip past him during the night, however, and take up position behind the fortifications at Franklin. Hood, irritated because Schofield had eluded him, rashly ordered an attack on Schofield's Corps on November 30. The Federals were behind carefully constructed permanent fortifications. The Southern attacking forces had to cross two miles of open plain that sloped gently up to the Union positions. This in itself made the assault foolhardly, but to make things worse Hood didn't wait for his artillery to get up. In the middle of the afternoon the Army of Tennessee launched one of the most violent and courageous attacks of the war. It was a magnificent sight as the waves of Confederate attackers crossed the open field with their colorful battle flags rippling on the autumn breeze, drums rolling and bugles blaring. The Rebels charged the Union works with vigor and persistence. They charged, reformed, charged and charged again. In some places they gained parts of the Federal works, but in the end the attack failed. According to Horn[7] one Federal officer said that his position in the line was hit by thirteen different assaults. The Confederate charge at Franklin made Pickett's charge at Gettysburg look like a Sunday School picnic. Horn makes a comparison in his book, The Army of Tennessee:

Pickett's loss at Gettysburg was 1354; at Franklin the Army of Tennessee lost over 6,000 dead and wounded. Pickett's charge was made after a volcanic artillery preparation of two hours had battered the defending line. Hood's Army charged without any preparation. Pickett's charge was across an open space of perhaps a mile. The advance at Franklin was for two miles in the open, in full view of the enemy's works, and exposed to their fire. The defenders at Gettysburg were protected only by a stone wall. Schofield's men at Franklin had carefully constructed works, with trench and parapet. . . . Pickett, once repelled, retired from the field. The Army of Tennessee renewed their charge, time after time.[8]

Hood's Army was badly battered, but the most disheartening thing was his loss of general officers. Six generals killed, including the gallant Pat Cleburne, one captured and five wounded.

Schofield moved out that night for Nashville, but Hood's rashness continued. He pursued the Union Army northward, determined to tackle it again at Nashville where Thomas had waiting, including Schofield's Corps, almost 70,000 men. Hood's force, after the casualties at Franklin, numbered about 20,000 effectives.

Hood intrenched his troops outside of Nashville and decided to wait and let Thomas make the next move. On December 15 the Union Army moved out of its works at Nashville and attacked Hood's tough but overmatched army. In a two-day battle which has gone down in history as a masterpiece of military strategy and tactics, Thomas broke Hood's army and drove it from Tennessee.

The men of the Army of Tennessee had never trusted Hood's strategic judgement. Both bold and courageous, but also rash and impetuous, Hood in the five months since he took command from Joe Johnston had lost 60 per cent of his men. There is a story that a Union scout returned from a patrol during the Atlanta Campaign on which he had seen Hood in a card game and he reported to Sherman, "I seen Hood bet $2,500 with nary a pair in his hand." This quality in Hood's character had served him well in many tactical field situations, but as supreme commander it had virtually wrecked the Army of Tennessee. Joe Johnston had always been a favorite of these men. They respected him. And as the gallant Army of Tennessee dejectedly retreated into Mississippi, they sang, to the tune "Yellow Rose of Texas," the following improvised words:

> So now I'm marching southward;
> My heart is full of woe.
> I'm going back to Georgia
> To see my Uncle Joe.
> You may talk about your Beauregard
> And sing of General Lee,
> But the gallant Hood of Texas
> Played hell in Tennessee.[9]

They soon got their wish. The Army of Tennessee was sent to North Carolina to challenge Sherman's march north from Savannah, and they got a new commander—Gen. Joe Johnston.

Sherman had arrived at Savannah on December 10. On Feb. 1 he moved north with his army, strengthened by Schofield's 23rd Corps which Thomas sent east. Grant was still involved with Lee at Petersburg. Sherman had taken the northern third of Georgia. Thomas had driven the Army of Tennessee from the mid-south. But still on the loose was Gen. Forrest and his cavalry command. Territory still in southern hands was all of Alabama and the southern two-thirds of Georgia in which remained some of the most important arsenals and war plants in the south—Selma, Ala., West Point, Columbus and Macon, Georgia, and Montgomery, Alabama. They were all protected by sizeable garrison forces. For the task of taking this tremendous territory, the Union command called on Gen. James H. Wilson.

Gen. Wilson had had a meteoric career thus far in the war. Graduating from West Point in 1860, he was Aide-de-Camp under McClellan at Antietam, Assistant Engineer and Inspector-General under Grant at Vicksburg and had led a cavalry division in the east from the Wilderness to Petersburg in 1864. He made Brigadier-General in October 1863, only three years out of the

Academy. When Grant sent Wilson to Sherman in October of 1864 to head up the Cavalry Corps in the West he said, "I believe Wilson will add 50 per cent to the effectiveness of your cavalry."[19]

Soon after the first of the year, Wilson began organizing his cavalry force for his raid through Alabama and Georgia. He brought together the largest and best armed cavalry force ever assembled anywhere on earth. Twelve thousand well-mounted men, most of whom were armed with the new Spencer Carbine, consisting of the 1st Div. under Gen. McCook, the 2nd Div. under Eli Long (recently made Brig. Gen.), the 4th Div. under Gen. Upton and the 5th Div. under Gen. Hatch. Gen. Long had replaced Garrard as commander of the 2nd Cavalry Division and his command was made up of:

Wilder's Brigade	*Minty's Brigade*
17th Indiana Mtd. Inf.	7th Pennsylvania Cavalry
72nd Indiana Mtd. Inf.	4th Michigan Cavalry
98th Illinois Mtd. Inf.	3rd Ohio Cavalry
123rd Illinois Mtd. Inf.	4th Ohio Cavalry

Wilson set the assembly point for his force at Gravelly Springs in the extreme northwest corner of Alabama.

The Second Cavalry Division left Louisville on the 28th of December and travelled down the Bardstown Pike about 20 miles where they went into camp that evening along Floyd's Creek near Mount Washington. This was not very good mileage, but the weather was very cold and they got a late start because some of the horses were not well broken.

In addition to new horses, each company had been issued four pack mules. They were young and frisky and although they had been broken to halter and lead, they had not had the experience of carrying a loaded pack until the campaign got under way. The pack saddle consisted of a wooden tree with high pommel and cantle. On either side were large containers made of canvas or wicker that held four or five cubic feet of supplies—ammunition, rations, cooking utensils, intrenching equipment, etc. As long as the load was evenly distributed weight-wise, the mule could carry an enormous load. Mules could live on more exotic food than horses, prefering dried weeds, cornstalks, and a little corn to fine hay and oats. But mules did have to eat something and when they got hungry they were just as apt to chew up the wagon tongues or a knapsack as not. Not as excitable as horses, mules were especially reliable in rough and mountainous country. It was said that a mule would work hard and perform peaceably for twenty years just to get one good kick at his master, but as a member of the 1st Ohio Cavalry said. ". . . for a service of so many years—a part of the time no doubt feeding on weeds and wagon-tongues, should entitle him to some privileges and a little pleasure as he is about to wind up his useful career."[11]

The horses themselves were pretty well loaded down, too, for that matter. A member of the Lightning Brigade described how he loaded his mount:

Our knapsack was cut to pieces and remodeled so as to fit closely and compactly to the cantle of our saddle; our haversack we had never carried, and it was fastened to the near side of the pommel; our canteen was hung to the other side of the pommel, as was also a good hatchet. When on a march our cartridge box was swung loosely to the pommel, and if we had five day's rations, it hung on the right side, and if our rations were out it hung on the left, but was never fast, so that any moment we could dismount and sling it over our shoulder. The muzzle of our gun, up to the first band, was stuck into a boot at the right side by the saddle girth, and a strap around our shoulder held it up by our side when riding, and this was the only article strapped or fastened to us. Under our saddle we carried two good sleeping blankets, a dog tent, and a gum blanket. In our cartridge box we carried 40 rounds of metallic cartridges, and in our saddle pockets 40 to 60 rounds more, an extra horse shoe, some nails, etc.[12]

Rations were carried in the haversack and the knapsack contained extra clothing, paper, thread, and personal items such as pictures, books, etc.

The Brigade moved out before sunup on the 29th and travelled through snow and a sharp winter wind to Bardstown. It moved to New Haven on the 30th and to Elizabethtown on the 31st. New Year's Day was the coldest and most miserable yet, but the Brigade got on the march by the middle of the morning and moved to Sonora. Next day they moved to the Green River near Munfordville. It had warmed up during the day and it rained. The rain together with the melting snow caused flooding conditions on the river and it took the division two days to cross by pulling a small flat bottom boat back and forth by means of a rope. Up before sunup on the 4th the Brigade moved to Rocky Hill Station, Kentucky, on the Louisville and Nashville Rail Road, to near Bowling Green on the 5th and traveled through rain which turned to snow on the 6th until going into camp four miles west of Mitchellville that evening. When the Brigade awoke on the 7th they found themselves blanketed by four inches of snow. Everything was frozen, the horses tails were frozen masses of mud and snow. Snow was frozen to the tents; the bridles and saddle girths were stiff. It was almost noon before the entire Brigade got underway. By the middle of the afternoon, however, the sun came out warm and bright. The division went into camp early near Tyree Springs, Tennessee, so the men could get their clothing and equipment dried out.

The Brigade was out of forage and rations and they were still a long day's march from Nashville where supplies could be had. Many of the men were tempted to go out foraging, but experience had taught them that Kentucky and Tennessee were full of Rebel guerrillas and this being the case, foraging was prohibited unless authorized and organized by the Brigade Commander. Col. Miller knew that the Brigade had been followed by a band of bushwhackers ever since they left Louisville. Two officers of the 7th Pennsylvania, Minty's Brigade, had been murdered by them on the 29th of December. But there are always a few men in every military outfit that never can seem to stay within the rules laid down by proper authority. That evening six men, two from the 17th Indiana and four from the 98th Illinois, and most of them recruits who had recently joined their regiments, went out foraging. Shortly after leaving camp they were captured by the guerrilla gang, tied together in pairs and set down on a log. The bushwhackers then fired into them, robbed their bodies and left them for dead. Five of them were dead, two from Co. F, 98th, two from Co. H, 98th and one from Co. K, 17th Indiana. But the other man from the 17th was only shot in the shoulder and feigned death until the bushwhackers left. He rejoined his command at Nashville where they had arrived on the evening of the 8th.

The division wagon train arrived the next day with rations, forage, supplies and the division artillery, the Chicago Board of Trade Battery. The division rested until the 12th just outside Nashville. Thursday, January 12th, the division renewed its trip, travelling through rain and with short rations until met by its commissary train at Columbia, Tennessee, on the 18th. Here they drew six days' rations. The Brigade moved on toward Gravelly Springs, stopping near Cyprus Creek on the evening of the 23rd, out of rations and forage. Wilder's Brigade remained in camp on the 24th while Minty's Brigade continued the march. The men couldn't understand why they didn't move this day. As one of them said, "both rations and forage were out, and we were full 25 miles from any supplies, and in this God-forsaken country there wasn't enough food to make a square meal for a whipporwill."[13] They reached Gravelly Springs late in the evening on the 25th where they remained in camp until March 13.

This period was the most difficult that the Brigade was forced to endure during the entire war. Gen. Wilson was a firm believer that the horses should be taken care of first and the men second. During the stay at Gravelly Springs the horses always had a full ration of oats, corn and hay, but during this whole time the men got nothing but a few crackers, two issues of fat pickled pork and an occasional pint of corn meal. Almost every personal account of this camp makes a daily mention of the scarcity of food. A typical entry is one from February 10 recorded by a man from the 123rd Illinois, "In camp near Gravel Springs in Louderdale Co, State of Alabama. We are still working at our horse sheds. The boys are grumbling because we have no rations. Hardly nothing but hardtack and a little coffee and but very little of that. . . ."[14]

Occasionally some of the men would steal corn from that stockpiled for the horses and parch it. One of the cavalrymen with a sense of humor took a piece of rope and hitched four of his buddies up like mules and drove them past General Wilson's headquarters, encouraging their movement with a long black-snake whip. When asked by one of Wilson's staff officers what he was doing, the cavalryman replied, "Doing? Can't you see? Why, I have just fed my mules and now I am driving them down to water. Get up there, Jack! And the mules answered 'Ah-heee!' as they started off."[15]

On the evening of March 13 the Brigade began crossing the Tennessee River on boats. It took all night to get the entire division across. The 5th Cavalry division was sent to Eastport, Mississippi for garrison duty, and the 1st, 2nd and 4th division remained at Chickasaw Landing where they completed their preparations for the raid through Alabama and Georgia. Each man was issued five days' rations for his haversack and five days' forage to be carried on the horses. The pack train was loaded with 45 days' rations of salt, sugar and coffee, and each man was issued 100 rounds of ammunition. On Tuesday, March 22, Gen. Wilson and his three divisions set out toward Selma, Alabama.

"Babylon Is Fallen"

WILSON'S THREE DIVISIONS MOVED SOUTH IN THREE COLUMNS with Upton's 4th division on the left, Long's 2nd division in the center and McCook's 1st division on the right. The three columns were separated by several miles so as to deceive the enemy and mask the real intent of the campaign. The Lightning Brigade, with Long's Division, passed south of Tuscumbia on the 23rd and camped six miles south of Russellville on the evening of the 24th. From this point they immediately sent out foragers to get forage for the horses and to procure a two day supply of meat. This was rich farm country and food was plentiful. The forages came back with a sizeable haul of hogs and chickens, but the several weeks of slim rations at Gravelly Springs and the sudden acquisition of such a supply of fresh meat was more than many of the men could stand with any reasonable degree of moderation. They gorged themselves on pork and chicken and their systems, being unaccustomed to it, rebelled with some violent cases of diarrhea, or as the men of the Brigade called it, "the Tennessee quick step."[1]

The Brigade crossed Bear Creek on the 25th and a branch of the Black Warrior River on the 26th. On the 27th they crossed a huge swamp and travelled through a torrential rain to the Jasper Road. They arrived at Jasper on the 28th where the 1st, 2nd and 4th divisions rendezvoused. Next day the entire force crossed the Black Warrior River. It was very swift with a rock bottom and high steep bluffs on either side, making it extremely difficult to ford. A rainstorm on the previous night had swollen the river somewhat and this added to the danger. The 4th division lost four men and all the regiments lost horses in crossing this river. They then travelled only ten miles farther when they were forced to cross another stream, the Locust fork of the Black Warrior, not as wide or as swift but much deeper. The 17th Indiana had a man drowned in this crossing and the brigade surgeon nearly lost an ambulance full of sick men. Next day the men were up early, still soaked to the skin, and although they had trouble getting breakfast fires started because of the rain, they were on the road by daylight. As they passed through Elyton (now known as Birmingham), Croxton's Brigade of the 1st division was detached to move west to Tuscaloosa. It was dark before they camped that night but the sky was red for miles around from the fires set by the 4th division who had moved ahead and burned the factories and foundries at Montevallo.

In the afternoon of the 31st the force met their first sizable resistance by the Confederate army. Upton's 4th division ran into a part of Roddey's Rebel Cavalry and a short but lively fight followed that resulted in Roddey's withdrawal and his loss of 100 captured.

At 9 o'clock the next morning, April 1, two couriers were captured with dispatches from Gen. Forrest's headquarters. These papers gave Gen. Wilson information as to the disposition and intentions of Forrest's Cavalry divisions and Wilson promptly sent McCook's other brigade west to assist Croxton near Tuscaloosa in challenging Gen. W. H. Jackson's Rebel cavalry division. The remaining two divisions, Long's and Upton's, moved on toward Plantersville. Long and Upton took different roads, these two roads converging into one at Ebenezer Church, five miles north of Plantersville. Before noon the advance of Long's division, the 72nd Indiana, ran into Rebel skirmishers. The Confederate force in their front consisted of about 2,000 men under the personal command of Gen. Forrest and made up of parts of Crossland's and Roddy's Brigades, Forrest's escort and a small detachment of Alabama militia under Gen. Dan Adams. The Union advance drove the Rebel skirmishers ahead of them until the middle of the afternoon when they came upon Forrest's main force in line of battle with three pieces of artillery near Ebenezer Church. All of Wilder's Brigade was then placed in line of battle except four companies of the 17th Indiana which were held in reserve. These four companies under Lt. Col. White had been issued sabers as well as Spencer carbines at Louisville and, although they had trained continually and worked hard at perfecting their saber techniques, they had never before used them in combat. They were eager to get the chance. The usual tactics were to order a saber charge to add the finishing touches to an already successful assault by the riflemen, but today these saber-wielding men of the 17th Indiana were too anxious. They didn't wait for the riflemen to attack first. Suddenly the men in the line heard a yell and the pounding of hoofs from their rear. To their surprise here came Lt. Col. White and his battalion charging past them into the Confederate position. The battalion slashed its way into the Rebel artillery position where Col. White, realizing that the Rebel force was much larger than he thought, wheeled to the left and fought his way back out in order to save his men from capture. But Captain Taylor of Company G did not hear White's order to wheel left and he, with sixteen of his men, charged directly into Gen. Forrest and his escort. A surviving member of the 17th Indiana wrote later, "On went the brave captain and his men, charging through the lines of the enemy, seemingly regardless of the roar of artillery and musketry."[2] Captain Taylor, small and weighing very little more than 100 pounds, spotted General Forrest and headed for him. A member of Forrest's escort recorded, "We soon got into a mix-up, and they began to overlap us in every direction. The bulk of our little band was fighting and falling back in an effort to clear a passage, when we discovered that the enemy was making a move to cut General Forrest off from his troops. About ten of us went to his assistance. They had him surrounded, and he was fighting like a lion at bay."[3] Captain Taylor singled out Forrest and assailed him with a shower of saber strokes, wounding him in the face and arm. Forrest dug his spurs into his horse's flank and bolted away from the Yankee saber. Forrest then drew his pistol and shot the brave young Captain Taylor dead. Concerning the affair, General Wilson wrote,

. . . for a moment it looked as though he would kill or capture the fleeing chieftain. So closely did the boy captain follow him and so nearly were their horses matched in strength and speed, it was several moments before Forrest could open space enough to allow him to turn and shoot his pursuer from the saddle. Speaking of it a few days later, under a flag of truce, with his arm still in a sling, he said, reflectively, 'If that boy had known enough to give me the point of his saber instead of its edge, I should not have been here to tell you about it.'[4]

Captain Taylor and the sixteen men who accompanied him on his attack of Forrest's party were all casualties. The captain and six of the men were killed, five men wounded and the other five captured. But the Confederate force withdrew hastily, pursued by the remaining six companies of the 17th Indiana and the 4th Iowa Cavalry of Upton's division which had arrived at the church by the other road. Forrest's entire force moved south and entered the fortifications at Selma and Gen. Wilson's Union force went into camp at Plantersville.

April the 2nd was a day of shining glory for the Lightning Brigade. Nineteen miles away was Selma, the primary objective of the campaign, defended by 5,000 Confederates. General Forrest was in command and his force consisted of his own escort of 200 men, Roddey's Brigade, Armstrong's Brigade of Chalmers Division which had joined Forrest between Selma and Plantersville, and 2,500 militia under General Daniel Adams. Selma was the most important industrial city in the mid-south, a humming complex of factories, ironworks and foundries. It was also one of the most elaborately fortified cities in the south and the fight for its possession was to be the last western battle of any consequence of the Civil War. And the honor of making the assault was to be given to the Lightning Brigade.

At 8 P.M. the evening of April 1, General Wilson issued his field orders for the following day:

SPECIAL
FIELD ORDERS,
    No. 13

HEADQUARTERS CAVALRY CORPS,
MILITARY DIVISION OF THE MISSISSIPPI
Plantersville, April 1, 1865—8 P.M.

The Cavalry Corps will resume the pursuit of the enemy tomorrow in the following order:

I. The Second Division will move at 5:30 A.M. by the direct Selma road. Unless Colonel Minty's brigade can reach this place by 7 A.M. to-morrow, General Long will begin his advance with his other brigade.

II. The Fourth Division will follow the Second Division.

III. Should the enemy show a front requiring more than one division to drive him from his position, General Long will move his division to the right of the Selma road in order to allow the Fourth Division to form on his left. As the corps approaches the city General Long will

incline toward the Summerfield Road, and both divisions will, if
practicable, march in columns of brigade.

By command of Brevet Major-General Wilson:

E. B. Beaumont
Major and Assistant Adjutant-General[5]

The force got underway at daylight on Sunday the 2nd with
Minty's Brigade in advance. At noon foragers were sent out

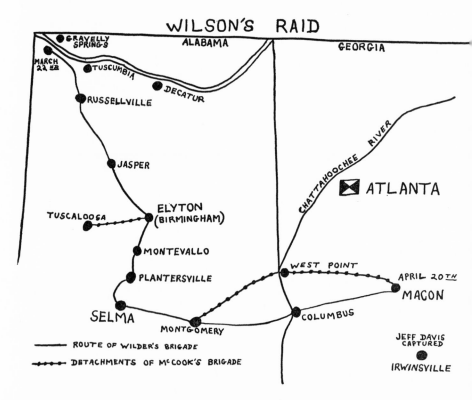

WILSON'S RAID

with instructions to return to the column as soon as they had
procured one day's rations. This was open country—cotton land
—and the gin mills could be seen on every plantation. Shortly
after noon Gen. Wilson sent for Col. Miller and told him that
he wanted his Brigade to make the assault on the works at
Selma. Miller was delighted by Wilson's confidence in his Brigade's ability, but Wilson had not made this decision because
of personal favoritism. It was the logical thing to do, militarily,
because as Gen. Long stated in his official report, the Lightning

Brigade had had longer practice at infantry type fighting and was "most accustomed to fighting on foot." General Wilson said further, ". . . If we would take the place it would be among the big things of the war—that Sherman had started twice for that place and failed. Sturgis lost all his forces in a similar effort."[6] The plain truth is that during the entire war General Forrest had never lost a battle in which he was in complete command and General Wilson wanted his best men to make the assault.

At 3 P.M. the foragers returned to the column just as the division advance reached a stream two or three miles west of Selma. At near 4 o'clock just as the last of the division was crossing the bridge, General Chalmers with two more brigades of Forrest's Cavalry approached from the rear. Long sent the 72nd Indiana except Co. D to the northwest to meet Chalmers' advance. A short time later the 3rd Ohio Cavalry of Minty's Brigade was dispatched to help the 72nd and four companies of the 98th Ill. were sent to chase a Rebel wagon train. This was Forrest's old trick—to draw the enemy into a fight and then bring a force in on their rear. Shortly before 5 P.M. Wilson was ready to make the attack on Selma.

Long's Division was to attack to the right of the Summerfield Road and Upton's division was to penetrate a swamp some distance to the left. As the regiments lined up for the attack Chalmers increased his pressure on the units guarding the rear and General Long sent the 4th Michigan back to assist them. A round from Upton's artillery was to be the signal for the beginning of the assault. General Long had his division lined up as follows:

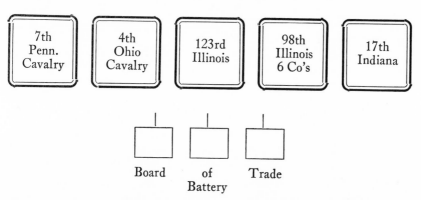

The total assaulting force numbered 1,546 officers and men.

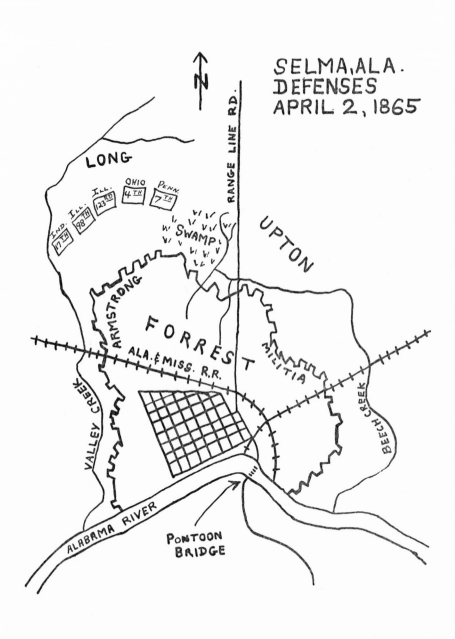

SELMA, ALA.
DEFENSES
APRIL 2, 1865

The Confederate defenders totalling 5,000 men were behind formidable works. Armstrong's Brigade, Forrest's best, was manning the works where the regiments of the Lightning Brigade were to hit. It was 600 yards from where Wilder's Brigade lay poised for the attack on the Rebel works. Two hundred yards from the works was an abatis of fallen trees, their branches pointed out from the fort and sharpened. The works themselves consisted of a line of earthworks eight to twelve feet high and fifteen feet across at the base. In front of the earthworks was a ditch ten to twelve feet wide containing five feet of water with the back slope lined with posts sticking out of the ground and sharpened at the ends. A string of forts with artillery were positioned along the works that covered the 600 yard approach and between the abatis and the works were scattered wire, "sheepracks," and an occasional torpedo.

Before Upton was up in position, General Long became concerned that Chalmer's attack on his rear guard might become serious enough to deter his attack so without waiting for Upton's signal he moved his men forward. They moved steadily across the open field through heavy artillery fire, fought their way through the abatis in the face of heavy musket fire and then, rapidly firing their Spencers on the run, they tore through the entanglements and climbed over the earthworks, completely mauling the Confederate defenders.

The main assault took only 25 minutes and the Rebels were on the run into the city proper. But the Yankee invaders paid a terrible price for their victory. One hundred fifty yards from the works General Long fell wounded in the head and the command of the division was turned over to Colonel Minty. Shortly Colonel Miller leading the Lightning Brigade was wounded in the leg, command being assumed by Colonel Vail of the 17th Indiana. At about the same time Colonel Biggs, commanding the 123rd Illinois, was wounded in the breast and Colonel McCormick, commanding the 7th Pennsylvania, was wounded in the leg. As the force entered the works, Colonel Dodd, commanding the 4th Ohio was killed. Captain Wiley of the 123rd Illinois assumed command after Colonel Biggs was hit because Captain Adams, second in command, had also been wounded before they entered the works.

The enemy then moved behind some partially completed fortifications at the edge of the city proper. Colonel Vail lined

up the 17th Indiana, the 4th Ohio, the 4th U. S. Regulars and
the Board of Trade Battery for this assault. They moved out
just as Upton's division entered the works and came upon their
left. The enemy was driven on through the city. Forrest, Roddey,
Armstrong, Adams and a part of their force jumped their horses
into the river and escaped. The fruits of the Union victory at
Selma included 2,700 prisoners, 31 field guns and a 30 pound
Parrot Rifle that had been used against them during the assault.

Forrest had gotten away but he had suffered his first and only
decisive defeat of the entire war. The Lightning Brigade pre-
served their record of never having been whipped, but they suffered by far their heaviest casualties of the war. In less than half
an hour the assault force lost over 20 percent of its men. A
breakdown of the regiments shows how hard they were hit,
especially the officers of whom 40 per cent were casualties:

Regiment	Number engaged		Killed		Wounded		Percent
	Off.	Men	Off.	Men	Off.	Men	Casualty
17th Ind.	17	404	0	12	7	72	21.6
98th Ill.	11	161	0	11	5	31	27.3
123rd Ill.	14	239	1	7	6	42	22.9
7th Penn.	13	353	1	1	4	47	14.4
4th Ohio	16	318	2	5	1	50	17.3
TOTALS:	71	1475	4	36	23	242	19.7*

* Casualties in the division and brigade staffs bring the percentage to
over 20 per cent.

The percentage of casualties suffered by the three regiments
of the Lightning Brigade are an indication of the bloody and
vicious fights required to take the works and break Armstrong's
Brigade—Forrest's finest. General Forrest's Confederate Cavalry put up a strong and violent resistance to the assault and,
although they were doomed to eventual defeat at Selma, it must
be said in all fairness to this fine Rebel cavalry corps that their
fate was hastened by the desertion of the works in other parts
of the line by the militia troops and the civilians who had been
hurriedly armed for the defense of the city.

The Lightning Brigade had put out a maximum effort. Captain
Robinson, in command of the Chicago Board of Trade Battery

supporting the attack, hardly got a chance to fire his guns at all because of the rapid advance of the assault force. In his report he stated, "I moved my whole battery forward to the advanced position referred to, replying rapidly to the fire of the enemy's artillery until it was silenced by the close approach of our men to the works, which in a moment more were in their possession."[7] After the attacking force had scaled the parapet and moved inside the works, Captain Robinson sent one section of his artillery in to engage the Rebel artillery at the edge of the city and as Captain Robinson reported, "opened upon the inner line of works, which, like the first, was soon in the possession of our troops, and rendering further firing unnecessary."[8] Captain Wiley of the 123rd Illinois described the advance, ". . . at General Long's, 'Forward,' the entire line started up with a bound, yelling, shooting and all pushing forward under a most terrific cannonade and through a perfect storm of bullets, losing officers and men at every step, until we cleared the high picket fence, crossed the ditch, and scaled the high earth-works. . . . When we struck and scaled the works the Rebels, who had fought us so desperately as to club their guns on some of our men. . ."[9] The Lightning Brigade had a burning desire to succeed in this assault. Maybe it was because they could smell the end of the war close at hand; or maybe it was the result of months of conditioning and fighting and training; or possibly it was due to the excellent leadership of Long, Miller and Wilson. But no matter what the hidden or unseen force that motivated an almost superhuman effort, the Brigade fought as though the future of the entire world was resting on the outcome of their assault. Individual acts of bravery and resourcefulness were innumerable. Captain Thistlewood of the 98th Illinois, after being severely wounded on the leg, led his company for over a mile before he would turn over his command to a subordinate and receive medical attention. Lt. Jenkins and eight of his men of Co. B. 98th, became separated from the regiment after passing the enemy works, but instead of wandering around looking for their command, they moved forward and fought with the 17th Indiana.

The impetus of the Union attack was so great in fact that it even resulted in a skirmish between two of their own units. As they gained the inner line of defenses at the edge of the city, a squad of men under Lieutenant Wheeler of the 98th Illinois along with two squads from the 123rd Illinois and 4th Ohio captured a fort and took possession of the four guns inside. Just as they had secured this position and were moving toward their next objective, they came under fire of a large force of mounted troops which was charging toward them. It was General Upton's 4th division who had mistaken them for the enemy. As soon as Upton discovered the error he charged on into town after the retreating Confederates.

In addition to the large number of prisoners taken by the Union troops at Selma, the Rebels lost an enormous amount of supplies, arms and equipment. The 17th Indiana made one of the better hauls, capturing two of Armstrong's ordinance wagons and 300 prisoners, including most of the 1st Mississippi Cavalry with its colonel, a lieutenant colonel and a major, and large portions of two other Mississippi regiments. For all practical purposes Forrest's excellent cavalry force had disintegrated. He, along with Generals Armstrong, Roddey and Adams, however, had escaped with a small part of their men and moved westward The first friendly face they saw after their escape was Sergeant Newton Cannon, 11th Tennessee Cavalry of Bell's Brigade who had been sent toward Selma by General Jackson to get orders from Forrest concerning the disposition of prisoners taken from Croxton's Brigade near Cotton Port. Cannon met Forrest on the road near Selma and learned of the defeat of Forrest's command. The defeated Southerners then moved on to link up with Jackson's Division and a few days later, as recorded by Sergeant Cannon, "General Forrest collected his command together and prepared to surrender."[10]

The capture of Selma was an amazing military feat. It did not involve the huge numbers of men that did many larger battles during the war, but it was no less sanguine than Antietam, Gettysburg, or The Wilderness; and it was much more decisive. The Battle of Nashville in December of 1864 has gone down in history as the "perfect battle," but it could hardly have been more perfect than the assault of Selma, Alabama. Colonel Miller, commander of the Lightning Brigade, summed up his brilliant victory in his official report when he stated, ". . . and the history of the war will not show another instance where such formidable works, well manned and defended with men and artillery, have been stormed and captured by a single line of men without support."[11]

The Confederacy was now teetering on the brink of com-

plete and total collapse. Sherman, although having been fought
to a stand-off at Bentonville, North Carolina by General Joe
Johnston and remnants of the Army of Tennessee, was pushing
that badly outnumbered Rebel army on north toward Virginia.
Grant's flanking maneuver had caused Robert E. Lee to evacuate
his Army of Northern Virginia from Petersburg and Richmond.
On April 1 General "Little Phil" Sheridan had decisively defeated the Confederates at Five Forks. Lee then started his
withdrawal toward Appomattox Court House with Grant in
close pursuit. General Wilson, after the fall of Selma, set his
sights on his next three objectives, the industrial towns of West
Point and Columbus, Georgia, and the fortified city of Macon.

The Union Cavalry Corps remained at Selma until the 10th,
destroying the arsenals and shops, resting and waiting on their
wagon train. General McCook with LaGrange's Brigade arrived
on the 5th with the wagon train and on the morning of the 10th
Wilson's entire force crossed the Alabama River on a newly
constructed pontoon bridge and moved toward Montgomery.
General McCook received the surrender of Montgomery on the
12th and took West Point, Georgia on the 16th. General Upton
and his 4th Division took Columbus the same day. Near noon
on the 20th General Long's Division (under Col. Minty) with
the Lightning Brigade in advance ran into a small enemy force
twenty miles from Macon. The 17th Indiana, advance guard of
the Brigade, drove them from their rail barricades and followed
them at a fast trot as far as the bridge across Tobesofkee Creek.
The Rebel force tore some of the planking from the bridge, set
it on fire and took position on the other side. Colonel White dismounted his regiment and, after fighting the fire with blankets
and water carried in their caps, moved across the bridge and
routed the Rebel defenders. Thirteen miles from Macon, Colonel
White was met by Confederate Brigadier-General Robertson
under a flag of truce, and carrying a dispatch from General
Howell Cobb stating that Sherman and Johnston had agreed on
an armistice. Colonel White sent the dispatch to Colonel Minty
who sent a staff member back to tell General Robertson that he
was relaying the message to General Wilson and that Robertson
should return to Macon to await a reply. Robertson refused to
accept Minty's message except in writing. This irritated Colonel
Minty as he felt that he was being intentionally delayed. He
wrote out the message for Robertson and added, "I have directed

the officer commanding my advance to move five minutes after this is handed to you."[12] Colonel Minty then ordered Colonel White to "give the flag of truce five minutes's start, and then to push forward, and if General Robertson and his party did not keep out of his way to take them prisoners."[13] Two miles down the road the 17th Indiana came upon the flag of truce in company of about 250 cavalrymen moving very slowly along the road. The 17th charged into them, capturing three and driving the rest of them on to Macon. On arriving at Macon, General Cobb approached under a white flag and asked what terms Colonel White was demanding. Colonel White demanded unconditional surrender to which General Cobb readily submitted.

The Union command had not received any word about the truce between Sherman and Johnston and they weren't going to take a Confederate's word for it. They took Generals G. W. Smith, Mackall and Mercer prisoners along with Generals Cobb and Robertson. The 72nd Indiana arrived inside the works at dark and went into camp with the 17th Indiana. The 98th and 123rd Illinois soon arrived and camped just outside the Rebel works. Next day the Brigade went about rounding up 3,500 prisoners, 60 pieces of artillery and 3,000 stands of arms. The battle flag of the 6th Arkansas Regiment was captured aboard a train that was standing in the depot. The most unusual acquisition was made by Corporal Bottorff of the 17th Indiana. On information obtained from a Rebel prisoner, Corporal Bottorff found four unmounted brass cannon boxed up and buried in a smallpox graveyard. These guns were known as Travis guns and were 2-pounder smooth bore breech-loaders intended for presentation to General Forrest. Late in the day General Wilson received official word that Sherman and Johnston had indeed declared an armistice for the purpose of arriving at an agreement of surrender terms. Lee had surrendered to Grant on the 9th. Except for the final formalities, the war was over.

13

"When Johnny Comes Marching Home"

ONE BY ONE IN RAPID ORDER THE VARIOUS MAJOR COMMANDS of the Confederacy surrendered to the North and the war was officially over. The usual procedure for ending a war, according to past history, was to end the fighting and then the heads of state would draw up a treaty which would lay down the procedures for the division of spoils and to set the price of defeat. The American Civil War, however, ended on a different note. The end of the fighting was immediately followed by two of the most widespread, dedicated and persistent manhunts in the history of America. The eventual victims of these hunts were of as widely different types of personalities as could possibly be imagined. Jeff Davis, President of the Confederacy, was attempting to make his escape through Georgia to west of the Mississippi in order to make an attempt at forming a new Rebel government. Davis, hated by the North at the time but both admired and pitied by the South, managed to make his way into history as an idealistic martyr. History was not so kind to the other man on the Union wanted list. John Wilkes Booth had sneaked up behind President Abraham Lincoln at Ford's Theatre on the night of April 14 and fired a lead ball into the brain of the beloved President. Although Booth was no doubt a complete neurotic, his was not an individual effort; he was part of a weird and sinister plot, born but not nurtured by the Confederacy. A brief hero only to himself, he left to posterity only cowardice and hate and the memories of a despicable and mentally deranged eccentric.

Booth was killed by a Union cavalryman in a Virginia barn on the 26th of April, 11 days after the death of the President. The capture of Jeff Davis took longer and it required the use of many more troops. The Union picket net was scattered all over Georgia and the Lightning Brigade was a part of this force.

Mrs. Davis and other members of President Davis' family along with some of his aides and assistants and a cavalry escort preceded Davis on his trip south from Virginia. By May 2 Mrs. Davis' party had arrived at Washington, Georgia while her husband's party was still several miles away in South Carolina. Late that morning Davis' secretary, with his wife's party, sent a message to Confederate military authorities:

> We are ready to move as I have said, and should have done so this morning, but Major Moses has just returned from Abbeville (South Carolina) which place he left at 2 P.M. yesterday, and tells me that he saw a quartermaster who left the President at Unionville night before last. . . . We have thence supposed that the President is in Abbeville today and that this town may be in his line of march. If so, he will probably be here tomorrow. . . . Mrs. Davis is very anxious to see him if she can do so without embarrassing his movements, and I wish to receive his instructions. She is willing to start without seeing him however if necessary. . . . It is not necessary, therefore, for him to change his plans or to allow them to be influenced on our account. . . . Please give me by return courier the information you may have which may be useful to me, and please give me your counsel.[1]

Davis and his party joined that of his wife's at Washington and on the 5th of May continued their journey together. Two officers of Davis' cavalry escort took different routes with sizeable detachments of cavalrymen to serve as decoys to the Davis party. That night, however, some of the Rebel soldiers deserted and reported Davis' movements to the Union authorities at Macon. General Wilson had already set up a line of pickets from the Chattahoochee River south to the Florida line. When he learned of the approximate route of the Confederate President's movement, he sent out additional troops, including detachments from the Lightning Brigade, to pick up Davis' trail. Several detachments of the pursuing troops struck Davis' trail or picked up information concerning his whereabouts and the entire chase turned into a race to see who would be first to capture the Rebel leader. The winner was the 4th Michigan of Minty's Brigade who surprised Davis and his party in camp at 2 A.M. of May 10 near Irwinsville, Georgia. The victory of the 4th Michigan was somewhat tainted, however, by an unfortunate incident arising from the intense competition of the race.

Ten or fifteen minutes after the detachment of the 4th Michigan had taken possession of the camp a detachment of the 1st Wisconsin Cavalry of McCook's Division approached. The men of each regiment mistook the other for enemy and a brief exchange of rifle fire took place between the two with the 4th Michigan losing two men killed and both regiments suffering some wounded. They soon discovered their mistake and Jefferson Davis and party were taken to Macon and then to Washington, D.C.

Macon was an exciting place in the days immediately following the surrender of the Confederate Armies. The 17th Indiana and the 98th Illinois were assigned to provost guard duty there after its capture with Lieutenant Colonel Kitchell of the 98th as Provost Marshal. In addition to the capture of Jeff Davis, detachments of the Lightning Brigade assisted in the apprehension of Captain Wirz, the cruel "whip" of Andersonville Prison. Both of these important personalities were brought into Macon for disposition. Many a veteran of the Lightning Brigade was able to tell his children and grandchildren that he had seen Jeff Davis.

On May 23 the regiments of the Lightning Brigade, having fought together for two and one-half years, headed northward and started on their separate ways for home. It had been nearly three years for most of the men and almost four years for some since the members of Colonel Wilder's Lightning Brigade had enlisted in "Father Abraham's" Army. They had been typical army enlistees—short and tall, thin and fat, grown men in their forties and youngsters who could hardly grow a beard; they had the usual number of loud mouths and shy ones and the moral and obscene, and like all armies the customary percentage with two left feet. But Colonel Wilder had molded them into one of the most effective fighting forces in the Union Army. As the first Spencer-armed Mounted Infantry force in the Army, they had set the example for Sheridan, Custer, and the other Union Cavalry leaders who became so successful in the latter part of the war by using the modern cavalry principles developed by the Lightning Brigade.

Their long months of fighting and campaigning had been filled with hundreds of individual instances of heroism and suffering and of comedy and comradeship. Many a story could be told . . . of John W. Richards, 98th Illinois, and William M. Spencer, 72nd Indiana, who met in a Georgia prison, shared their few possessions and then escaped together, spent 33 days in the Georgia swamps until they arrived at Union-held Savannah in January of 1865. They went by ship to New York and then by rail to Indianapolis and Nashville and arrived at Gravelly Springs, Alabama, in time to move with their regiments on Wilson's raid and participate in the capture of Selma[2] . . . of Captain Eli Lilly, 18th Indiana Battery, who fearlessly exposed himself to enemy fire by personally carrying ammunition on his horse to his battery in order to help stop a near breakthrough by the Rebels on the first day at Chickamauga[3] . . . of the forager of the 72nd Indiana who had his hat shot off when surprised by a Rebel scouting party[4] . . . of the audacity and resourcefulness of Lt. Col. White of the 17th Indiana in taking Macon, Georgia, with a small detachment of men[5] . . . of the aggressiveness and bravery of the men of the 123rd Illinois who were the first to hit the enemy works at Selma[6] . . . and of the two Morey brothers of the 98th Illinois who tangled with an angry colored woman in middle Tennessee during the Wheeler Raid. The Brigade was out of rations and an enterprising Negro lady came in to the regimental area carrying a griddle and the makin's for hot cakes. She built a fire and began selling hot cakes to the soldiers. George Morey was broke but hungry and when the woman turned her head he stole the cakes off the griddle. The woman was after him in a second, swinging the hot griddle at his head. George couldn't make very good time because the cakes were so hot that he had to juggle them as he ran, but brother Charles saved him from his eventual fate by grabbing the woman and paying her for the cakes.[7]

The men returned to their homes and went to work. Most of them were farm boys and they returned to the farm, but many of them made a name for themselves in other fields. Captain Lilly founded what became a multi-million dollar pharmaceutical business. Colonel Miller practiced medicine at Lebanon, Indiana. Colonel Wilder regained his health and became a wealthy industrialist in Chattanooga, and was one of the founders of the University of Chattanooga. At least one of the Brigade members, Captain Funkhouser, 98th Illinois, volunteered for service in the Spanish-American War, serving as a Lieutenant-Colonel.

They had been a close-knit unit and for forty or more years after the war the Brigade held regular reunions. They were proud of their service and they had a right to be . . . there wasn't a man in the army, Confederate or Union, who hadn't heard of the exploits of Wilder's Brigade.

Notes

1
"How Are You, John Morgan?"

1. S. C. Williams, *John T. Wilder*.
2. Howard Swiggett, *The Rebel Raider*.
   Morgan's wedding was most certainly attended by the leadership power of the Army of Tennessee. General Hardee had spent 24 years in the Regular Army. Breckinridge, from Kentucky, had been Vice-President of the U. S. under Buchanan. General "Bishop" Polk was a West Pointer but had resigned from the army six months after graduation to enter the ministry. Cheatham, a veteran of the Mexican War, was a very competent non-West Pointer.
3. Personal Recollection.
4. B. F. McGee, *Regimental History of the 72nd Indiana Volunteer Infantry*.

2
"I Can Whip the Scoundrel"

1. *Harper's Pictorial History of the Civil War*.
2. *Ibid*.
3. B. F. McGee, *Regimental History of the 72nd Indiana Volunteer Infantry*.
4. *Ibid*.
5. *Adjutant General Report—Illinois*.
6. *Photostat*.
7. J. O. Buckeridge, *Lincoln's Choice*.
8. *Campbell's Diary*.
9. *Photostat*.
   General Wharton, a Texas lawyer, had been Colonel of the 8th Texas Cavalry before assuming brigade command. He was killed in 1865 in a private feud. General Van Dorn was a West Pointer from Mis-

215

sissippi. In 1863 he was also killed in a private affair by a doctor who claimed that Van Dorn had "violated the sanctity of his home."

10. Col. A. S. Hall had formerly commanded the 105th Ohio Infantry. Col. Long, only 25 years old, had graduated from a Kentucky military school and moved up to brigade command from the 4th Ohio Cavalry. Rodman guns were named for Brig. Gen. T. J. Rodman who had invented the method for manufacturing this type field piece.

11. *Personal recollection.*

12. *Photostat.*
General John J. Reynolds was Wilder's division commander at the time. A West Pointer from Kentucky.

13. R. Gerald McMurtry, *Ben Hardin Helm.*

14. Major James Connolly, *3 Years in the Army of the Cumberland.*

15. Gen. Gordon Granger was commanding the Union Reserve Corps. Stanley was Rosecrans' Chief of Cavalry. The commanders of Rosecrans' three main infantry corps had widely varied family relationships. McCook had nine brothers and a father in the Union Army. Crittenden's brother was a general in the Confederate Army while Thomas, a native Virginian, had married a northern girl and remained loyal to the Union.

16. *Campbell's Diary.*

3
"Glory Hallelujah"

1. General Rousseau was a prominent criminal lawyer in Louisville, Kentucky, before the war. General Negley was a former Brig. Gen. in the Pennsylvania Militia.

2. Ed Porter Thompson, *History of the Orphan Brigade.*

3. General Bate refused the governorship of Tennessee during the war but after the war served as both governor and U. S. Senator. Bushrod Johnson was a West Pointer and former college professor. He died in poverty in Macoupin County, Illinois, in 1880.

4. Ed Porter Thompson, *History of the Orphan Brigade.*

5. *Official Records of the War of the Rebellion,* Vol. 23.

6. B. F. McGee, *Regimental History of the 72nd Indiana Volunteer Infantry.*

7. S. C. Williams, *Gen. John T. Wilder.*

8. *Ibid.*

9. Major James Connolly, *3 Years in the Army of the Cumberland.*

10. *Personal Recollection.*

11. S. C. Williams, *John T. Wilder.*

12. *Ibid.*

13. *Official Records,* Vol. 23.

4
"The Brass Mounted Army"

1. B. F. McGee, *History of the 72nd Indiana.*
2. William M. Lamers, *Edge of Glory.*
3. *Ibid.*
4. *Campbell's Diary.*
5. Major James Connolly, *3 Years in the Army of the Cumberland.*
6. W. H. H. Benefiel, *History of the 17th Indiana.*
7. *Campbell's Diary.*
8. W. H. H. Benefiel, *History of the 17th Indiana.*
9. *Campbell's Diary.*
10. *Official Records,* Vol. 30.
11. B. F. McGee, *Regimental History of the 72nd Indiana.*
12. Minty's cavalry brigade was commanded by Col. R. H. G. Minty, an Irishman and veteran of the British Army. Brig-Gen. William B. Hazen's brigade was a member of Gen. John Palmer's division of Crittenden's Corps and Brig.-Gen. George Wagner's brigade belonged to Gen. Thos. Wood's division of the same corps.
13. *Official Records,* Vol. 30.
14. Glenn Tucker, *Chickamauga.*
15. Brig.-Gen. Frank C. Armstrong was one of Forrest's most able commanders; a veteran of Wilson's Creek, Pea Ridge, Iuka, Corinth and Stones River.
16. Wyeth, *That Devil Forrest.*
17. Henry, *First with the most Forrest.*
18. Wyeth, *That Devil Forrest.*
   General Pegram, a West Pointer from Virginia, went east after Chickamauga. Wounded in the Wilderness, he fought in the Shenandoah Valley and around Petersburg. He was killed at Hatchers Run in February '65.
19. General Strahl was an Ohioan who had practiced law in Tennessee before the war. He was killed at the Battle of Franklin in November, 1864.
20. B. F. McGee, *Regimental History of 72nd Indiana.*
21. *Battles and Leaders,* Vol. 3.
22. *Ibid.*
   Major-General D. H. Hill was formerly in the Regular Army and fought in the Mexican War. A veteran of Antietam, Seven Day's Battles and the Peninsular Campaign. After the war he was President of the University of Arkansas.
23. *Ibid.*
24. Boatner, *Civil War Dictionary.*

5
"Root Hog or Die"

1. Gen. W. H. T. Walker's military career had been somewhat erratic because of poor health resulting from severe wounds suffered in the Mexican War. A capable leader he was killed in the Battle of Atlanta in July 1864.
2. *Campbell's Diary.*
3. A. P. Adamson, *Brief History of the 30th Georgia.*
4. *Official Records,* Vol. 30.
   General Liddell had served on Hardee's staff. General Govan, a North Carolinian had gone to war with the 2nd Arkansas. Gen. Walthall was one of the south's most competent "civilian" generals and he served admirably to the end of the war.
5. Joseph G. Vale, *Minty and the Cavalry.*
   Gen. John Bell Hood had arrived earlier in the evening with part of Longstreet's force from the Army of Northern Virginia. Hood had the reputation of being a daring and vicious fighter and this admirable trait served him well at the division command level.
6. *Ibid.*
7. *Ibid.*
8. *Ibid.*
9. William Andrew Fletcher, *"Rebel Private, Front and Rear."*
10. B. F. McGee, *Regimental History of the 72nd Indiana.*
11. *Ibid.*
12. Glenn Tucker, *Chickamauga.*
13. *Campbell's Diary.*
14. *Ibid.*
15. *Battles and Leaders,* Vol. 3.
16. *Ibid.*
17. W. H. H. Benefiel, *History of 17th Indiana.*
18. *Official Records,* Vol. 30.
19. S. C. Williams, *John T. Wilder.*
20. *Battles and Leaders,* Vol. 3.
21. *Official Records,* Vol. 30.

6
"Riding a Raid"

1. Gen. John B. Gordon, *Reminiscences of the Civil War.*
2. James K. P. Blackburn, *Terry's Texas Rangers.*
3. John Percy Dyer, *From Shiloh to San Juan.*
4. *History of Richland, Cumberland and Jasper Counties, Ill.*
5. B. F. McGee, *History of the 72nd Indiana.*

6. *Ibid.*
7. W. H. H. Benefiel, *History of the 17th Indiana.*
8. *Diary of Henry Campbell.*
9. James K. P. Blackburn, *Terry's Texas Rangers.*
10. B. F. McGee, *History of the 72nd Indiana.*
11. B. F. McGee, *History of the 72nd Indiana.*
12. George B. Guild, *A Brief Narrative of the 4th Tennessee Cavalry Regiment.*
13. *Ibid.*
14. *Official Records,* Vol. 30.
15. B. F. McGee, *History of the 72nd Indiana.*
16. *Official Records,* Vol. 30.
17. B. F. McGee, *History of the 72nd Indiana.*
18. *Ibid.*
19. George B. Guild, *A Brief Narrative of the 4th Tennessee Cavalry Regiment.*
20. *Ibid.*
21. *Official Records,* Vol. 30.
22. B. F. McGee, *History of the 72nd Indiana.*
23. *Official Records,* Vol. 30.
24. *Diary of Henry Campbell.*
25. *Official Records.*

7
"Wait for the Wagon"

1. B. F. McGee, *History of the 72nd Indiana.*
2. *Ibid.*
3. *Memoirs of U. S. Grant.*
4. *Official Records.*
5. *Letters of William Hammer.*
6. *Diary of Henry Campbell.*

8
"Johnny Is My Darling"

1. *Official Records.*
2. W. H. H. Benefiel, *History of the 17th Indiana.*
3. *Ibid.*
4. *Ibid.*
   Gen. J. H. Kelly had commanded an infantry brigade at Chickamauga. After his promotion to Brig-General he commanded a division of cavalry under Wheeler until he was killed in the summer of 1864.
5. *Ibid.*

6. *Sherman's Memoirs.*
7. W. H. H. Benefiel, *History of the 17th Indiana.*
8. *Sherman's Memoirs.*
9. Brearly, *East Tennessee Campaign.*
10. W. H. H. Benefiel, *History of the 17th Indiana.*
11. *Ibid.*
12. W. F. Curry, *History of the 1st Ohio Cavalry.*
13. *Ibid.*
14. *Official Records.*
15. *Letters of Tighlman Jones.*
16. B. F. McGee, *History of the 72nd Indiana.*
17. *Letters of William Hammer.*

9
"We'll Fight for Uncle Abe"

1. Joseph G. Vale, *Minty and the Cavalry.*
2. B. F. McGee, *History of the 72nd Indiana.*
3. *Ibid.*
   McGee was referring to the incident involving Sheridan's division on the first day at Chickamauga as described in Chapter V.
4. *Official Records.*
5. B. F. McGee, *History of the 72nd Indiana.*
6. *Official Records.*
7. B. F. McGee, *History of the 72nd Indiana.*
8. *Ibid.*
9. *Ibid.*
10. Ed Porter Thompson, *History of the Orphan Brigade.*
11. *Ibid.*
12. Stanley Horn, *Army of Tennessee.*
13. *Sherman's Memoirs.*
14. B. F. McGee, *History of the 72nd Indiana.*
15. *Sherman's Memoirs.*
16. *Official Records.*
17. Joseph G. Vale, *Minty and the Cavalry.*
18. B. F. McGee, *History of the 72nd Indiana.*
19. *Ibid.*
20. *Sherman's Memoirs.*
21. Stanley Horn, *The Army of Tennessee.*
22. *Official Records.*
23. B. F. McGee, *History of the 72nd Indiana.*
24. *Ibid.*
25. *Ibid.*
26. Joseph G. Vale, *Minty and the Cavalry.*
27. B. F. McGee, *History of the 72nd Indiana.*

28. Stanley Horn, *The Army of Tennessee.*
29. *Sherman's Memoirs.*
30. B. F. McGee, *History of the 72nd Indiana.*
31. *Letters of Andrew Bleakley.*

10
"Hard Time in Dixie"

1. Marlin, Rev. Lloyd G., *History of Cherokee County.*
2. B. F. McGee, *History of the 72nd Indiana.*
3. *Ibid.*
4. *Letters of Capt. John Funkhouser.*
5. B. F. McGee, *History of the 72nd Indiana.*
6. *Ibid.*
7. *Official Records.*
8. *Ibid.*

11
"Here's Your Mule"

1. *Official Records.*
2. B. F. McGee, *History of the 72nd Indiana.*
3. *Ibid.*
4. *Diary of Forrest Farley.*
5. *Ibid.*
6. *Ibid.*
7. Stanley F. Horn, *Army of Tennessee.*
8. *Ibid.*
9. *Ibid.*
10. *Official Records.*
11. W. F. Curry, *History of the 1st Ohio Cavalry.*
12. B. F. McGee, *History of the 72nd Indiana.*
13. *Ibid.*
14. *Diary of Forrest Farley.*
15. W. F. Curry, *History of the 1st Ohio Cavalry.*

12
"Babylon Is Fallen"

1. B. F. McGee, *History of 72nd Indiana.*
2. W. H. H. Benefiel, *History of the 17th Indiana.*
3. *Recollections of Thomas D. Duncan.*
4. Gen. J. H. Wilson, *Under the old Flag.*
5. *Official Records.*

6. *Ibid.*
7. *Ibid.*
8. *Ibid.*
9. *Ibid.*
10. *The Reminiscences of Newton Cannon.*
11. *Official Records.*
12. *Ibid.*
13. *Ibid.*

13
"When Johnny Comes Marching Home"

1. *Official Records.*
2. B. F. McGee, *History of the 72nd Indiana.*
3. *Campbell's Diary.*
4. B. F. McGee, *History of the 72nd Indiana.*
5. *Official Records.*
6. *Ibid.*
7. *Personal Recollection.*

Bibliography

Adamson, A. P., *Brief History of the 30th Georgia*, Mills Printing Co., Griffin, Ga., 1912.

Adjutant Generals Report, Confederate Kentucky Volunteers.

Battles and Leaders of the Civil War, The Century Co., N. Y.

Benefiel, W. H. H., *History of the 17th Indiana Volunteers*, Revised Edition.

Blackburn, James K. P., *Reminiscences of Terry's Rangers*, Univ. of Texas, 1919.

Boatner, Mark M. III, *The Civil War Dictionary*, David McKay Co., Ind., N. Y., 1959.

Brearly, ——, *East Tennessee Campaign*.

Bryant, Will., *Great American Guns and Frontier Fighters*, Grosset & Dunlap, N. Y., 1961.

Buckeridge, J. O., *Lincoln's Choice*, Stackpole, 1956.

Catton Bruce, *Terrible Swift Sword*, Doubleday & Co., Garden City, N. Y., 1963.

Connolly, Maj. James A., *Three Years in the Army of the Cumberland*, Edited by Paul Angle, Indiana Univ. Press, 1959.

Curry, W. F., *Four Years in the Saddle, History of the 1st Ohio Cavalry*, 1898.

Diary of Forrest Farley, 123rd Ill. Mounted Infantry.

Diary of Henry Campbell, 18th Ind. Battery.

Dyer, John Percy, *From Shiloh to San Juan*.

Fletchef, William Andrew, *Rebel Private, Front and Rear*, Univ. of Texas Press, 1954.

Gordon, Gen. John B., *Reminiscences of the Civil War*, N. Y. & Atlanta, 1904.

Guild, George B., *A Brief Narrative of the 4th Tennessee Cavalry Regiment*, Nashville, 1913.

Harpers Pictorial History of the Civil War.

Henry, Robert Selph, *"First With the Most" Forrest*, Bobbs-Merrill, 1944.

History of Richland, Jasper and Cumberland Counties, Illinois.

Horn, Stanley F., *The Army of Tennessee*, Bobbs-Merrill, 1941.

Lamers, William M., *The Edge of Glory*, Harcourt, Brace and World, Inc., N. Y., 1961.

Letters of Andrew Bleakley, 98th Ill. Mounted Infantry.

Letters of Tighlman Jones.

Letters of William Hammer, 123rd Ill. Mounted Infantry.

Marlin, Rev. Lloyd G., *History of Cherokee County*, Walter W. Brown Publishing Co., Atlanta, 1932.

McGee, B. F., *Regimental History of the 72nd Indiana Volunteers*, S. Vater & Co, Lafayette, 1882.

McMurray, W. J., M. D., *History of the 20th Tennessee Volunteer Infantry*, Nashville, 1904.

McMurtry, R. Gerald, *Ben Hardin Helm*.

Memoirs of Gen. U. S. Grant, Charles L. Webster & Co., N. Y., 1886.

Memoirs of Gen W. T. Sherman, Civil War Centennial Series, Ind. Univ. Press, 1957.

Oates, Stephen B., *Confederate Cavalry West of the River*, Univ. of Texas Press, 1961.

Official Records of the War of the Rebellion.

Recollections of Thomas D. Duncan, McQuiddy Printing Co., Nashville, 1922.

Reminiscences of Newton Cannon, Edited by Campbell H. Brown, McCowat-Mercer Press, Inc., Jackson, Tenn., 1963.

Report of the Adjutant General of the State of Illinois, Springfield, 1901.

Swiggett, Howard, *The Rebel Raider*, Bobbs-Merrill, Indianapolis, 1934.

Terrell, W. H. H., *Adjutant General Report of the State of Indiana*, 1885.

Thomas, Benjamin P. and Hyman, Harold M., *Stanton, the Life and Times of Lincoln's Secretary of War*, Alfred A. Knopf, N. Y., 1962.

Thompson, Ed Porter, *History of the Orphan Brigade*.

Tucker, Glenn, *Chickamauga*, Bobbs-Merrill, 1961.

Uniform Regulations for the Army of the United States 1861, Smithsonian Institute, Washington, 1961.

Vale, Joseph G., *Minty and the Cavalry*, Harrisburg, Pa., 1886.

Wilder Letters, Photostats loaned by Eli Lilly.

Wilson, Gen. James H., *Under the Old Flag*, N. Y., 1912.

Williams, S. C., *General John T. Wilder*, Indiana Univ. Press, 1936.

Wyeth, John Allan, *That Devil Forrest*, Harper & Bros., N. Y., 1959.

Index

Abbeville, S.C., 212
Ackworth, Ga., 150, 179, 180, 181
Adairsville, Ga., 142, 143, 144, 148, 185
Adam's Brigade, 67
Adams, Captain, 205
Adams, General Dan, 199, 201, 206, 208
Adamson, A. P., 73
Alabama Troops:
  17th Inf., 69; 19th Inf., 69, 96; 22nd
  Inf., 69; 24th Inf., 69, 88; 25th Inf.,
  69; 28th Inf., 69, 88; 34th Inf., 69,
  88; 39th Inf., 69; 50th Inf., 69;
  58th Inf., 37, 40; 2nd Cav., 144;
  4th Cav., 101, 116; Eufala Ar-
  tillery, 37; Fowler's Batt., 68, Rob-
  ertson's Batt., 69; Water's Batt.,
  69; Garrity's Batt, 69
Alexander's Bridge, 65, 70, 71, 73, 74,
  76, 91
Allatoona, Ga., 145, 180, 181
Allen, General W. W., 170
Allisonia, Tenn., 44
Alpine, Ga., 60
Anderson's Brigade, 67, 87, 88, 156,
  157, 170
Anderson, Colonel R. H., 109
Anderson, Tenn., 49
Andersonville Prison, 117, 131, 169, 170,
  213
Antietam, Battle of, 13, 192, 208
Appomattox, Va., 209
Arkansas Troops:
  2nd Inf., 68; 3rd Inf., 68; 4th Inf.,
  69; 5th Inf., 68; 6th Inf., 68, 210;
  7th Inf., 68; 8th Inf., 68; 13th Inf.,
  68; 15th Inf., 68; 25th Inf., 69, 79;

31st Inf., 69; 1st Mtd. Rifles, 69;
  2nd Mtd. Rifles, 69
Armstrong's Brigade, 60, 62, 68, 181,
  201, 205, 206, 208
Armuchee Creek, 141, 182
Army of Northern Virginia, 64, 74, 83,
  138, 159, 209
Army of Tennessee, 11, 67, 137, 138,
  159, 165, 173, 176, 177, 178, 179,
  180, 190, 191, 192, 209
Army of the Cumberland, 11, 12, 14,
  17, 26, 27, 28, 30, 34, 44, 51, 54, 64,
  66, 70, 94, 112, 115, 117, 118, 122,
  137, 138, 142, 145, 158, 160, 166,
  167, 176
Army of the Ohio, 11, 18, 137, 139, 162,
  166
Army of the Potomac, 11, 13, 59, 110,
  115, 122, 137, 140, 159
Army of the Tennessee, 122, 137, 139,
  143, 145, 150, 153, 160, 165, 168
Ashby's Brigade, 170
Athens, Ala., 114, 134
Athens, Tenn., 126
Atkins, Colonel S. D., 51, 59
Atlanta, Battle, 168, 177
Atlanta Campaign, 131, 136, 137, 138,
  148, 192
Atlanta, Ga., 165, 166, 167, 169, 170,
  171, 172, 173, 174, 175, 176, 177,
  180, 181, 186, 187, 188
Audenried, Major, 127
Augusta, Ga., 95

Baird's Division, 66, 76, 84
Baldwins Brigade, 66
Bardstown, Ky., 193, 194

227